BUILDING BLACK

Before you start to read this book, take this moment to think about making a donation to punctum books, an independent non-profit press,

@ https://punctumbooks.com/support/

If you're reading the e-book, you can click on the image below to go directly to our donations site. Any amount, no matter the size, is appreciated and will help us to keep our ship of fools afloat. Contributions from dedicated readers will also help us to keep our commons open and to cultivate new work that can't find a welcoming port elsewhere. Our adventure is not possible without your support.

Vive la Open Access.

Fig. 1. Detail from Hieronymus Bosch, *Ship of Fools* (1490–1500)

BUILDING BLACK: TOWARDS ANTIRACIST ARCHITECTURE. Copyright © 2022 by Elliot C. Mason. This work carries a Creative Commons BY-NC-SA 4.0 International license, which means that you are free to copy and redistribute the material in any medium or format, and you may also remix, transform, and build upon the material, as long as you clearly attribute the work to the authors (but not in a way that suggests the authors or punctum books endorses you and your work), you do not use this work for commercial gain in any form whatsoever, and that for any remixing and transformation, you distribute your rebuild under the same license. http://creativecommons.org/licenses/by-nc-sa/4.0/

First published in 2022 by punctum books, Earth, Milky Way.
https://punctumbooks.com

ISBN-13: 978-1-68571-028-6 (print)
ISBN-13: 978-1-68571-029-3 (ePDF)

DOI: 10.53288/0372.1.00

LCCN: 2022938771
Library of Congress Cataloging Data is available from the Library of Congress

Book design: Vincent W.J. van Gerven Oei
Cover image: Piranesi, "Frammenti di Marmo della Pianta di Roma antica scavati, saranno due secoli, nelle Rovine dell Tempio di Romolo, et ora esistenti nel Museo di Campidoglio" (1835).

spontaneous acts of scholarly combustion

HIC SVNT MONSTRA

Elliot C. Mason

BUILDING BLACK

Towards Antiracist Architecture

p.

Contents

0. Memories   17
1. Cities   25
2. Sights   67
3. Spaces   121
4. Fantasies   155
5. Bodies   205

Bibliography   241

Acknowledgments

For years, I wrote exclusively in spite of myself. I wrote everything as if no author was present. I wrote poems from the points of view of medieval monks, rich women in New York, and Olaudah Equiano. I wrote a play about sailors on a ship, a novel about a German retiree alone in a forest. I could get none of it published. My ego — a tiny tangle of motored razors — couldn't handle the rejection, and I raged for years. I was cycling with my laptop one day and my bag fell off my shoulder, thankfully smashing the hard drive and deleting all my memories — photos from trips with old friends, and hundreds of pages of unreadable literature from an absent author.

The broken laptop forced me to start again. To keep this little myth to less than a page, I will distort the timeline. When I got off my bike, I met Eugenia, who emerges sometimes in this book. Shortly afterwards, I was commissioned to write a book by the head teachers of a south London academy. These events themselves, as well as the surrounding changes they facilitated, made me realize the duplicitous ethics of never writing about oneself. To avoid any mention of oneself is not safety against egotism or self-obsession. Everyone looks at the thing that no one mentions. As I say later in this book, if a wall is missing from a building, it's the only wall you notice.

Instead, I have come to think that a more ethical practice of writing is one that focuses honestly on the production of self inevitably at play. I could write throughout with the pronouns "we" and "us" instead of "I" and "me," but who would my collaborators be? Who gets the author royalties for this book's sale, whose name is on the cover, and who has been sitting at desks and on sofas for a year and a half writing this? To name the subjectivity bringing these words together as "we" would only emphasize the absence of collaborators. By using "I" and focusing on myself, I attempt to critically confront the impossible position that is individual subjectivity, to demand explanations from it, and to reveal the instability and multiplicity that is always in silent operation around any use of "I." I do not want to claim that the people in silent operation around my use of "I" were active co-writers for the same reason that I do not want the council architect of the flat I am in to claim me as a co-designer, because I would then be responsible for the creaky floors, wasted hallway space, and drafty windows.

Many people helped the writing of this book. However, I am not sure that "acknowledgment" is the word that best describes how I want those people to be included here. My acknowledgment of other people seems to affirm my position as singular commanding author. The author can give out thanks to others only on the condition that the author was the ultimate creator of the text. The point of my positioning within the aporia of "I" is precisely to make that commanding authority unstable, surrounding the demarcated border of the subject by ensembles of collective questions that individual subjectivity cannot answer. To be doubtfully and critically "I" while acknowledging the support of others for "my" project seems like duplicity.

In resistance to acknowledgement, I thought first of using Oulipo's N+7 method of rewriting, which replaces a chosen word in a text with the word that appears seven words later in the dictionary. The word I find is "acolyte" — a religious servant, a follower of the priest — which perfectly emphasizes the limitations of acknowledgment. In order to acknowledge the input of someone else, I must already hold the position of giver; I must be the one who can dole out the accolades.

In this book, I focus on the personal conditions that result in a book, rather than presuming a logic in which I am always already the presupposed Author, and others work like acolytes to set up the ceremony of my arrival — the spectacular event of my publication. I am an acolyte among acolytes and what we serve is sociality itself. We have no priest, but we believe. We cannot invest in the singularity of any text — including ourselves — but we are deeply dedicated to the practice of text-making that is sociality and its ethics of sharing. In *Building Black,* I talk about myself and how it came about that I wrote a book about space and race and architecture and Blackness. To not mention how this work emerged would be to presume its nature, and any authorial and singular nature is always an imperial pursuit.

The way I attempt to move out of the presuppositions of acknowledgment is by focusing on openings that already exist, that go on around and despite me. What I want to point out and sing for in this acknowledgements section is that the people who have made this book possible did not work in order to make this book possible. That is not the temporality of this text. Instead, many people are playing and performing in an ongoing operation. Into that operation, I stuck my own work for a while. All I can say here is what I have learned from those whose work is ongoing.

Certainly, *Building Black* would not be possible without Eugenia Lapteva. Her support, knowledge, and love has opened up every side of the little box I lived in. The book's possibility was also materially opened by the head teachers who commissioned me to write: Mona Taybi and Judette Tapper. Their commission gave me the time, space, and money to write this book, as well as the one they commissioned. Without that luxury, it would not have been possible.

The possibility for this was also opened by those who helped to edit it. The following book has no resemblance to the document I first wrote and submitted for publication. It is now a readable and hopefully useful text because people told me what I did badly and showed me how to do it better. Among these people are Ben Spatz at Advanced Methods, Livy Snyder, Eileen A. Fradenburg Joy, and Vincent W.J. van Gerven Oei at punctum books, Victoria Hindley at the MIT Press, and my friends

Melanie Vasselin and Caitie Lawless. Other peer reviewers were anonymous. While they did not directly deal with *Building Black,* German Primera Villamizar and Giovanni Marmont's edits of my essay "Thing: A Fugitive In( )Operation" also opened crucial insights into how to edit and rewrite this book.

Throughout my studies, many academics have supported my projects and made my writing possible. The most instrumental in opening the possibility of Building Black are Francis Wilson, Katy Beinart, Seb Franklin, Jane Elliott, Amy De'Ath, and — for opening theory itself to me, and for showing me its poetry — Ivan Callus.

This book would not be possible without the direct and indirect help of my friends, who have supported and encouraged me, as well as directly offering their knowledge and expertise to improve my writing projects. They are: Saifoor Rahman, Patrick Moore, Gabriel Cabral, Pepe Chozas, Carlos Lozano, Grace Porter, Klara Kaliger, Bruno Vilhar, and Jorge Alvar.

I am also certain that none of my writing would ever have emerged if I had not learned how to tell a story from the matriarchal fabulists of my family: Janice Gordon, Jessica Dentice, and Rebecca Mason.

For Genia

0

Memories

While working for an academy of state schools in south London, researching and writing a book about its architectural and pedagogical history, I begin to use some of the deleted sections as another book. In this second book, the refuse of the institutional first, I keep hitting the same dead end while planning the objects of study. How can I write about Black space, antiracist architecture, and radical practices of building? What can I say when I no longer have the excuse of having been commissioned and told what to write by school managers and head teachers?

At the insistence of my wife Eugenia, who is a psychotherapist, I begin psychoanalysis. When I read Frank B. Wilderson III's new book and he says that he was in psychoanalysis for years before formulating his self-critical mode of Afropessimist radicalism I take it as a sign, a good omen of thinking.[1] Through psychoanalysis, I realize that the only valid object for this study is myself. What can possibly explain and criticize the position of the white, British man — neither an architect nor a professional philosopher, still working on his PhD — in Black Studies and architectural theory? It is a position that can be approached by self-critical readings of architecture, which means the practice of understanding architecture as a constituent agent in my

---

1 Frank B. Wilderson III, *Afro-pessimism* (New York: Liveright Publishing, 2020).

own construction. To resist the book becoming only a theory of whiteness in architecture, or only pseudo-philosophical autobiography, other possibilities are listened to and allowed to emerge, forming the procedure and plans for earths that are built without the conflation of race and space that I read here in European and North American design. The opening of other earths is approached, is heard and felt, but is not turned into an object of study.

I turn to what I see as the only ethical practice for a book on this topic: write about myself as white architecture. I write about my memories of home, the many spaces I grew up in as we moved constantly around the same town, a repetition that became complete difference—everything so similar it was all forgettable. My mum woke me and my four siblings up to move somewhere else, escape unpayable rent. I write about my best friend throughout adolescence, our petty criminality, our regime of bicycle-thieving that made us enough money for years of drug use. I write about what separates us now, the spatial borders constructed around differently racialized subject-positions. I write about the architectural codes surrounding a decade of alcohol addiction; the dark bars and canal paths, the bright lights of all-night off-licenses, the positioning of lager advertising, and the balance between paying rent and buying booze.

When a section of the book gets shortlisted for a prize, my ego's grandiose fantasies of literary stardom are charged with excitement and the book turns into a presumptuous theory of the possibility of Black architecture. As I move into the writing of the second chapter, dedicating every day to it amid the paralysis of a pandemic, the book oozes out of my own containing structures. It is dragging me through the pages and eventually, while trying to explain the project to a friend, I realize that I have written *Building Black: Towards Antiracist Architecture* as if I were a Black architect. I am neither Black nor an architect.

I abandon the manuscript.

In *Otherwise Worlds: Against Anti-Blackness and Settler Colonialism,* Frank Wilderson and Tiffany Lethabo King discuss white people's involvement in Black Studies. Whiteness is presented as a structuring force that creates codes of coherence in certain congregations — the congregations of buildings and privatized spaces that form a city, the congregations of citizen-subjects who claim themselves as the effects of individuation, and the city as an effect of that subject-position. Whiteness formulates and regulates zones of internal coherence, centered on the European white man, with orbital spaces of exclusion for Indigenous, colonized, gendered, dis-ablized, and queered group formations, and all constructed on this world's — which, in its commanding proclamation, as an expansive imperial form, is called *World* — antithetical reliance on the impossibility of Blackness. "There is so much work that can be done on whiteness and how its coherence requires parasitism in order to survive," King says. "I think white folks have so much to do in that respect. There is this ongoing and enduring question of how does whiteness require Black death. Deal with that. What's with this obsession with us?"[2]

For Wilderson, it is only the method of questioning that is Blackness that can provide openings into antiracist liberation. The structure of whiteness is not limited to governmental policy or the pseudo-biology of skin tone. Its racializing structure is implicit in everything, in the form of global links given as modern ontology and epistemology. Its totalizing structure requires complex procedures of thinking to escape; it requires another kind of reason, antecedent to modernity and ongoing despite its genocidal regime. "I think this structure of feeling is hegemonic, that no matter how good the argument is, folks refuse to be authorized by a Black ensemble of questions," Wilderson says. "[W]hat you get out of Blackness is a politics without claim. And no one seems to be taking that on."[3]

---

[2] Tiffany Lethabo King and Frank B. Wilderson III, "Staying Ready for Black Study," in *Otherwise Worlds: Against Settler Colonialism and Anti-Blackness,* eds. Tiffany Lethabo King, Jenell Navarro, and Andrea Smith (Durham: Duke University Press, 2020), 56.

[3] Ibid., 65.

I return to the abandoned manuscript with the questions, "Why do architectural theory and practice need to rely on racism to exist?" "Why is the internal coherence between whiteness and architecture so hard for us to imagine and understand?" and, "How has architecture maintained itself as a white thinking practice and why does it rely on colonial foundations that implicitly affirm the non-being of Blackness?"

None of these questions is intended to establish a new foundation. I am not in the game of writing manifestos. Instead, the intention is to open ongoing sites of resistance; to listen to the sound of otherwise rhythms and formulate a theory — of both space and race — that allows these present knowledges to emerge, to open the totalizing structure of whiteness to a Black ensemble of questions. This book is a critique of the implicit whiteness of architectural theory, mostly focused on the British tradition, but also involving substantial discussions of the North American context. Where I live in south London, the spatial meaning of race mostly centers around the oppositions of whiteness and Blackness. In my PhD research, and in my writing generally, I read and think about Black Studies, so the focus of *Building Black* is mostly an internal criticism of whiteness with a dedication to openings of Blackness in antiracist urban forms. Indigenous, Brown, Asian, Jewish, Arab, Aboriginal, and other racial subject positions are therefore left somewhat to the side, not to suggest lesser importance, but because I do not know enough to write a book about them. There is some discussion of Indigenous theory and conceptions of land, but the book is really about the two parts of one question, in two subject areas: How is architecture involved in the mechanisms of racialization (architectural theory), and how can the built environment be thought otherwise (Black Studies)?

Following this preface, Chapter One, "Cities," presents the book's central antagonism with Kantian subjectivity and then provides a critique of a particular British architectural project, attempting to reveal the subtle mechanisms of racialization at work in buildings. The huge Motion development of apartments in Leyton, east London, is constructed according to what I claim are the archetypal principles of racialization in architectural history. First, liberal inclusivity is proudly stamped all over the project's advertising, proposing the eradication of difference as the initiation of inclusion, as the working-class residents of the area are pushed out by direct destruction and price increases in order for the purportedly diverse, bourgeois hipster residents of the new development to reproduce the scenes of Motion's advertising copy. Second, the project is narrated by its developers as a personal aspiration, coded as the telos of human life through property ownership, which gives an architectural project a remarkably Kantian character, with its appeal to a projective way of seeing the world through transcendental epistemology. The new residents come to know the world through the projective imagining of themselves as the expansive owners of the space they inhabit. Third, the architectural features of the building restage important moments in the development of modern design, with blocks of smoothness representing a cleansing of social life. Where the midcentury council estates of the rest of Leyton develop according to the agency of those who live there, Motion is built as the establishment of a homogeneous space in which each resident is nothing but a personal project of self-realization through property ownership.

Chapter Two, "Sights," sets up the fundamental Kantian criticism that forms the principal impulse of this book. Revealing the undercurrent of Kant's transcendental ideality of space and time in the trends of urban planning and design since the Enlightenment, I conduct close readings of modern architectural theory and its reliance on a racializing logic of space, focusing on the World's Columbian Exposition, in Chicago in 1893. I relate the history of Christopher Columbus and the colonization of the Americas to the architectural principles developed through the Exposition, interpreting the aesthetics of Louis Sullivan and Frank Lloyd Wright through my critiques of Kant and Hegel.

Chapter Three, "Spaces," furthers my architectural critique of Kant in the specific context of Westfield, a global chain of shopping centers of which there are two in London. When I moved to London at the age of nineteen, my first job was at a restaurant in

Westfield. This chapter is a personal, authotheoretical critique of the subtle violence of the built environment, engaging with my own experiences of addiction. I weave this personal criticism into a reading of the Kantian epistemological edifice behind the brilliant but disturbing thinking of Gaston Bachelard.

In Chapter Four, "Fantasies," I attempt to complicate what I have proposed as the ubiquitous whiteness of architecture through two propositions. One is a notion of the Black witness, which I develop through Jacques Derrida, Fredrick Douglass, Frantz Fanon, and Paul Gilroy. The other is an understanding of the shopping centers Westfield London and Westfield Stratford City as sites of Orientalizing and ornamentalizing, which I develop with the work of Anne Anlin Cheng. Then, through an engagement with contemporary Black Studies scholarship, I develop a proposition for the possibility of "Blackitecture," the intention of which is to confront the implicit whiteness of global architectural theory and practices.

Chapter Five, "Bodies," returns to the basic questions of this book: How can we understand the racializing function of architecture? How are cities complicit in the dispensation of racializing violence? How can the built environment be developed differently? "Bodies" investigates a thinking model for critical white architecture. I move with the philosophy of Saidiya Hartman and Denise Ferreira da Silva into a mode of confronting architectural theory and practice that is immanently unable to ignore its own constituting whiteness. In this final section of *Building Black,* I abandon the method of critiquing theory, and move towards an experimental imagining of building as a form of dance. Building, in opposition to the institutional epistemology of Architecture, is constant spatial manipulation and the undoing of its central positioning in relation to itself. I call this "building as love-of-dance." Attempting to exceed the limitations of Kant's spatial theory of self-consciousness through a sustained engagement with Ferreira da Silva's abandonment of spacetime, I initiate a decompositional (po)ethics of building without Architecture. This involves positing the ancient ruin, after Pier Vittorio Aureli, as the architectural analogue of Blackness, definable by its language of survival against the imperial expansion of urbanization/whiteness. The last chapter opens numerous possibilities for thinking architecture otherwise, beyond the expansive and consuming World of European urban subjectivity.

I

Cities

Mathematical Repetitions at the Ethical Borders of the Unbearable Self

As teenagers, my Brown best friend would endlessly take the piss of my whiteness, designating my social position as inseparable from white supremacy and racist violence. The position of being white became inherently racist. I imagined whiteness as an encroaching sea, a massive wave of pain permanently suspended just beyond collapse. At any moment it could be released. The whole regime could end in a final spectacle of genocidal rage. I waited for it.

Meanwhile, my best friend and our other Brown and Black and Muslim friends seemed to have other ways of relating, other modes of speaking under the tracking devices of a white bourgeois society. At his mosque, men participated in exchanges that delinked from the coordinates of reason I could understand. There was another kind of language, another way of making worlds. Even my dad seemed to build incomprehensible structures of dad jokes with his best mate, the rabbi.

My best friend's memories were of a burning hot Bangladesh, which he did not need to remember in order for the memories to construct him. My transcendent memories responded with an opposing extremity: I remembered my pre-birth in snow, all white. I was as far as possible from the languages of my friends.

In fury, in wanting fetishized and whitening access to the spaces beyond my understanding, I turned to any mode of destruction that would leave my whiteness unquestioned. I became a communist, an anarchist, a socialist, a communist again, circling the icy patches of my gated territory. I raged at everything, drank away the impossibility of escaping, tried to burn the boundaries of established epistemology.

And then, some uncountable time before writing *Building Black,* I fell in love with a Swedish woman, and she fell in love with me. We moved in together, to her little flat on a council estate in south London, where I wrote this book. And then we decided to move to Sweden. At some point I would have to undo the simple geographical fantasy of race I had lived my life with. I called my old best friend now distanced from me in his fatherhood. He laughed and couldn't believe I was moving to Sweden, like some reverse process of Black nationalism; a white concentration in the far north.

My psychoanalyst, however, is completely unconvinced. I try to set up coherent lines of reason. *My teenage dreams of racial polarity were a long-running joke between young people trying to understand the perverse positioning of racialized subjectivity. In the smashed-up trading floor of Britain after Brexit, I can get Swedish citizenship and remain European. My Swedish partner anyway is a foreigner in Sweden — neither of her parents is Swedish.* All excuses, says my psychoanalyst. Focus on yourself, on your internal causes, she says, but without the words. She speaks, psychoanalytically, with silence.

At the same time, this book is not an autobiography. Readers have no reason to want to know about me. But it is a universal modernity that has constituted me, so a critique of myself and my constituting violence is a critique of the violence that constitutes me. That violence, as I keep repeating throughout the book, is fundamentally Kantian. To criticize the world-forming philosophy of Kant and its afterlives in the architecture of contemporary cities I make some Kantian linguistic distinctions through capitalization. I talk of World and world, Subject and subject, and Human and human. World with a capital-W is the specific space created by Subjects rather than the neutral planet, and Subjects are the creators of World rather than any people subjected to a particular manifestation of power. Capital-W World is formed in modernity through the projection of an anthropocentric expansion of the self into the earth, the world, making a planet for humans in which the production of capital and its racialization of human life-forms is the central goal of being. The form of human produced in the dialectic between World and (Kantian) Subjects is the Human with a capital H.

In the long genocide of modernity and its racializing logic of cartography, my internal signifiers are a particularly imperial form of coherent reason. My internal design gives me away already to a fully Kantian architecture of ontological becoming. The structure of World designates me as all the traces of what whiteness is, what whiteness did, what masculinity and Britishness have always meant.

My givenness to these structures is a givenness that I can no longer reject. I cannot speak in the language of my friends or build the house of my neighbor. When Hamid Dabashi asks, "Can non-Europeans think?"[1] I want to stop saying like a happy liberal, "Yes, you can!" and affirming our individualized separateness from each other. I do not want to make us the same, to absolve our internal structures, our histories. Instead, I want to sit beside Dabashi, head in hands, and wonder how I got here. I want to ask how my life became a series of borders demarcating the proper territory of thinking; to ask, "How can I think?" "*Can I* think?" and "In this architecture of modernity's raciality, how can my social referents — white, man, British — sever their direct line to the institution of Thinking?"

I intend to fall inside the givenness that is already given. I want to lose myself inside its rationality and trace the etchings of violence it was built upon, the violence I was born inside, I was born as.

---

1 Hamid Dabashi, *Can Non-Europeans Think?* (London: Zed Books, 2015).

The City of Kant

Throughout this book, Fred Moten will provide many of the openings into my foremost questions. In the case of architecture and Kant, Moten is already there. Here are "a couple of realizations that are impossible for Kant: (1) that black is a gathering of chance in the submerged city, ready to erupt, at the city's unruly, disagreeably ornamental outskirts, where the [foreigner] is homelessly at home," says Moten, "and (2) that in this city there are no men, there is no Man."[2]

This is the most important sentence that can ever be written in the newly founded cartographies of *Building Black* and its internal subsumptions within Black architectures and radical Kantian ethical propositions. Moten continues:

> To inhabit this marginal, underground city, where the informal is the condition of possibility of form, has required a shift of emphasis — from the resistance of the object to the insistence of things; from the existence of the freedom drive to the persistence of escape — in the interest of voiding state-sponsored normativities and the statist anti-state shade they project.[3]

The city that Kant cannot know, where Moten talks and plans with his friends, is informal in the sense that its form is not constructed around a narrative of progressive time. It is not conditioned within the narratives of national time that buildings tell. The building says it grew out of modern industry, out of iron production and oil extraction, out of the excavation of artifacts in the archaeology of empire and out of the glassy contemporaneity of smooth neoliberal advertising.

---

2 Fred Moten, *Stolen Life* (Durham: Duke University Press, 2018), 39–40.
3 Ibid., 40.

The other city, submerged, underground, undercommon city,[4] does not set up temporal signifiers of progress, trying to show who is enslaved and who is free on a timescale that gradually perfects itself, on a line that leads to an ideal. Architecture in the city where we live, any global city where anyone lives, is held around a narrative of time. Sigfried Giedion theorizes the progressive time of architectural space in his massive classic of 1941, *Space, Time & Architecture*. It is a temporal urban theory that Kant would be pleased with.

To Giedion, the city is not only a signifier and carrier of the metaphysical notion of progressive time. It is its initiator. "The city will not disappear," he writes. "It has been an ineradicable phenomenon since the very beginning of higher civilization."[5] The possibility of such a thing as a "higher" civilization — or even of such a thing as a "civilization" — is constructed within the physical form of the city. It is where the time flow from barbarism to civilization is physically manifested.

Over the five centuries of imperial modernity, since Europeans began colonizing the world through a new philosophical conception of the ocean, of land, and of humanity, as well through material violence, the codes of the city and of bodies have turned around each other. Together, they form an epistemology constructed on the raciality of bodies that are meaningful specifically in relation to the city, to architecture, and to the urban ethics that uphold the ontological structure affirming

---

[4] Moten refers to "the undercommons" as a space of sharing before — in the sense of antecedent to and in the face of — sharing's subsumption into the expansive and possessive logics of modernity's capitalist subjectivity. The undercommons, and that which is undercommon, is the architectonics of intrasubjective sharing without subjectivity, of giving oneself to the other without a prescriptive and absolute border between self and other. What this opens is the possibility of realizing that the self is always constituted as the other, and that constant sharing is the anticapitalist site Moten speaks of, often with Stefano Harney, as the undercommons. See Stefano Harney and Fred Moten, *The Undercommons: Fugitive Planning and Black Study* (New York: Minor Compositions, 2013).

[5] Sigfried Giedion, *Space, Time & Architecture*, 5th edn. (Cambridge: Harvard University Press, 2008), xxxvi.

race's veracity. The codes of bodies and the city merge, mix, slosh back and forth, and become impossible to neatly trace in the teleological spacetime of modernity or its ground of subjectivity. For Zakiyyah Iman Jackson, "[i]magining a new world […] demands the reimagining of the human body."[6] This reimagining of something already imagined, the already unbearably present body, occurs through an urban, spatial designation, its accommodation within and through the ontological limits of singular corporeality, and its attendant notion of possessive individual subjectivity. To reimagine the body is to resituate the body out of the city. Drawing on Octavia Butler, Jackson imagines the

> (social) body […] as a discursive and multiscalar complex system of bodies inside of bodies that have differential capacities, powers, activities, and aims. Butler's revision of human embodied subjectivity as multispecies interactivity is a provocative call for a praxis of being/feeling/knowing that can accommodate accommodation and challenges […] forms of dominance […] including but not limited to slavery, conquest, colonialism, and imperialism.[7]

The body is the single-scalar form managing and regulating the spatial limits and ideological coherence of subjectivity. The body, World, and the building are not neatly separable, Jackson's work states, in any pursuit of uncovering the racializing constitution of architecture.

Buildings and bodies have merged their meanings throughout modernity. In those merged codes, the defining ontological feature of the city is the people's and the buildings' mutual acts of self-presentation. The buildings and the people present themselves as present, commanding their presence into action as signifiers of each other.

---

[6] Zakiyyah Iman Jackson, *Becoming Human: Matter and Meaning in an Antiblack World* (New York: NYU Press, 2020), 158.
[7] Ibid.

The higher civilization of the city, in Giedion's World of Universal Europe, also means the higher civility of the body in the city. The bodies surrounding what has been physically constructed as the white, marble edifice of civilization are redeemed, ushered into a category that, in this Kantian modernity, means more than the immortality of the Grecian gods: subjectivity. These bodies are converted out of the flesh of animal-being and reconstructed according to imperial architectural principles as subjects who belong to a city. These are the citizens, the civilized beings who are not bodies — they live beyond that crude biological designation, for Giedion and everyone in his colonnaded atrium.

Once this process of civilizing European being and architecture itself has taken place, the only premise on which such a thing as civilization — let alone a higher civilization — can be conceived is by the foundations of Europe. There is no way of imagining what a progressive human form could assume once there is a singular trajectory of building — of building as any act of creation — that develops from Ancient Athens to Euro-American High Modernism, unless that progressive form moves with the European body/building itself. In the construction of a singular universal proposition of race, marking white as the summit of architectural perfection and human being, cantilevered by the ferrous weight of Black as a necessary antithesis, there is always this circular logic: the Kantian Subject emerges as an effect of Kantian Subjectivity; "the transparent I, the subject of freedom, is but an effect of the rules of production of truth, of the modes of power," as Ferreira da Silva says.[8]

Maybe even more so than Kant, it is G.W.F. Hegel who establishes a singular timescale of progressive becoming that ultimately aims for whiteness — a perfecting being is a being on the way to becoming perfectly white. The long and difficult first section of Darell Wayne Fields's *Architecture in Black* is focused on this trajectory and its significance for architecture.

---

8   Denise Ferreira da Silva, *Toward a Global Idea of Race* (Minneapolis: University of Minnesota Press, 2007), 23.

Slightly before Hegel, Kant's third critique, *The Critique of Judgment,* lets out his theory of the paradox of fine art. Judgments of beauty must be independent of concepts, for Kant. Concepts are the unity of understanding and imagination; they are the categorical forms created in the rational Human mind after receiving sensations from external objects. These concepts are too limiting for fine art, since they are categorical, while fine art must create new sensations. Kant responds to this philosophical aporia with a vastly insufficient answer. The work is *guided* by concepts, but carries an inherent "genius" that pushes the work beyond the understanding of the artist. The inspiration of originality is then passed on to successive artists, while leaving behind the conceptual rules, which the artwork has surpassed.[9]

The name Kant gives to this force that carries the inspiration on, presupposing Hegel, is *Geist,* or Spirit. Kant's architectural theory still offers what are essentially Vitruvian propositions: buildings should contain three necessary elements — *firmitas* (strength), *utilitas* (functionality), *venustas* (beauty). However, by freeing somewhat the principles of architecture from singular, deterministic use, Kant opens the possibility of later developments. The main propositions in philosophy that take up this opening in the generations following Kant's life are F.W.J. Schelling's theory that architecture should express its own function, Arthur Schopenhauer's theory that architecture should express the nature of its physical construction, and Hegel's theory that architecture should express the Spirit of metaphysical ideas.[10]

Hegel fit this metaphysical call to architecture's Spirit into three stages. The first is *symbolic,* which is the architecture of Egypt and the world before Ancient Greece. In this architectural form, a structure is created which is sufficient to its aims, intending only to connect beauty and use through a symbolic representation of form and function. The pyramid's form, for

---

9 Immanuel Kant, *Critique of Judgment,* trans. Werner S. Pluhar (Indianapolis: Hackett Publishing Company, 1987), §§43–53.

10 For more, see Paul Guyer, "Kant and the Philosophy of Architecture," *The Journal of Aesthetics and Art Criticisms* 69, no. 1 (2011): 7–19.

example, does not extend and complicate its function. Its triangular mass serves as a point of meaning around which a nation's mourning of their leader can cohere.

In Hegel's general scheme, the intention of Spirit is to attain the gradually perfecting abstraction of beauty. Each stage must make beauty a purer metaphysical idea. But since the symbolic stage of architecture places its meaning in the people who use it, it does not generate an independent beauty that abstracts Spirit into a purer form.

The second stage is *classical*, which "clears up," as Hegel writes in his lectures on aesthetics, the "defect" of the symbolic stage through the fact that the classical is "the free and adequate embodiment of the Idea in the shape peculiarly appropriate to the Idea itself in its essential nature."[11] This stage allows the artwork to present to consciousness the actualized Idea, producing an independent development of the artwork as Spirit. The purpose of art, for Hegel, is to "bring the spiritual before our eyes in a sensuous manner," which Spirit completes "in a satisfying way only in its body."[12] The Idea as the pure abstraction of Spirit must be able to present itself in an embodied form that is meaningful to the people sensing it. Therefore, the classical stage leads Spirit on to the next level of History, making it more developed than the symbolic stage in Hegel's formulation.

The great moment of the classical stage is Ancient Greek sculpture, which is not simply a symmetrical and formulaic mimesis giving physical form to a social need, as Hegel says of architecture in the symbolic stage, but is rather an embodied expression of the sensuous body of Spirit itself. Most crucially, sculpture in the Ancient Greek style is sufficient to itself, not relying on the continued participation of those who created it for its meaning, where Egyptian pyramids need to be used in order to maintain their social meaning.[13]

---

11 G.W.F. Hegel, *Hegel's Aesthetics: Lectures on Fine Art*, Volume 1, trans. T. M. Knox (Oxford: Oxford University Press, 1975), 77.
12 Ibid., 78.
13 Ibid., 85.

The third stage is *romantic* and is represented by the paradigms of painting and music. Strictly speaking, for Hegel, the classical is the highest form of art because it most accurately embodies the form of Idea itself as Spirit. The purpose of art is to take "as its subject-matter the spirit [...] in a *sensuously* concrete form," which is exactly what classical sculpture achieves.[14] However, this does not represent Spirit in its "*true nature*. For spirit is the infinite subjectivity of the Idea, which as absolute inwardness cannot freely and truly shape itself outwardly on condition of remaining moulded into a bodily existence as the one appropriate to it."[15] What happens when this is revealed to people is beyond the classical revelation of the being of the gods in the form of humanity. Instead, humanity realizes itself as its own essential form of being, a being that is beyond a mimetic form of the gods. Man realizes "the *inwardsness of self-consciousness*."[16]

Romantic music and painting, according to Hegel, are art forms that have superseded use. Architecturally, this stage's paradigm is the Gothic cathedral, which has a use, but the use is of no importance. Its beauty, and the pure abstraction of that beauty, supersedes the form of function. Romantic painting and Gothic architecture are dematerialized representations of conceptual realms that ultimately free the abstract idea of beauty from the vulgarity of physical forces and the constructed world in reach of all living things. This artistic development of Spirit is the attainment of History, the dialectical movement towards the end of History, in which humanity is finally fully realized, or sublated. The synthesis of beauty is the full sublation of human reason, having abstracted itself into pure thought. Here, for Hegel, philosophy is the final stage; the end of History: the full realization of Spirit.

Darell Fields finds in this architectural formulation a grand leap in the theory of race. "In essence, Hegel's philosophical system of representation — thesis, antithesis, synthesis — eclipses

---

14 Ibid., 79. Original emphasis.
15 Ibid.
16 Ibid., 80. Original emphasis.

Vitruvius's theoretical scheme of 'firmness, commodity and delight.'"¹⁷ Hegel has established a theory constructed on proximity to the abstraction of History. Any human grouping outside of this dialectical process is dismissible in Hegel's philosophy. So, in order to afford Egypt at least the label of being the beginning of the journey of Spirit, Hegel has to balance the racism of his other theories that explicitly impose barbarism and nonhumanity on Black people and Africans. He does this by qualifying the cultural meaning of Egypt.

> Egypt will be considered as a stage in the movement of spirit from east to west, but is no part of the spirit of Africa,' [Hegel writes.]¹⁸ […] 'Egypt,' for Hegel, is the example of *the* symbolic form of art. Furthermore, this definition of symbolic art is compatible with the definition given for 'original' history. […] 'Egypt' is defined as being 'artistic,' but its art is 'mysterious and dumb, mute and motionless.'¹⁹

Egypt is the historical designation of a point in History before the possibility of Hegel's self-recognition within the means of artistic production. The world Hegel recognizes as World, as European modern being, is one in which a particular logic of abstractions must be employed. That requirement is founded on a principle that is built in every direction, on every side, in the logics of race. Since Africa is the impossible non-history that cannot even be considered as a constituent part of History and Art's beginning in Egypt, it is only by its reliance on that nothingness that Hegel can conceive of the teleological and beautiful mode of being that is the European Historical trajectory. Humanity and architecture — as much as Hegel and Kant can conceive of their meaning — are equally reliant on their definition against Blackness. As Fields puts it, "If the symbolic cat-

---

17 Darell Wayne Fields, *Architecture in Black: Theory, Space, and Appearance* (London: Bloomsbury, 2015), 28.
18 Ibid., 29.
19 Ibid., 33.

egory is 'Egypt,' and 'Egypt' is defined in the context of [Hegel's] *The Philosophy of History* as a negatively affirmed Black racial subject, and architecture is placed within the same category, it is difficult to continue to maintain that blackness has nothing to do with architecture."[20]

This relegation to a pre-History incapable of abstraction has, as Fields point out, great significance for Hegel's philosophical categories, as well as the aesthetic categories explicitly constructed through the stages of architecture and art. In the philosophical categories, it is only through access to this process of abstraction that takes place between Athenian sculptors and Romantic German painters that the perceiving subject can emerge as a self-representing subject within the schema of History's Spirit. It is, then, by being European, or being white, that one can access the abstraction of History that defines what the Human is.

> In essence, a racially determined geopolitical scheme was used to legitimize an aesthetic scheme whose categorical splits were constructed from the same theoretical paradigm. And it was "consciousness" as derived from the "spirit" that constituted the limits of Hegel's categories [...] This absence of consciousness is the same absence used to define the symbolic category ("Egypt"/architecture) of art. In essence, the absence of consciousness in Hegel's philosophical and aesthetic models is blackness.[21]

Giedion's proposition that Europe *is* architecture is easier to understand when seen in relation to a history called History, in which Giedion is irrefutably contained, that is necessarily Hegelian. The Hegelian notion of History is what has defined European being since his philosophical works became the founding principles of an industrializing global Empire of European colonies. By the time Giedion is writing, in the height

---

20 Ibid., 35.
21 Ibid., 41–42.

of Modernism's fetishistic excitement, architectural and artistic practice outside Europe are beginning to be focused on by European theorists and artists, which negates the strict Hegelian end of History prophesied by the abstraction of philosophy and pure thought. However, Giedion's era's fixation on African aesthetic forms and Asian ornament is not a fixation with a genuine will to listen, to learn, to communally form a synthesis of different practices. It is, rather, the confusion of an imperial throne whose Empire has lost any self-convincing reason. The white bourgeois producers of World could no longer justify the tidy telos towards whiteness, since whiteness anyway was now ubiquitous, so there was nothing left to subsume within the temporality of colonial progress.

Achille Mbembe describes the result of this Euro-American boredom.

> The renewal of an anticolonial critique within aesthetics and politics shaped the re-evaluation of Africa's contribution to the project of a humanity to come. The surrealist movement and the proponents of primitivism were key contributors to the critique. André Breton in the 1920s declared that surrealism was connected to "people of color" and that there were affinities between so-called primitive thinking and surrealist thinking. Both, he argued, aimed to eliminate the hegemony of the conscious.[22]

He goes on,

> the aesthetic critique of colonialism never fully departed from the myth of the existence of "superior peoples," and therefore the danger or fear of degeneration, or the possibility for regeneration. It did not distance itself enough from the idea that "Black blood" could play a central role in the awakening of the imagination and artistic genius. In many

---

22 Achille Mbembe, *Critique of Black Reason*, trans. Laurent Dubois (Durham: Duke University Press, 2017), 41.

ways the conceptions of art developed between 1890 and 1945 were deeply shaped by the idea that civilization had exhausted itself.[23]

At the end of civilization, beyond the self-eclipse of History, all that's left to do is for the overlords of Being to play with the others they defined themselves in opposition to.

Giedion makes this clear by affirming that these extra-European architectures are not architectures as such. Rather, they are exciting but ultimately primitive attempts at becoming European. "In the last quarter of a century Europe has not been the only source of breezes freshening the development of contemporary architecture," he writes, clearly suggesting that for all time before twenty-five years ago, Europe did it all. "A universal civilization is in the making but it is by no means developing in every country at the same pace."[24]

For Giedion, and for so many Modernist thinkers in architecture, it is unquestionable that there is a singular timescale of progress, and it expands out of Europe and envelops the earth as World. All forms of life become caught up in this great movement of progress, and finally in some mythical, ideal future everything will be just like Europe.

This is the fundamental narrative of modern European capitalism, its urban ontology and its architecture. It is this narrative that I write inside, attempting to understand it in collective pursuit of its abolition.

Forward/Outward Motion

A couple of miles north of Westfield Stratford, in east London, is a huge new development of apartments. On Google Maps it's called "ENTERPRISE PARK," but there's no reference to this name anywhere else. Its name much more precisely captures the movements in spacetime that these apartments perform. Eve-

---
23 Ibid., 42.
24 Giedion, *Space, Time & Architecture*, xxxvi–xxxvii.

rything nowadays is an enterprise. I'm sure I've bought shoes that shopkeepers claimed were enterprising, made for the feet of entrepreneurs.

This development is about pushing time forwards. It intends to designate an entire area of London as pre-modern, as set in a spatial logic that is behind the forefront, and the forefront is a £350 million union of the development giants Hill and Peabody.[25] The area is Leyton, right beside Lea Bridge Overground station, and this development marks it as lagging in time. Lagging also in space, but, like Giedion says, inevitably to be pulled forwards into the European thrall that defines the progress of spacetime. The development is called Motion.

Motion is built in a different style to most new developments. The new towers in Elephant & Castle, in central south London, are stock blocks, exactly the same as 1960s council housing but with plastic panels replacing bricks. The enormous Nine Elms development in south-west London, meanwhile, is formed of a completely uniform architectural aesthetic, a style that seems to abolish itself with its own blandness. It is exactly the same as blocks in Singapore, Tel Aviv, Dubai, and New York.

Motion in Leyton, though, has an early Modernist feel. With brown plastic paneling resembling a Nordic wooden frame, the main theme throughout is large blocks of smooth white lines. Each floor of the towers is underlined by a thick white frame.

This whiteness and smoothness has a long-standing connection to the colonization of the Americas. In Modernist American buildings since the end of the nineteenth century, as I investigate at length in Chapter Two, these features signify far more than habitation. They are not just places to live. These are signifiers of aspiration, of goals and go-getting attitudes and personal success. To have one of these apartments also means that one of these apartments has you. It has you inside its progressive logic

---

25 "Hill and Peabody Enter into £350m East London Regeneration Joint Venture," *Hill News*, March 30, 2017, https://www.hill.co.uk/news-press/hill-and-peabody-enter-into-%C2%A3350m-east-london-regeneration-joint-venture.

at the forefront of time. The brochure for the Motion development makes this abundantly clear, calling itself the "HEIGHT OF ASPIRATION," in huge bold and all capital letters.[26]

It is your aspiration to have one of these apartments, in fact, that gives you your cultural capital. This is more than a financial investment. It is a personal, cultural investment in becoming what is signified in the history of this building. These smooth white lines have, since the height of industrial architecture in the nineteenth century, meant the reformation of classical purity and the forwards-thinking, forwards-moving, progressive industrial dreamers. This is the Leyton version of the American Dream, and, as Adrienne Brown writes, the "American Dream is built on the premise of upwards mobility, pulling yourself up by your bootstraps and working toward a singular reward of a home, the ultimate symbol of peace of mind."[27]

The peace of mind provided by this narrative and this building is the security of not only having a future but also being the future. These "apartments provide comfortable living in a development which will stand as a landmark in a forward-moving, forward-thinking London borough," the brochure says. And "it's right here where your future plans are set to into Motion."[28]

Motion as a development is very proud of its position as prime mover. Their first act of redevelopment in an area is to call it underdeveloped. Motion does not simply follow the gentrification projects of other key zones of London's architectural profit, like Shoreditch, Hackney Wick, Peckham, and Brixton. It is the first slice in the stone, which it redefines as a "fabric" because a fabric must be fixed when it is broken, unlike a stone. It is the genesis of a force that will abolish difference in Leyton.

---

26 Peabody, *Motion: Lea Bridge London E10,* brochure PDF, no date, 6: https://www.peabodysales.co.uk/media/110599/motion-lifestyle-brochure-compressed.pdf. See also *Motion E10,* https://motionlondon.uk/.

27 Adrienne Brown, "'My Hole Is Warm and Full of Light': The Sub-Urban Real Estate of Invisible Man," in *Race and Real Estate,* eds. Adrienne Brown and Valerie Smith (Oxford: Oxford University Press, 2016), 186.

28 Peabody, *Motion,* 7.

"Welcome to the beginning of something special," the website says. "Motion marks the start of the regeneration of Lea Bridge and Leyton in the London Borough of Waltham Forest. A catalyst for the renewal of the area."[29] Precise scientific language. Trust the experts. This language cannot be separated from the architectural style of the buildings, which is drawn from the American Modernism of Louis Sullivan and Danmark Adler, and Sullivan's later pupil Frank Lloyd Wright. Motion reinscribes the previous industrial heterogeneity of the area with simple smoothness, the colorless clarity of white lines over timeless brown, as Sullivan commanded in 1892:

> I should say that it would be greatly for our aesthetic good if we should refrain entirely from the use of ornament for a period of years, in order that our thought might concentrate acutely upon the production of buildings well-formed and comely in the nude. We should thus perforce eschew many undesirable things, and learn by contrast how effective it is to think in a natural, favorous and wholesome way.[30]

Motion, as Sullivan decrees, in its own vernacular is not really *adding* anything to the area, but rather taking away its excess. It is stripping the area back to a form that is "comely in the nude," uniting as "one bright future" in the central light of the racial/architectural cosmos. Whiteness right in the middle of everything, the Copernican Sun. Motion is the purifying mill making sure the right bodies fit the right buildings, and vice versa.

Essential to both Motion and Sullivan is that, while this unifying ritual of racial purification is underway and all the excess of dark outside is being whitened, there is a hero leading the narrative. One hero must bring this purity forward to both an architectural and social ideal in what Sullivan calls the "una-

---

29 Ibid., 1.
30 Louis Sullivan, *Ornament in Architecture*, 1892, cited in Kenneth Frampton, *Modern Architecture: A Critical History* (London: Thames and Hudson, 2018), 51.

dorned masses." As the architectural critic Kenneth Frampton says:

> Sullivan, like his pupil Frank Lloyd Wright, saw himself as the lone creator of the culture of the New World. Nurtured on [Walt] Whitman, [Charles] Darwin and [Herbert] Spencer and inspired by [Friedrich] Nietzsche, he regarded his buildings as emanations of some eternal life force.[31]

Calling itself a "catalyst," "the beginning of something special," Motion is invested in these same principles of a hero-figure pulling the stagnant past into the future at the center of the light. The future in this narrative is light, it is bright, it is alive and white. The past is dark, a Black pathology resisting its inevitable subsumption in Giedion's progressive force of time.

Exactly what Motion is a catalyst of, though, is quite peculiar. It is not a new kind of architecture, and it does not claim to be. It is not at the forefront of architectural styles, performing the newest thing of chalky-colored plastic panels surrounding big windows with external shutters, and whatever else. Motion is Modernist; it draws from a style a hundred years before its time.

Architecturally it is not a catalyst. It can only be an *ethical* catalyst, attempting to claim the initiation of a new ethics of the city, and these ethics of the city are old: they have been said already by Sullivan, by Giedion, and, long before them, by Christopher Columbus.

Motion is the ethical catalyst of a new kind of temporal project. And exactly what makes it so new is that it never ended, not since 1492 when Columbus arrived on islands he decided were insufficiently developed, or since 1707 when the first industrial iron production began, or since the emergence of an impossibly complex army of architectural, imperial, social, and economic forces converged to mutually produce these bizarre things, so hard to know and define, that we call "the city" and "race."

---

31 Ibid., 56.

Motion's ethical movement is progressive time, and what it is doing to the space of Leyton is to set that time into geography. Columbus was doing the same thing when he arrived in the "New World." The progressive time of Europe's imperial pursuits could never work if it was not settled in the form of land itself. Some land is backwards, and so are the bodies coded as the produce of that land: Africans, Native Americans, Aboriginals — the products of a backwardness that must be brought into the developing future of the bright light of the racial/architectural universe's center.

It is spaces like Motion and the temporal logic it sets into land that bring out the constant question that is never asked: where do race and architecture converge? What is included in such illusive referents as the city, race, and Blackness? How do we find the racial signifiers of buildings and the architectural meaning of skin? We know these things are built together. We cannot understand the social referent race without understanding how the theory of buildings has commanded societies.

Life here in Motion's ethics of the city is primordial if it is not in motion. It is closer to nature; an innocent, pure, but totally stupid form of life. It doesn't know the competitive rigor of the city, or the complex logics of capital accumulation. But it is comfortable. A noble savage. This spatialized horde of natural atemporality, a non-time zone of pre-modernity, is presented as primitive relaxation for the laboring capitalist who is heavy with accumulated labor-time and the itching brutality of capital.

Oh, Walthamstow, tell me how it is that you have suffered? Has Motion forced you forwards from your comfortable Nature?

No, my time exists and continues to exist in Black spaces beneath all this, in the belly of the undertoad, where Blackness sings and plans without the imposition of a single time that pulls it into profit production forever.

Love, and the Relation of History — A Fantasy

While writing this book, I moved from a single rented room in Hackney, where I had lived for three years, to my partner's flat in Borough, south of the Thames, on the tenth floor. The flat faces south, looking over a few nearby six or seven story social housing estates from the middle of the twentieth century, then the new towers of Elephant & Castle. Beyond that, slightly to the west, you can see the cranes of the infamous Nine Elms development. If you stretch your head out, you can see the houses of parliament and the Big Ben tower. The other way, at the top of the distant hill, you see the television transmitters of Crystal Palace.

When I moved in with Eugenia, coronavirus had pretty much paralyzed everything. Pandemics had been mythical aggressions of the unbelievable past, like wars with swords, real ale, democracy, and waistcoats. Pandemics were a constituent feature of all the things that ended before I was born.

I cornered my own aggression in an out-of-tune pessimistic future, packing it into a Marxist drinking schedule that took me back to about the age of twenty-one, when getting pissed was resistance to the violence of capital. If society was forced to be a fabric, if a man had to be iron, if the steel frame of skyscrapers unwound the epidermal mythology of race, then I would destroy myself and redden my surface of iron ore and collapse the structural support that masculinized me and my anger.

I lost my job and stopped getting paid at the start of the pandemic. I had just started a new job, after finishing a long research project for an educational academy in south London. In the new position, I had only been put on shifts for two weeks while they planned how to go about working longer term.

Two days in, everything was closed, and I was told not to come in. Emails were sent to everyone who worked there, assuring us that we would be paid for those two weeks. The two weeks passed, and I stopped receiving emails. I wrote to a couple of people who work there, and they said they were still getting emails.

They had erased me because I had only just started. The management scratched me — and presumably others — off the table of their responsibility.

There are constant sirens on Borough High Street. Beer flattens the longer you leave it, unlike something the news reader calls pandemic spikes. Stand up with me, hold my hand Eugenia, pour the dusty remnants away. Let's walk somewhere. Our love is our only protagonist. Even while the collapse of our murderous symbolic father is staged around us. The economy, in our Stockholm syndrome, falls apart and we fall too. Got no money left, just a master.

I thought for a while the economy's control over me was premised on my possessions, but it remains while all else is lost. Saved up for months while researching with those schools. Always chose the cheapest beer. Stopped smoking in the autumn. And then the money poured away. How do you respond to the imposition of poverty when you're caught in contradictory social codes?

Our love though. Let's take it for a walk.

And then, in a similar scene, we look over the city. The surface drifted off from the spools of a hot iron core. Bits of torn fabric blew through evacuated streets, and little memories arose in gusts of warmer days.

Unwound from the central spool of the machophallic architectural economy that cradles its paid subjects, forcing their embroilment in its imperial schemes and sneering at those without employment, without homes, I began looking for any work.

I saw on the news that the Co-op supermarket needed staff, and they recommended going in to the nearest store. So I walked a few minutes to Southwark Bridge Road, went in and asked if I could start packing shelves. The woman in a Co-op uniform told me to apply online. I said that the website instructed me to go into the shop. I showed her the website, but she didn't look at the screen on my phone. She just kept filling up the tobacco shelf behind the counter. Then she stopped and asked me what I wanted, as if I hadn't just said. I repeated myself and she shook her head, realizing it was still me, asking the same thing, and she was still she, packing tobacco in a pandemic. The madness was too much and all we had left was humor. We covered our mouths and laughed like people laughing.

I went into Tesco and they asked for my curriculum vitae. I deleted all the writing work, the master's degree and the ongoing PhD, keeping only the years of service work I had done to maintain the other life — the bourgeois secret I was hiding from them, perversely.

They never called. I wrote to some translation companies, but no one responded. An echo in a rusty iron chamber, muffled like the macho core was woven into spools of social fabric with its back turned to me.

A bicycle courier company told me I "was not right" to be a cyclist. I have cycled my whole life. I cycled to primary school. I cycled to secondary school and sixth form. I cycled to work. I cycled to the ceremony of my mum's second marriage. But then I realized, in the moment of my not-rightness, that I just cycled; I wasn't a cyclist. I hadn't constructed the right aesthetic surface to convince the collection of social fabrics that I had been woven for their particular market stall. My interior was incorrectly decorated, revealing filthy glimpses of an iron core.

There was building work going on all around the new flat, or the old flat that was new to me. Eugenia and I sat on the balcony drinking wine and beer and eating a bag a day of those apparently healthy crisps, stamped with the marketing insignia of the economic survivors.

The fantasy of the city and its endless growth did not stop for a moment. In the collapsing folds of becoming, where the plateau of being smoothens off and there is nowhere else to go, the physical movements of the economy — these plastic panels of paradigm capital — maintained the horribly tangible fantasy that all goes on. The order of the Empire rises, regardless of what happens in the experience of being. Pandemics do not close the mighty call of steel shafts that chant the chorus of absentee financial investment.

Investors endure pandemics. That was painfully obvious from the first Covid-19 death.

Buildings continued to blindly construct empty space, accumulating the open-mouthed and virus-breathing labor of material city bodies and encasing the value of their labor force around the rebounded shell of *terra nullius,* space unused, space useless as only exchange, as the physical ceiling pounding the city down and covering its breathable air for the abstract concept of investment.

Between the bodies and the buildings of the city there is a relation that synonymizes their distinction. Since classical antiquity it is not quite possible to say what is the civilized body of the citizen and the civilized building of the city. Where are my entablatures, columns, and marble stairs? Where is the red-brick wall of my inherited body, and its upholding steel center, its skeletal iron frame?

It would be presumptuous to presume that the problem here might not be relation itself. Nothing is excluded from the possibility of being *the* problem, including my own authorship of this sentence. Relation in the institution of critical thinking, the established and signed-up practice of Cultural Studies at funky gentrifying university campuses, is picked up like a pint of IPA. It's just *not possible* not to like it.

But a relation, anyway, presupposes unrelatedness and covers up the possibility of its emergence. As Georg Simmel writes in his study of bridges and doors, "we can only sense those things to be related which we have previously somehow isolated from one another; things must first be separated from one another in order to be together. Practically as well as logically, it would be meaningless to connect that which was not separated, and indeed that which also remains separated in some sense."[32] The bridge, Simmel notes, disguises this duplicity in the act of relation, concentrating the experience of *crossing* as one of forming connective relations, distracting from the operation of separation that it simultaneously and necessarily maintains. The door, on the other hand, emphasizes the co-constituency of separat-

---

32 Georg Simmel, "Bridge and Door," in *Rethinking Architecture: A Reader in Cultural Theory,* ed. Neil Leach (Abingdon: Routledge, 1997), 66.

ing and uniting in the operation of relation. "Whereas in the correlation of separatedness and unity, the bridge always allows the accent to fall on the latter, and at the same time overcomes the separation of its anchor points that make them visible and measurable, the door represents in a more decisive manner how separating and connecting are only two sides of precisely the same act."[33]

In a world — this *World* — of relations, the possibility of opening an unrelatedness between non-antagonistic forces or beings is eclipsed by the totality of relations and discourses on relation. How can I even think that two things can have no relation and yet not be antagonistic to one another? Forever in modernity, in the long, long antecedence to modernity that Hegel stoutly establishes, there is a relation between bodies and buildings. That relation is marked by an underlying ontological assumption of difference; the solidity, the permanence of that European relation between bodies and buildings requires a hushed whisper of the fact that they must necessarily not be the same. However, that difference has been collapsed into the fundamental principle of post-Enlightenment modernity's reigning ethics: *universality*.

The implicit difference that structures the relation between bodies and buildings is eclipsed by two stages in the marking of universality. The first is Kant's transcendental ideality of space, which posits all external life as animated by the Human mind, which receives the stimuli of objects as sensations, or intuitions, and then processes them in the faculty of reason that defines the Human, configuring sensations in the already-given a priori categories, ultimately projecting them back onto the world as understanding; a spatial synthesis of Human and World. Kant's cartography of the mind is an internalization of difference, masticating everything into a single nodal point that is the proof of rational beings which, for Kant, always means white, European men: the faculty of *universality*. "The second transformation," Ferreira da Silva writes, is "G.W.F. Hegel's rewriting of formal

---

33 Ibid., 67.

(transcendental) reason as a living (self-developing) force,"³⁴ resituating Kant's spatial synthesis of self-consciousness as an external, *temporal* pursuit of universal Spirit. The Human mind, Hegel agrees, is an animating faculty for the reception of sensations and their transformation into understanding — a process which is both the cause and the effect of being Human and proof of universality as European Man. Hegel develops this, though, by attaching this epistemological form onto a universal ontological mode, the Spirit, which carries life towards its completion as the final stage in the dialectic of Human and World. Once bodies and buildings have said everything they can to each other, they exist as pure relation and as abstract beauty in romantic perfection. As Ferreira da Silva says in her always complex and magnificent poetic philosophy,

> The writing of transcendental reason as spirit, the self-producing, self-knowing, living force, transforms universality (and along with it self-determination [freedom]) into an ontological descriptor, on which signifies […] a particular spatial/temporal juncture, namely the moment of transparency, where the revelation of transcendentality announces the end of the temporal trajectory of spirit.³⁵

Ancient Athenian architectural practice built buildings in the abstract likeness of the values of a new concept of the Human. This merging of the symbolic meanings of bodies and buildings defined the emergent proposition of the rational Human. The mathematical relations of Apollonian reason were displayed in the countless temples dedicated to the god of rational thinking and order. The material form of reason is given its originary conditions, which, many centuries later, will be appropriated into the teleological framework of Hegelian time and the ration-

---

34 Denise Ferreira da Silva, "No-bodies: Law, Raciality and Violence," *Meritum* 9, no. 1 (2014): 137.

35 Ibid.

ality of the Kantian subject, figuring the connection between Athens and Germany/Prussia as direct and progressive.

Once this trajectory has retroactively been posited by modern philosophers and architects, employing a whitened and rationalized concept of Grecian Man as the new foundation of imperial Europe, every movement is set in the sense of relation. The thesis is the Human, a single form of Man that is inherently superior, based on territorial markers such as climate and color; the antithesis is the city, the collection of stone porticos and monochrome columns that designate the space of Human reason but also, scandalously, exists for anyone to walk through — the building's door is open, and cannot, without the intervention of Human subjectivity, police its borders of reason. The synthesis, of course, is reason itself. Apollo represents the potential of this universal faculty.

Recent attempts to counter these teleological formations of relation with relational syntheses that liberate an antecedent subject still seem somehow to get caught in the temporal arch of that originary relatedness of modernity. Édouard Glissant's *Poetics of Relation* is possibly the most influential example of this. In the context of the postcolonial Caribbean, Glissant argues for the construction of an identity built on a relation between the subjects who refuse history. Caribbean history in isolation from its people is a violent imposition, and release from that is attained through an ongoing, shared epistemological Relation. "Peoples do not live on exception. Relation is not made up of things that are foreign but of shared knowledge. This experience of the abyss can now be said to be the best element of exchange," as Glissant writes.[36]

While I am deeply influenced by Glissant, the problem I find with his poetics of Relation is that it always presupposes the individual and autonomous creation of two separate things that form — with some kind of independent agency — a contractual obligation between them. Within the given logic of Rela-

---

[36] Édouard Glissant, *Poetics of Relation*, trans. Betsy Wing (Ann Arbor: University of Michigan Press, 1997), 8.

tion, there is always the presupposition that these two parties have some agency as distinct things. Given that these distinct agencies also contains a reason to operate their agency into a contractual obligation with each other, the logic of Relation can never be separated from the logic of contract, of contractual obligations. This reveals the violence always implicit in the logic of Relation. How can you imagine what it is to have a relation to something without implying the simultaneous proposition of a status as a subject relating to an external and non-co-constitutive object? How can there be such a thing as a relation between two things that are not distinctly constructed, and presupposing a non-givenness to each other? *Relation* itself could be the force stopping our ability to imagine what exists behind the synthesis of the city.

Being, as Giorgio Agamben engages with ontology, is already presupposed in relation and yet exceeds it. Being is, for the history of philosophy up to Kant, a necessary and constitutive mode of relation, and neither exists without the other. "We can therefore define relation as that which constitutes its elements by at the same time presupposing them as unrelated," Agamben writes in *The Use of Bodies*.[37]

The mechanism at work in the foundation of the city, then, is one which operates by retroactively positing the synthesis as the foundation. A synthesis of body and building is achieved, which then acts as the foundation of the city: the polis is where the building and the polity are united as one, creating one another — a causal synthesis of Architecture. In many paradigms of social violence, the same mechanism is at work. As Agamben states a little earlier in the same text,

> the *archè* [which "means both 'origin' and 'command'"[38]] is constituted by dividing the factical experience and pushing down the origin — that is, excluding — one half of it in order

---

37 Giorgio Agamben, *The Use of Bodies*, trans. Adam Kotsko (Stanford: Stanford University Press, 2016), 270.
38 Ibid., 275.

then to rearticulate it to the other by including it as foundation. Thus, the city is founded on the division of life into bare life and politically qualified life, the human is defined by the exclusion-inclusion of the animal, the law by the *exception* of anomie, governance through the exclusion of inoperativity and its capture in the form of glory.[39]

The *relation* is the exclusionary premise of Architecture. The city itself, its manifold of material constructions and their synthesis as the city, is based on the premise that only *citizens* (Humans who are coded as belonging here) are constitutive of and constituted by this city. The relation between buildings and bodies is premised on the exclusion of some forms of life necessarily not entering the ethics of this synthesis, otherwise the city would be everywhere, undefinable, and meaningless.

The relation of the city, then, is inscribed in the narrative of History as the foundation of race. The demarcation of difference in bodies is written as non-compliance with the synthesis of the city. What it is to be outside or to be different is to be not constitutive of the relation of the city. However, it is equally as necessary to the city and this exclusionary premise that no one recognizes it. If the city were knowingly formed on its exclusion of life defined as non-life by exclusion from the city, then the illusion of the ethical synthesis would collapse, and the city would end.

The city functions as a ban on the revelation of its presupposed non-relation. The city disallows the contact of body and building, instead constructing them abstractly as the synthesis of relations, which is always and necessarily the functional prohibition of a non-relation: the relation's principal decree is that any doubt in the synthesis of this relation will undo the state of relation, and thus its constituent forces, which ultimately is life: buildings, bodies, and beings.[40] One can never say that there is a non-relation because those living beings of non-relation who

---

39 Ibid., 265.
40 Ibid., 237.

exist as racialized life would emerge into the precarious and yet permanent construction of the city's synthesis of relations.

After Kant this relation becomes explicitly internal. The projections of the superior beauty of Gothic cathedrals and Neoclassical domes is only a confirmation of the superior understanding of the Human who perceives this beauty and turns it into meaning. The building itself loses any autonomous architectural meaning and becomes a constitutive proof of the architectonic faculty of internal Human reason, laying down the final claim that universalizes the History of Europe. This claim is formed of three parts, as I have attempted to describe above. First, all things that *are,* are in the Human mind and its faculty of reason. Second, the Human mind is rational because it constitutes the white, European male body, which is itself the external sign of reason. Third, the given synthesis of the city is universal proof that the Human is universally superior, since all other forms of life are not constitutive of the relational synthesis, and therefore are not rational and therefore are not white.

Remembering the Line

The illusion of the city's relation also creates teleological links along the trajectory of Hegelian time, in which each one of the city's participants is game. I am a product of this relation, in this city's synthesis, and so I form constitutive relations with all the other Humans presupposed by the ethics of this relational synthesis. Our necessary and underlying non-relation is ignored as a presupposition of existing in this city, of being white and Human (which are synonymous) in World.

Try proposing the oppression of the temporal logics of modernity and you get snapped back. What I look at is what I construct a notion of *relation to.* I remember seeing myself pour the coffee this morning. I watched the cup. Whose cup are you? Who paid for this casket to carry my beans? How private is the internal zone of my own mug? The mug is mine, for I saw it. I *saw it first.* But I also constructed relations of sight long outside the immediacy of today's memory. I re-member happenings otherwise, at other points of the same timeline. If time is constructed solely as a simplistic line drawn from then to now, then of course I trace my sight back along it and reveal glimpses to myself, sticking sections of experience together with *my having seen,* my having been there; I make myself there by seeing it now, tracing lines of time. The members of experience are parted by some underlying break, but I re-member them. Turn the underlying lapses of experience into a single member. A member of a private club called seeing.

I remember whipping my slaves two hundred years ago. They were picking cotton, cutting sugarcane. I was on a horse. I saw it for myself. Time as a line commands me to re-member this. I remember the factories. I lived in slums and shoveled coal. I died of syphilis, of cirrhosis, I killed myself and they killed me too. I was also the foreman. I told myself where to go, who to be, and shut up ask no questions. Red brick, we lived in for the working years, generations parted us from the immediate contemporary of our slave-owning selves. I was the first white to arrive in Africa. And I was my wife waiting at home, milking the cows and sewing socks for the children. I was the original condition of individuation, the first myth of self, and I told myself that I was me, exchanging labor time and building little patches of privatized relation. What's like me? I asked in my little space. Everything, of course. That's the world I work to sustain, that I exist to continue. The only World I've ever known.

Building continues, but the fabric must be wound, wounded, the core that holds the surface up must not be allowed to open. The surface presents the ornaments of self, and without them we do not understand what we are. Without the surface, peeled away, our fury and disappointed poverty would gain access to the steel structure that maintains the smoothly-packed away but enduringly ancient pillar that rose out of the Black history of Greece, before history was whitened in the Enlightenment cultural consciousness and everyone pretended we'd all been capitalist and Christian and white and hetero for two and a half thousand years. History arose from the millions of stolen African bodies turned into machines of labor to justify their own enslavement. It pushed up from the industrial consumption of the planet, its universalizing ideology of a single world which can be entirely consumed, and the white bourgeois environmentalist movement that resulted from that destruction, constructing care of the city in an inseparable tangent from disgust at racialized flesh occupying urban space.

The line of time coordinates the experience of individuated beings — whitened life turned into the specter of European Empire. Simultaneously, individuation creates the condition and the language of the individual against another way of being that precedes and exceeds the limitations of this strictly singular form. In *Black Marxism*, Cedric Robinson calls this antecedent form "the ontological totality" that inheres in a radical mode of obligation to the structure of feeling, a social duty to the meaning of meaning.

> And long before the advent of the "madmen and specialists" (as Wole Soyinka phrased it), the military dictators and neocolonial petit bourgeoisies who in our own time have come to dominate Black societies in Africa and the Caribbean, the Black radical tradition had defined the terms of their destruction: the continuing development of a collective consciousness informed by the historical struggles for liberation and motivated by the shared sense of obligation to preserve the collective being, the ontological totality.[41]

The ontological totality is the constant undercurrent of Black Studies as a discipline within the academy and Black study as a form of fugitive sociality. Contemporary Black Studies scholars from the generation proceeding the originary legend of Professor Robinson — Nahum Chandler,[42] Sarah Jane Cervenak, J.

---

41 Cedric Robinson, *Black Marxism: The Making of the Black Radical Tradition* (Chapel Hill: The University of North Carolina Press, 2000), 171.
42 Society for the Humanities, "Nahum Chandler, 'Paraontology: Or, Notes on the Practical Theoretical Politics of Thought,'" *Vimeo*, October 29, 2018, https://vimeo.com/297769615.

Kameron Carter,[43] Fred Moten[44] — call this "paraontology." As Moten writes, "What is inadequate to blackness is already given ontologies. The lived experienced of blackness is, among other things, a constant demand for an ontology of disorder, an ontology of dehiscence, a para-ontology whose comportment will have been (toward) the ontic or existential field of things and events."[45]

This book, this attempt at making a practice of writing books about Black space, attempts a certain approach towards the paraontological disorder that is ongoing in the someplace-else sociality of Black study, while also attempting to resist the constraints of positionality. *Building Black* is always lingering under subtitles like "How (Not) to Write a Book about Black Space" and then leaning away from them. I try to move around, to lean back, to dance a little, to shake off the scripted procedure of approach, precisely because the ontological totality is re-membered into a deadly telos when pinned to positionality. As Claudia Rankine says, "space itself is one of the understood privileges of whiteness."[46] I spread my legs out, as I've been taught to, but then my mum — or the ontological totality, or some fugitive member otherwise; I can never tell which — slaps me and I curl up on the floor. I sink in to somewhere else.

How (Not) to Write a Book about Black Space — An Apology

In her PhD dissertation, Bryony Jane Halpin argues that gentrifying developments are acting according to two colonial logics, *fantasy* and *apology*:

---

43 Sarah Jane Cervenak and J. Kameron Carter, "Untitled and Outdoors: Thinking with Saidiya Hartman," *Women and Performance: A Journal of Feminist Theory* 27, no. 1 (2017): 45–55.
44 Fred Moten, "The Case of Blackness," *Criticism* 50, no. 2 (2008): 177–218.
45 Ibid., 187.
46 Claudia Rankine, *Just Us: An American Conversation* (London: Allen Lane, 2020), 33.

> I contend that revitalization projects reveal the *fantasy* that the settlement dispossession / violence is long over now, and that there is a "pastness" to the injustices of settler colonialism. Therefore, the *fantasy* that informs how we plan and envision our urban spaces positions settlers legitimately and unquestionably on the land — in perpetuity. This *fantasy* is related to, and in tension with, the apology, which I argue is also revealed in urban revitalization and works to foreshadow the search for state-sponsored reconciliation in the present day. The *apology* represents the way in which urban revitalization makes insincere attempts to address the violent dispossession of Indigenous peoples and to apparently facilitate Indigenous agency in the present day. As a result, the *apology* ends up marking the erasure of Indigenous sovereignty in urban space.[47]

Developers resolutely build on the "pastness" of colonial violence, lightening up the heavy violence of the past with sparkly neoliberal buildings that elicit social participation. The social participation is entirely in the orbit of profit; there is only one way to exist in these spaces and it is *make profit,* revealing again the "nightmare of participation" that Markus Miessen derides, proposing instead a "post-consensual practice."[48] To construct the glistening facade of liberal neoimperial architecture over a site of settler colonial violence is to mask the autonomy of Indigenous history and turn it into a performative show for white audiences.

In the case that Halpin discusses, the murder of a First Nations family took place at the central waterfront in Toronto in 1796. The same spot as the gentrifying development she is criticizing in 2017. The murder of Chief Wabikinine and his wife is spun into plastic panels and hung balconies suspended fashion-

---

47 Bryony Jane Halpin, "Unsettling Revitalization in Toronto: The Fantasy and Apology of the Settler City," PhD diss., York University, 2017.
48 Markus Miessen, *The Nightmare of Participation: Crossbench Praxis as a Mode of Criticality* (Berlin: Sternberg Press, 2010), 13.

ably on stainless steel cables. Fantasy, as Halpin says, requires ongoing reaffirmation to assure that everyone keeps believing in its necessity.[49]

Halpin's notions of fantasy and apology are also useful for thinking outside the context of Indigenous land in North America. The fantasy that forms the operation of expansive subjectivity, intent on constructing its own reflection in every mapped and charted space, is conducted worldwide in the ubiquity of neoliberal capitalism, as is the subsequent movement of apology—the fantasy's accompanying world of cover-ups, smiling politicians, and cute marketing campaigns by developers.

As Glen Coulthard notes in *Red Skin, White Masks*, Karl Marx's notion of "primitive accumulation" has been criticized by Indigenous and Black scholars for attributing its initial and ongoing violence to a particular capitalist operation in industrial England, and for being reliant on the economic relations of value that Marx proposes in *Capital*. However, "the escalating onslaught of violent, state-orchestrated enclosures following neoliberalism's ascent to hegemony has unmistakably demonstrated the *persistent* role that unconcealed, violent dispossession continues to play in the reproduction of colonial and capitalist social relations in both the domestic and global contexts."[50] The principally *territorial* pursuits of British colonizers in North America eclipse the operation of value-reproduction in the factories of northern England, establishing a manifold of violences that has continued as the "escalating onslaught" of neoliberalism and its urban project. Neoliberal architecture, indeed, comes to appear as the apology for the fantasy that is colonial domination.

There are at least two simultaneous timescales to these mechanisms. One involves the fantasy of global colonial domination and its apology in the long development of neoliberalism since the Chicago School economists. The other operates within single projects, such as Halpin's focus on the Toronto waterfront

---

49 Halpin, "Unsettling Revitalization in Toronto," 3.
50 Glen Sean Coulthard, *Red Skin, White Masks: Rejecting the Colonial Politics of Recognition* (Minneapolis: University of Minnesota Press, 2014), 9.

or my focus, below, on the area surrounding Manchester train station, in which fantasy and apology are constantly operating over and within each other, justifying violences yet to be enacted, and violating the scenes of ongoing apology.

By focusing on the operations of neoliberal architecture that violate Indigenous land in Canada and working-class land in northern England, despite the enormous differences between these contexts and histories, the trends in the sociality of resistance and refusal emerge as connected and simultaneous without, crucially, any relation or participation. Working-class resistance to neoliberal developments in Manchester is not explicitly eliciting the precedent of Indigenous resistance to projects in Canada, but still the sociality of each resistance, and the onslaught of each neoliberal operation, is connected.

Coulthard writes:

> I believe that reestablishing the colonial relation of dispossession as a co-foundational feature of our understanding of and critical engagement with capitalism opens up the possibility of developing a more ecologically attentive critique of colonial-capitalist accumulation, especially if this engagement takes its cues from the grounded normativity of Indigenous modalities of place-based resistance and criticism.[51]

While in the British context there are no site-specific Indigenous histories and modalities, this method of understanding the violence of architectural developments still opens up the possibility of seeing the global and centuries-long operation of these mechanisms of power. It is in this way that I engage with Indigenous scholarship in *Building Black*: not to remove its context, nor to ignore it because there is no direct parallel of its situation in the UK, but rather to learn from Indigenous scholars in order to understand the global operation of imperial and neoliberal architecture and urbanization.

---

51 Ibid., 14.

I will discuss more the links between Indigenous studies, Black Studies and antiracist space in the British context in Chapter Two, "Spaces."

The development in Manchester is part of an unprecedented operation, transforming the city and turning every signifier of working-class pastness into a profitable machine for developers, involving a city-wide coherence that peculiarly re-animates the job of city planning, a profession that was killed in the 2007–8 financial crash by neoliberalism's ideology of affectless glass towers with no context and occasional Insta-ready starchitect monuments.[52] Over sixty big developments and 15,000 properties are upcoming or recently opened in Manchester. Not a single one of these houses in 2018–19 met the government's definition of "affordable," which is, at 80% of market price, not what anyone else would call affordable. In 2018, only twenty-eight social houses were built for the 13,500 people on the social housing waiting list, and these are subject to Right to Buy, inevitably setting up their loss in the near future to private ownership.[53]

The fantasy is strongly enforced by those who profit from the new developments. The fantasy concentrates dually on the supremacy of *seeing* over *living,* and on the introspective development of self as the principle that justifies any social destruction. The "breathtaking views of a rising global destination" show that, when a property-owning subject *looks* at the city, the city grows in accordance with the subject's sight. By looking as a property owner in one of these new luxury properties, with the eyes of a property owner, the city itself rises globally, tectonically shifting and gaining a superior standing in the imperial competition of global finance.

It is important that a hierarchy of viewing is stamped into these new Mancunian structures, in order to uphold the fantasy

---

52 See Bob Colenutt, *The Property Lobby: The Hidden Reality Behind the Housing Crisis* (Bristol: Policy Press, 2020), 92 ff.

53 Oliver Wainwright, "Welcome to Manc-hatten: How the City Sold Its Soul for Luxury Skyscrapers," *The Guardian,* October 21, 2019, https://www.theguardian.com/artanddesign/2019/oct/21/welcome-to-manc-hattan-how-the-city-sold-its-soul-for-luxury-skyscrapers.

that property ownership is a constituent feature of *being Human*. It enhances Human senses, making the inhabitant literally see more. This is, as the architects say, "a true epitome of exclusivity and architectural grandeur."[54] It is the exclusivity that grows the city, that enforces growth on a stagnant population.

Before this, before the opportunity to oversee and raise the city that is granted by Manchester's new glassy skyline, the city was submerged. It was a place without rise. That is the new coding stamped on the city by the fantasy of these mega building projects.

The central cog of the logic that upholds the continuing fantasy is the imposition of *terra nullius* — useless, unused land. As Halpin says, "Urban renewal and revitalization provide an ideal platform to re-assert settler belonging and at the same time, acknowledge vanished Indigenous sovereignties. This is achieved by claiming the land to be yet again a *terra nullius* and re-narrating the land, again and again. The chief tool, therefore, in this fantasy of settler belonging is the use of the concept *terra nullius*; the empty land."[55] Not to mention the irony of it being the "chief" tool, when the site she is analyzing is the site of the murder of Chief Wabikinine.

The *apology* in Manchester comes firstly by direct lies. The architect of one of the buildings says, "There aren't enough expensive homes in the city."[56] The narrative, in the simplest way possible, is twisted to the favor of profit. *No, all those homeless and poor people aren't really there. Look at me. Look at the view from this building. The problem is that there are millionaires who aren't currently enjoying this view, OK?*

The second part of the apologetic logic is the neoliberal ethics of self-improvement. Poverty, this new ethics of the city dictates, is not really a material problem. It is not part of a social system that needs to be repaired, or destroyed and built differently, in order to correct the social flaw that is chronic inequality. Instead,

---

54 Ibid.
55 Halpin, "Unsettling Revitalization in Toronto," 3–4.
56 Wainwright, "Welcome to Manc-hatten."

the problem is that people's *interiors* are not at peace. The individual is unhappy in her or himself. Poverty, homelessness, hunger, destitution: these are, in the new urban ethics, conditions of a self that has not bought the right equipment to be happy.

"At Moda," says an Instagram post from one of the developers, beside a photograph of a muscular white woman doing yoga on the rooftop of one of Manchester's new racializing tombstones, "we understand mental health is just as important as physical health. All our developments will have space so you can focus on yourself. Space to connect. Space to be active. Space to reflect and talk. Here's to mental health. Happy, healthy and connected communities are an integral part of a Moda neighbourhood."[57]

For one thing, the post is written in the future tense. This development is the initiator of the future, the bearer of the torch of time, lightening and whitening the way for the submerged and dark city that preceded this development. Most importantly, though, the developers' logic of apology is presented by claiming that the development itself is the community. This building, built for millionaires in a city with thousands of people in desperate need of affordable housing, is presented as the neighborhood, making all else around it simply a disfigured pile of architectural and human debris. There's just unnameable stuff around here, but this building configures life together as a neighborhood caring for the mental health of its inhabitants. And anyway, why is everyone in here struggling so much with their mental health?

Here, in Manchester and in so many other British spaces, the "chief tool" of *terra nullius* is in play. Its rules are different to those by which it operates in Toronto, seizing Indigenous land and turning it into profitable territory, but it is one unending game, a deadly game that divides space by the ontological scales of race, class, gender, ability, and nationality.

---

57 Steve Robson, "'In what sense are they going to be Mancunians?'... The Five-star Flats Where Critics Say Residents Will Be Living in a Bubble," *Manchester Evening News*, June 2, 2019, https://www.manchestereveningnews.co.uk/news/greater-manchester-news/angel-gardens-moda-living-manchester-16306998.

Terra nullius has come back to haunt British city space. The empty land imposed on the colonized world has rebounded as a spatial specter haunting Europe. *Terra nullius* has become so acutely concentrated, with such a stingingly intense inequality and violence, that it now seems incompatible with the logics of property ownership still enforced by the neo-colonial state of Britain today. But at the apex of neoliberalism's spatial violence, unused land, the logics of property ownership and colonial expansion unite, in the space where Marx, Coulthard, and Halpin also come together. The prime minister has no idea what this encroaching ghost of *terra nullius* means. He thinks it's just another opportunity for profit. His hungry chancellor is also drooling at this opportunity — *yum yum, big empty luxury apartments withholding millions, empty blocks, unused space in the air above the city.* With no idea that this is *terra nullius* haunting its own grave.

Finally, the Chorus

On off days, I dream of being a regal theorist making branded neologisms for the academy's box of neologism-suggestions, all from the comfort and beautiful views of my Moda apartment, my happy and healthy and connected community of property owning brethren, my long-forgotten colonial past and my gleamingly glassy present. My neologisms will define the rectangular glass monument they construct in my honor when I die of peace and satisfaction after another Moda Yoga Class on the Overlooking Rooftop: *terra quicumque,* whatever land, land to be used for anything, deconstructed, free of all imposed meaning; *terra animax,* alive land, land that lives and breathes and co-constitutes the cultural category of human life, a nonhuman being that allows my white and European body to appropriate Indigenous knowledge that makes me famous and loved and carried like an imperial king through the blossoming lecture halls of emancipatory theory and all the debt that got me here; *terra copia,* a land of fullness, of abundance, a land like

Olaudah Equiano's African soil,[58] so full of redness and aliveness that no one ever stops and everyone rejoices in the land, with the land, as the land, for the land, a land that carries the possibility of life without and against the horror of profit and its land-killing overlords.

I learn about the walls of this apartment from the words they say, from the fact that all the words they say are "Me." And that sounds like me. In the space of that learning, I do not exactly build Black. Rather, I move around in a chorus I cannot understand. However, the chorus grows, the ontological totality expanding and making walls seem to sink. The sound gets louder.

> The chorus bears all of it for us. The Greek etymology of the word chorus refers to *dance within an enclosure*. What better articulates the long history of struggle, the ceaseless practice of black radicalism and refusal, the tumult and upheaval of open rebellion that the acts of collaboration and improvisation that unfold within the space of enclosure? The chorus is the vehicle for another kind of story, not of the great man or the tragic hero, but one in which all modalities play a part, where the headless group incites change, where mutual aid provides the resource for collective action, not leader and mass, where the untranslatable songs and seeming nonsense make good the promise of revolution. The chorus propels transformation. It is an incubator of possibility, an assembly sustaining dreams of the otherwise. *Somewhere down the line the numbers increase, the tribe increases.* The chorus increases.[59]

The sound is incredible. I cannot believe the movements of these walls. I feel myself approaching a dance. In Chapter Three, "Bodies," in body, we dance, but before that all I hear is laugh-

---

[58] Olaudah Equiano, *The Life of Olaudah Equiano, or Gustavus Vassa, the African* (New York: Dover Publications, 1999).

[59] Saidiya Hartman, *Wayward Lives, Beautiful Experiments* (New York: W.W. Norton & Company, 2019), 347–48.

ter. Not an ironic sound, not that riff on trodden bodies. Something else, confrontational and present. The laughter of finding the chorus after all. I write for the purpose of proximity to the movements of the chorus, in opposition to why I live inside architecture.

The survival of the possibility of another kind of architecture, the trace of antiracist urban life and the construction of an island of being otherwise, is a chorus of joy inside the brutality of the expanding machine. And the inhabitants of the antiracist city — you, whoever you are — exist as evidence of it, as Ilya Kaminsky knows:

> Watch —
> Vasenka citizens do not know they are evidence of happiness.
> In a time of war,
> each is a ripped-out document of laughter.[60]

---

[60] Ilya Kaminsky, "A Cigarette," in *Deaf Republic* (London: Faber & Faber, 2019), 30.

2

Sights

Dekanting

A new book arrives, emerging already given to itself as the false prophet of a radical theory of architecture, pushing into a busy field it calls its own and opening its arms for applause — not only explicitly expecting, but indeed demanding to be happily accepted by all the colors alike. The book is written by a white man living in a house with Immanuel-in-a-Wig, and in the house, they sit at separate desks but play the same game without ever looking at each other. Of course, the mechanism of sight that each of their bodies operates is the very same. There are two bodies, distinguishable by the imperial naming ceremonies of individuation as *Elliot* or *Immanuel*. However, despite this appearance of duality, there is only one way of seeing.

The house they live in is built on a graveyard, which, in the binaries of their strict ontology, they call *community,* but supposedly in the basement it's referred to as *Blackness*. No one in the house knows what that means, and they are both unwilling to learn. Instead, one of them learns about whiteness, while the other learns about himself (who is whiteness). These impossible and endless pursuits cause sparky fissions between Immanuel and Elliot, and one of them always accuses the other of underpaying rent. Immanuel says he had to wait till he was in his sixties to afford his first house, and Elliot — writing *Building Black* at the age of twenty-nine — should shut his barking-hole and put that filthy tail between his legs. Immanuel has set up a hairy old rug in the corner for Elliot to sleep on. Elliot has filled it, despicably, with Immanuel's books.

In those books found in the scripter's crib is a truth that is both morally pure and purely universal: *The new book that arrived is wrong.* The book called "Cities," which was presented by its author as a self-denigrating and radical reformulation of the malleable materials of Black study and antiracist thinking, gets everything wrong because all it ever managed to formulate a plan for was the disjunctive logics of the author himself (underpaying resident of Kant's muddy sub-cage) and an undercommon sociality he dreams of but doesn't know and never will know and absolutely should not know. Nowhere in the poetic but ultimately disappointing novel — "Cities" — does the author ever approach a genuinely self-confrontational ethics of study with his own property-possessive epistemologies. He meanders, rather, into the scripted blues that sound pretty in their performance of anarchist radicalism and I-know-all-the-latest-Duke-Uni-Press-hits-isms, but fails at two specific elements of the book, without which "Cities" and its predecessor, "Memories," function as little more than a mediocre poetry-slam performance by a white bourgeois boy who obviously has a good degree from a hip university in the white institution of Cultural Studies and has read a significant number of books in Black Studies but understands nothing. These two elements are: (1) an actual, sustained, and practical synthesis of Kantian reason and its proposed part in constituting modern architecture; (2) a radical engagement that truly confronts the position of the author.

In this reasoned and considered response to what I propose as the failings of "Cities," I indulge in a full consideration of what Kant's philosophy means to modern and contemporary architectural practices, providing an outline of Kant's fundamental concepts, a possible spatial reading of their cultural and racializing codes, and an account of Kant's philosophical legacy worn subtly within the canon of architectural theory. In order to do this honestly and with the utmost consideration of how to be useful to the reader, unlike the author before me, I continuously confront the aporia (or, maybe better, unbearable coherence) of my presence in this space of study. While I journey into modern architectural theory and the difficulty of Kant's spatial significance, I take breathing breaks into myself, the staggered timescale of my bleached self-history, and establish a particular architectural focal point for the grand theorizing of this work, grandiosely titled "Spaces." The focal point is Westfield, a network of vast shopping centers in Europe, North America, and Australasia. There are two Westfield centers in London, one in the east (Stratford) and one in the west (White City), both styled architecturally as a unique tangent on the stock form of contemporary mass consumer spaces. They both resemble and yet significantly develop the familiar architectural forms of airports, apartment complexes, cultural hubs, and other shopping centers. I attempt to critically think the raciality of these huge buildings alongside Anne Anlin Cheng, the actor and model Anna May Wong, Gaston Bachelard, Kant, and my own memories of working in the shopping center as a waiter in my early twenties.

Towards the end of "Spaces," I dedicate a significant amount of time to the application of what I have been studying throughout. The previous author — the co-inhabitant with Immanuel of "Cities" — was satisfied with poetic gestures of critique, which were then discarded when the work became hot and sweaty and all the long words had already been said once, giving the author the cultural value he clearly seeks through writing "Cities." I, however, intend to fully dedicate myself to the unfashionable and frankly unsexy labor of applying radical philosophy to quotidian architectural practice. Denuded and borne in brazen sparsity before my audience, I formulate a tangible list of architectural and practical propositions towards the lived employment of these abstract elicitations of emancipation. They are the eleven suggestions in "Towards an Ethics of Blackitecture: An Opening," following a section dedicated to a transcendental synthesis of the preceding architectonic apperception (by which Kant means self-consciousness), properly Kantianly, titled "Blackitecture."

Modern TV Achievements

Seeing as an apparatus of being in the world has changed enormously between times, eras, places, cultures. There is no singular "natural" way of seeing, or a pure, innocent, unindoctrinated use of the eye that precedes its formation as a social apparatus. The eye is always folding into the spaces of the city, folding the city into itself, making phantom absences and projecting fantasies. The police make the city a fantasy of constant crime and racialized terrorism. They turn dark alleys into the setting of a Black-mugger monologue. They redress wide thoroughfares as the quiet anticipation of a car-chase, featuring working-class-car-thief, as seen on TV.

In her landmark 1977 book *On Photography*, Susan Sontag outlines her theory of what has now become a commonplace. She writes that photography is not just an additional technology of seeing; it fundamentally changes the way that seeing is known. It entirely reforms the apparatus of sight. As Sontag says on the first page:

> This very insatiability of the photographing eye changes the terms of confinement in [Plato's] cave, our world. In teaching us a new visual code, photographs alter and enlarge our notions of what is worth looking at and what we have a right to observe. They are a grammar and, even more importantly, an ethics of seeing.[1]

Holding a camera allows the holder to be removed from the world she sees. She is no longer present; she is the holder of an external technology of sight. Her own apparatus of seeing is disguised by the technology that brings her into a different temporal union with the world: she and the object of the photograph

---

1 Susan Sontag, *On Photography* (New York: Rosetta Books, 2005), 1.

exist, then, in the same moment, but with the camera acting as a new ethics of seeing between them, they are dropped from their suspension in the ongoing contemporary. Their nowness falls through, and they are trapped in a past that only one of them remembers. Only one of them — the photographer — knew that this entrapment in the past was happening, and only one of them has access to it later on. She can see it again and again. She can repeat trapped time ad infinitum.

The object of the photograph, meanwhile, has been grasped and flattened onto a screen, forced into a time that is not its own.

The photographer wields a technology that disguises the subjective ethics of her seeing apparatus: her eye is always uncannily different to the world, unlike the object of sight — so unlike it that the *peculiar institution* of the eye is obvious in every turn, every gaze; but the technology she shields herself with disguises the violence of the eye, introducing a new ethics of seeing.

This removed act of shielding the violence of sight becomes not just an individual ethical practice, but the visual basis of national temporality, of a telos for the nation-state, on which imperial nations were able to construct resolute and irrefutable ideologies of nationhood and their own internal racial supremacy. The United States is the exemplar of this use of visual cultures to assert a political practice of racism on heterogeneous populations. Elizabeth Freeman writes in *Time Binds* that photography produces the same timescale as writing, in that it inheres in a belief in the posterity of the user: the one who is photographing or writing is able to access a form of teleological belief, assured "that there will be a future of some sort, a 'Queer Time' off the battlefield of everyday existence, in which the act of reading[/viewing] might take place somehow, somewhere."[2] This produces a national timescale that demarcates boundaries between different bodies within the nation. Those bodies who can project themselves into a self-assured future by acting *now* in order to be viewed or read, in that future, gain the temporal

---

2   Elizabeth Freeman, *Time Binds: Queer Temporalities, Queer Histories* (Durham: Duke University Press, 2010), xxiv.

coding of future-oriented bodies. They are the bodies that survive, the bodies that are able to look back on now from the future. Freeman calls this form of socially constructed time *chrononormativity*, which "is a mode of implantation, a technique by which institutional forces come to seem like somatic facts."[3] These bodies projected into the future become not just beholders of a technology of seeing: they become, instead, inherently superior because they are in themselves technologies of seeing.

This ethics of seeing that designates racialized temporalities within the nation-state is an abstract ideological apparatus. It is also a lived, material, and very deadly practice. In her astounding 2006 study *A Spectacular Secret: Lynching in American Life and Literature*, Jacqueline Goldsby traces the material and murderous reality of photography as a developing technology and its employment in the establishment of a racist state post-1865.

For Goldsby, lynching has a unique significance in the history of America because it dominates through two functions. First, it is a state-sanctioned act of racialized murder. It is used by white vigilante mobs to impose the already-given-death-penalty of Black life in America's postbellum state of free range slavery. Second, it is a visual spectacle, used by American communities to bring the whites together, cathartically watching the internal enemy swing. Lynching photography was a popular practice around the turn of the twentieth century in the USA. Photographs of lynched Black people, surrounded by crowds of celebratory whites post-feast, were distributed widely across the country. Lynching became such a crucial mark of America's development because, as Goldsby writes, it "bridges the fields of history and literary studies because it is itself an act and a sign, a literal thing and a symbolic representation to which the violence refers. […] However, […] lynching's cultural logic changes over time, and does so (in part) as forms of mediation refashion the representation of the violence."[4]

---

3 Ibid., 3.
4 Jacqueline Goldsby, *A Spectacular Secret: Lynching in American Life and Literature* (Chicago: University of Chicago Press, 2006), 42.

The conflation of sign and act is a great development in the understanding of the inherent racist visuality of America and this late modernity based on America's unethical standards. Throughout the end of the nineteenth and early twentieth century, lynching as a visual sign as well as a political act employs a technology that temporally moves the white photographing and lynching bodies into the future of spectators — they will one day look at this, meaning, implicitly, *they will exist in the future.* Meanwhile, the Black person lynched is marked as the past. However, as cinema begins to emerge — set around a very similar scene, in which festive and horny white bodies crowd around a spectacle to establish their own suspended futurity — the lynching photograph's meaning of pastness takes on a new layer; it also refers to a past that is not only the life of lynched person, but also the past of photography itself. Photography is a visual form that is static, unlike the quick-flash rate of films that make many photographs appear as a single continuous image moving into the future with its audience.

> If the promise of cinema was to make images move and through that motion to convey a sense of life, in photography the opposite was true. Making time stand still, photography promised to make memory possible by preserving that which could not keep its place in time. It is also true, though, that photography's images elude the fixity of documentary history; once taken, moments taken by still-capture pictures do not exist in the historical present. For lynching to be represented in this medium, then, made the violence easier to disavow because photography transformed it into a spectacle that would prove impossible either to ignore or to see. How could it be that photography could make lynching both appear and disappear in public?[5]

Photography, in Goldsby's study, takes on a complex ethical and ontological meaning. It is an external technology of seeing,

---
5   Ibid., 229.

merged into the white body in order to affirm a racialized and racializing temporality in which whiteness signifies futurity, posterity, while Blackness is a sign of being caught. It is not a coincidence, surely, that the verb a camera enacts on its object is *capture* — an image *captured* in its temporal space. This technology is this new ethics of observation, which creates a way of living out of the *visuality* of apparatuses. In this ontological mode, space becomes a complex layering of internal and external stimuli. Space is a real structuring force, within whose logics exist all knowable objects, and from which sensations emerge based on their relation to relative spaces. It is also a projection from the Human mind, leading lines of racialized signification out of the subject-grids with which racializing principles mark the subject: the subject of modernity sees himself as the creator of his own reality, so space is also ordered according to his own projections. Where he *looks* is where space *is*. The outer edge of the city is only its outer edge because the seeing subject who commands meaning into space is far from that edge; he is in the center — he is the center, a center which is the center because the seeing subject is (t)here.

This world-changing logic of space as both objective and subjective — both real and imagined — is the proud work of Kant.

A Very Long Engagement (to Kant)

Immanuel Kant was the philosopher who first set out a complete theory of how the mind is able to know objects in space without empirically observing space itself. Throughout European philosophy, thinkers held that there are two ways of proposing truths about the world. One is synthetic, and one is analytic. An analytic judgment only contains truths suggested by the meaning of the judgment itself, or within the statement itself. Humans are mammals, for example, is an analytic judgment because the meaning of human is contained within the meaning of mammal, so the truth of the statement is already contained within the judgment. Analytic judgments do not teach us anything about the world, because they are already true in themselves. However, a synthetic judgment relies on facts about the world that are not contained within the meaning of the judgment itself. Humans are greedy, for example, is a synthetic judgment because the meaning of human does not necessarily suggest greed, so the truth of the judgment requires knowledge of other things in the world, not just an understanding of the meaning of the statement itself. Synthetic judgments, in opposition to those that are analytic, can teach us about the world, because they contain the possibility of difference; they develop and change according to investigation.

This distinction in judgments functions alongside another distinction, which is in the way knowledge can be known. The distinction is between a priori knowledge and empirical knowledge. Empirical knowledge comes from the senses; it is something you observe in the world by hearing it, seeing it, smelling it, and so on. Scientific experiments are all empirical, for Kant, because they rely initially on the senses.

A priori knowledge, on the other hand, is known without any appeal to the senses. An a priori fact is something that is known only by the human's capacity for knowledge itself. Mathematics, according to Kant, is a priori because we *just know* that equations are correct without having to observe their truth in the world with our senses. The crucial point about a priori knowledge is that it is both *necessary* and *universal*. It is always right, everywhere, for everyone. Empirical knowledge is neither necessary nor universal because it is known by the senses, and they change according to so many factors constantly.

Kant's main three philosophical works were published over a decade, and are known as the Three Critiques: *Critique of Pure Reason*, 1781/1787; *Critique of Practical Reason*, 1788; and *Critique of Judgment*, 1790. Up until these pivotal works, it was held that these two distinctions in judgments and in knowledge always correlate. One distinction is that *synthetic judgments are always empirical* because you need to observe the world, using your senses, to be able to say whether humans are greedy or not, and it cannot simply be known by the truth of the judgment itself. The other distinction is that analytic judgments are always a priori because they are true in themselves, according to their own meaning, so they need no observation of the world or use of the senses.

The fundamental revolution in knowledge that Kant proposes is the existence of synthetic judgment a priori. That is, knowledge that relies on facts about the world that are not knowable only by the judgment itself, and yet that cannot be observed by the senses. Such a judgment, according to Kant, is geometry. The truth of the configuration of space is not contained within the judgment of space itself; it is not stuck, but rather teaches us about the world. Meanwhile, it is necessary and universal; geometrical knowledge is always true regardless of the situation.

If geometry is synthetic a priori, then space does not exist in the world but rather in the Human mind. Space is not a feature of objects; it is not contained within objects themselves. Space exists in the Human mind and is projected onto objects, and Kant says that this must be so because geometry is synthetic a priori. How would we know anything of geometry if it existed in objects and yet we know this knowledge without observing those objects?

Kant says, then, that the world and the Human mind are necessary for creating knowledge about the world. The way of accessing this knowledge is split into two fundamental cognitive powers of the Human mind: the transcendental aesthetic and transcendental logic. The transcendental aesthetic is the capacity to feel affect in response to objects, or the capacity for sensibility. The transcendental logic is the capacity for formulating concepts from particular material objects in the world, or for making categories. Kant's formulation of the transcendental, by which he means the rule according to which Humans can access objective knowledge even before perceiving any objects,[6] is one in which the mind *must* think in *categories*.

---

[6] Immanuel Kant, *Critique of Pure Reason,* trans. Paul Guyer and Allen W. Wood (Cambridge: Cambridge University Press, 1998), A12/B25. As is customary in Kantian scholarship, when citing *Critique of Pure Reason,* both

> If I take all thinking (in categories) away from an empirical cognition, then no cognition of any object at all remains; for through mere intuition nothing at all is thought, and that this affection of sensibility is within me does not constitute any relation of such representation to any object at all.[7]

For Kant, all of nature is subject to the rules of these categories, and these categories are a priori. These Kantian categories become very important when we think about how buildings as an urban apparatus of being and eyes as a Human apparatus of seeing come together to produce the social conditions of the city. Eyes and buildings are up to something. They are making racialized space. They condition the Blackness of certain zones and suspend white areas above the tangibility of risk.

This ethics of seeing is the transcendental ideality of space, in which space, and the Subject projecting it, is *ampliative*, which is also to say *synthetic*. The Subject's space grows, developing the epistemological engine or the transcendental ideality of the Subject, affirming by ampliative expansion his position as central Subject, defining what is central.

Color Quality

For Kant, space is the only "subjective representation related to something external that could be called a priori objective."[8] Space is the peculiar position of having both "empirical reality" and "transcendental ideality."[9] Space, in this way, is distinguished from other sensations given to Humans by objects. The objects that give Humans sensations are already laid out on a grid of space, and it is only by their positioning on that spatial projection that Humans can receive the sensation given to Hu-

---

the first (A) and second (B) editions will be referenced, using the cited passage's number in the German original, rather than page numbers in the cited edition.

7   Ibid., A253/B309.
8   Ibid., A28/B44.
9   Ibid.

man reception already contained within those objects. Color, revealingly, is one of the sensations contained within objects that does not ambivalently merge the borders of empirical reality and transcendental ideality.

> Colors are not objective qualities of the bodies to the intuition of which they are attached, but are also only modifications of the sense of sight, which is affected by light in a certain way. Space, on the contrary, as a condition of outer objects, necessarily belongs to their appearance or intuition.[10]

Color is then separable as a sensation from the ampliative powers of the mind that perceives color.

Color, however, for Kant is not only a neutral sensation in objects that is given to Human minds, ready for subjective interpretation and the formulation of judgments. Color also provides the condition for rational judgments, or rather judgments of the power of reason of external objects. In a later essay, Kant describes meeting a Black African man. After a description of the man's illness, he concludes, "but in short, this fellow was quite black from head to foot, a clear proof that he was stupid."[11] Color, then, is a quality of this (human?) object that gives itself to Kant's internal reason as an intuition of a category with the heading Stupid Things.

This reveals, in Kant's own theory, an element of Kant's own internal category-production machine, rather than any objective qualities about this Black man himself. His stupidity, as Kant describes the process of intuiting color and taste, is a constituent feature of Kant's ampliative logics, rather than any limitation in the man's intelligence.

---

10 Ibid., A28/B44.
11 Immanuel Kant, "Observations on the Feeling of the Beautiful and Sublime," cited in Darell Wayne Fields, *Architecture in Black: Theory, Space, and Appearance* (London: Bloomsbury, 2015), 135.

> The aim of this remark is only to prevent one from thinking of illustrating the asserted ideality of space with completely inadequate examples, since things like colors, taste, etc., are correctly considered not as qualities of things but as mere alterations of our subject, which can even be different in different people.[12]

The proposition of an object's color is immediately signaled as the Human mind senses the object within the spatial grid the mind projects. According to Kant, the grid all Human perception projects must follow the logic that it is impossible to know anything unless it is already placed on the ampliative and subjective logics of synthetic a priori space. The Human mind's sensation is then judged through the power of reason, sticking to a priori intuition that allows the Human to formulate a moral worldview. However, there is nothing in Kant that explains why these judgments do not also occur diachronically, or through time as well as across space. These judgments could also form the historical construction of a certain judgment formulated in response to certain senses, for example color.

In his 2017 response to Kant's universality of reason, *Critique of Black Reason,* Achille Mbembe presents exactly this possibility of historical judgment.

> On a phenomenological level, the term [*Nègre*/Black] first designates not a significant reality but a field — or, better yet, a coating — of nonsense and fantasies that the West (and other parts of the world) have woven, and in which it clothed people of African origin long before they were caught in the snares of capitalism as it emerged in the fifteenth and sixteenth centuries.[13]

---

12 Kant, *Critique of Pure Reason,* A29/B45.
13 Achille Mbembe, *Critique of Black Reason,* trans. Laurent Dubois (Durham: Duke University Press, 2017), 38.

Black is a semiotic designation marking a certain sensation of *nonsense* within the spatial projections of the Human mind. That nonsense, according to Kant's schema, has the effect of making the bodies to which these intuitions are attached non-human, since they do not have the internal capacity of reason (i.e., they produce sensations of nonsense; their internal reason is incoherent). As Mbembe goes on to say, "the Black Man is above all a body — gigantic and fantastic — member, organs, color, a smell, flesh, and meat, an extraordinary accumulation of sensations."[14]

The semiotic designation of Blackness as nonsense, in an incoherent antagonism with whiteness's ampliative logics of pure reason, is a revelation of the mechanisms of whiteness and white ontology more than anything else. What I am trying to uncover, to study, to chew over and masticate here in "Spaces," is the reason why white thinking requires Black nonsense to survive. Why — in my Kantian White House, my purely racializing, ampliative reason — can I not imagine the possibility of my own internal reason without it relying on its incoherent antagonism in the *nonsense* of Black (non)being. Mbembe powerfully brings forth this illusive specter of modernity's racist logics.

> From a strictly historical perspective, the word "Black" refers first and foremost to a phantasmagoria. Studies of the phantasmagoria hold interest not only for what they can tell us about those who produced it but also for what they say about the timeworn problematic of the status of appearances and their relation to reality (the reality of appearances and the appearance of reality), and about the symbolism of color.[15]

The very language of sensation requires an extractable zone to be pre-marked as a place where only profit-potential residue exists, in a form of life that is inherently and necessarily agonistic to the central designation of Life — that which is called Human

---
14 Ibid., 39.
15 Ibid., 39–40.

by virtue of being a Subject, itself by virtue of being white. This symbolism of the subjective projections of color emphasizes the phantasmagoria of the ghosts on which this production machine is built.

There are ghosts in the photographs we look at; ghosts of lynchings passed around America for the development of a visual ethics of whiteness. There are ghosts in the houses we live in; ghosts of rational constructions of subjective architectonics; ghosts of the deep foundations of individuation; ghosts of the extraction zones where nonlife is separated from a symbolic paradigm of Life. There are ghosts in the food we eat, the books we read, the people we live with in the house of the city.

The world of whiteness — which is called World — requires Black death, endlessly performed as a visual spectacle on which the modern ethics of observation is constructed, in order to exist at all. Why is the World unimaginable without the politics, architectonics, and visual spectacles of Black death?

Kantsy / Kant Sees / On the Kantian Seas / Kantxiety

The Human mind is a containing space, a space that contains the possibility of containing space; it is a repository of knowledge about the world, with which it constructs itself. By accumulating space, by bringing inside itself the knowledge of things it has spatialized, it is aggrandized; its space increases. The Kantian mind, I am trying to say, is a lot like a building. The building that orders space according to its own positioning, and that then exerts itself as the founder of space. The beautiful building *is* the completion of beauty; it *is* the reason for space, and it projects its spatial judgment onto the city surrounding it.

The building is just an idea, but it has accumulated the space of History and been built up solidly in the city, and the city is only called a city because its buildings have accumulated History. The city is the site of accumulated History. And Kant says, in the long introduction to the *Critique of Pure Reason,* something similar about his own project.

> Transcendental philosophy is here only an idea, for which the critique of pure reason is to outline the entire plan architectonically, i.e., from principles, with a full guarantee for the completeness and certainty of all the components that comprise this edifice.[16]

The edifice of his thinking, the building of his philosophy, is set in completeness.

This completeness, as he reveals much later in the book, is formed by the categories of reason. Everything that fits the categories is brought into the edifice of thought and allowed to aid its structure. Everything that does not fit is cast out because it "would render the completion of an edifice of cognitions entirely impossible."[17] These propositions and bits of knowledge that are antithetical to the construction of a solid edifice of rational thinking would break down endlessly, always coming out in smaller and smaller observations because they are not upheld in the categories; they do not fit into the tidy ordering within the edifice of thinking. They are furniture of a different style to the rooms within the building of thought. Human reason, then, seeks the assortment of proper knowledge into the set form of its categories. "Human reason is by nature architectonic."[18] It projects spatial completion onto the world by fitting all the knowledge that exists into its internal categories. "Hence the architectonic interest of reason (which is demanded not by empirical unity but by pure rational unity) carries with it a natural recommendation for the assertions of the thesis."[19]

For Kant, the mind is storing images of the world inside itself. The edifice of thought or the building of subjectivity; the Human-as-building, sees the world, projecting its spatial understanding onto objects. Having seen them according to its own architectural reason, it absorbs them into itself, into the

---

16 Kant, *Critique of Pure Reason*, A13/B27.
17 Ibid., A474/B502.
18 Ibid.
19 Ibid.

categories of its own internal reason. The building, in urban architecture, also projects its own spatial ethics onto the city, and absorbs the city into its internal form. Each building is the repository of architectural histories, of agencies developed through cultures and times, from Vitruvius or Palladio or Zaha Hadid, and a Neoclassical gallery in the center of a city imposes a certain kind of spatiality onto the city and absorbs the reflected urban ethics into its own way of seeing. In a different way, with a different ethical construction, the 10-story block of social housing projects its own eye onto the surrounding city, absorbing a different ethics. But each one is a mind holding in the sights of the city and constructing the world according to its own projection of space.

Where, in this Kantian schema, is the difference between knowing and seeing? That is what I want to know. Is there a difference between the architectonics of the mind and architecture itself? What I want to know is how this differs from the geography of Empire. John Ruskin, the infamous imperial architectural critic of the nineteenth century, was adamant that English colonizers had to build Gothic civic buildings in India in order to architecturally establish English superiority. However, that was not enough. That is still only one building; particular knowledge, manifest singularly. The rebellious Indian subject of Empire can still turn her back on the building and no longer see it.[20]

Instead, the very concept of the city must be imposed universally to achieve global imperial domination. The aesthetic category of knowledge that is the modern city must be stamped onto every ground, every geographical logic, until every space is marked as either civilized/white or defined solely by its lack of epistemological and ontological conformance with the universal system of knowledge that is the city.

---

20 For a history of English imperial architecture in India, see Ian Baucom, *Out of Place: Englishness, Empire, and the Locations of Identity* (Princeton: Princeton University Press, 1999), chap. 2, "English to the Backbone," 75–100.

City, I say to Kant, *is* Man, and reason is the universal application of the World onto earth — of the European capitalist logics of land onto otherwise spaces. Man, I say to Kant, is the urban eye; he is the visual police of a category of knowledge called "the city."

Taking on the thinking of Susan Sontag, Elizabeth Freeman, and Jacqueline Goldsby, I want to ask: What if the necessary condition of the city is the human's impossible pursuit of being suspended above it? What if all the city means is the space created by Man's attempt to rise out of his own habitat? What if the city is the space created by Man's impossible attempt at self-removal? That would mean that if Kantian modern Man ever achieved this suspension above the city, the city would no longer exist. It only exists in relation to modern capitalist Man's impossible attempt at escape.

Maybe, then, the way we see and know the city is premised on our attempt to separate ourselves from it. The city only really exists, as a conceptual totality, in response to Man's self-removal that never works. Man never gets away, necessarily, or Man would no longer be.

The Aggressive Justification of an Orbital Object Called Elliot C. Mason

Some academics have noted surprise at the suggestion that race and architecture exert a mutual force, an oppression in tandem. Their surprise adds vigor to my presumptions, and I try to give these philosophical/architectural bullet points a more scientific language. Pump up the haunting figures of philosophy with the gravitational pull of scientific sounding words and people tend to believe you more. I say that architecture and race are connected by a law of motion, a timeframe of the universe that Kant sent up in unknowing collaboration with Darwin. They are joined by a gravitational force directed along the lines of divergent objects who know each other only as objects in mutual suspension between each other. They know each other only as objects that are necessarily external, and necessarily in each other's orbit.

The academics nod and then see if it's time for the pub, which in the academy is at about four o'clock because it's permanently winter, our friendships and battles parted by six-month summers in isolation at cheap hotels near conference venues.

My stepdad, though, shakes his head and pulls the pint from his mouth. Eagerness to drink is yanked from beneath the solid customs of an Englishman, and he puts the beer down. "Architecture and race? No way. No connection."

That's that then.

A friend who works in marketing asks me why the subject I dedicate myself to is called "Black Studies." It sounds exclusionary — *racist*, even. Sounds like it's only for Black people. And I'm white, for fuck's sake.

A Black friend says to me: it seems offensive that I would look for her in buildings. Look for *you*? Yes, look for *me* and *my Black body* in buildings.

I don't know what I'm being accused of so I change the subject.

Yes, we have both seen that program and we like it.

She changes the subject again.

Eugenia, who is a psychotherapist, confronts me with my internal causes. Why am I studying Black architecture or whatever it is that I study?

The scenes between these lapses in my project crumble at the edges of my thinking city, and all I remember is what no one believes. I rage against their beliefs and I wander like an Ancient Greek around London, pointing out to myself the racial signifiers of buildings and public spaces, secretly privatized.

I have to represent this project to myself, as the achievement of my ego, because I'm a dirty neoliberal millennial who wants to be followed by far more people than I've ever met. I have to be the speaker of this theory, the body beholding the command to action. The precarious fragility of my ego is impossible to dodge in the presentation of this aggressive book, so I pretend I can't hear anyone and dress up in the ideology of my enemies: *bootstraps up, get on with it, number one knows best.*

Meanwhile I have to disguise my responsibility for what I say. I have to pretend it's not my fault if it all goes wrong. If I have to self publish — after stern dismissals from authorities that always begin emails with "Dear Mr. Mason" like it's the nineteenth century — then I'll do it under a foreign name, so no one suspects me. *Got published by Linn Tse Marañón. A very interesting publisher. No online presence so don't bother searching. Where's she from? Oh, erm, all over. A bit Finnish. Some Korean. And an Argentine uncle or something.* If it never gets published then I'll pretend I never wrote it. *That book? Ha-ha. Got you! Can't believe you believed that…*

There must be jobs in offices somewhere. People do that when they're not writing about race and architecture.

Just before four o'clock, when the philosophers sit on tiny stools with all the fur rubbed off from years of shifty arses, I take a long walk and end up in Westfield Stratford. Its wide open spaces, its imposing whiteness. There are police on the bridge between the station and the shopping center with a strange machine in their hands, tracking something. I don't know what part of me they are analyzing so I just continue. Nothing happens. They are clearly seeking subjects racialized in other ways by the surveilling power of the imperial police eye, and I am of no interest to them except as another example to be later used in court about how "normal people" go about their business.

Some people love Westfield and some people hate Westfield. People buy what they either love or hate. So I decide to write "Spaces" loosely around the shape of Westfield. As long as people are not indifferent, they won't question me. They'll just fume their hatred or their love, and it'll be nothing to do with me. I will ease myself out the door while they're arguing. Rile up the readers and they'll support me.

I had enough of a battle sitting through the rest of the pint after my stepdad's incredulous dismissal of whatever I do with my life. *But what the hell is Philosophy anyway? Didn't that end in like 1700 or something? Why don't you get a proper job?* I don't want to go through it all again on a national scale, prodded by LBC radio hosts about being a "race nut" or hearing reports of

Dominic Cummings dipping an effigy of me in petrol and doing whatever the Cummings' equivalent of laughter is, which presumably involves the same permanent suspension of expression as all his other feelings.

My stepdad will never read this book, but my ego frantically retaliates anyway by writing an aggressively self-justifying chapter that weaves Westfield into Kantian discourses and the philosophy of shopping centers. We won't even mention "the book" when it's time for another pint together, next Christmas.

What Does Space Say?

Benjamin H. Bratton writes that the structure of sight falls from buildings, from urban structures, and inspires the body's mimesis. The body takes on the structure of the building, performing its way of seeing, as if seen from a third position that is neither the building nor the body. The third position is the overseer of this scene, conducting relations between the building and the body. The structure writes into the body the laws of structure. The body mimes these laws and dictates them again to the structure. The third position oversees this binary command that screams one way and the other and each becomes a representative of universal structure.

"In essence," Bratton writes, "that structure is already dissimulation, as architecture endures its career as a metaphor for bodily form, as a prosthetic life-world or self-image, as a foundational referent for structure per se, as an original solid from which deviations might be developed."[21] The building and the inhabitant of buildings make the category of seeing together. In unison they achieve the geometrical act of sight, and they make it universal as the urban building claims to have achieved not only itself, but also the city, the life of the city: the individual/universal Human.

---

21 Benjamin H. Bratton, *Dispute Plan to Prevent Future Luxury Construction* (Berlin: Sternberg Press, 2015), 80.

Something brings together the apparatuses of seeing that unify in Kantian reason. Something acts as a binding agent that abolishes the sameness of buildings and bodies. That something is a kind of technology that allows these apparatuses to seem different, but to have a single pursuit together.

Why do we not all know that buildings and bodies create each other? What is stopping our knowledge of the fact that the city is just a remnant of Man's attempts at escape? What stops us from seeing buildings and bodies historically united?

The technology, what I call capital-A Architecture, is, a unifying agent of the categories of reason, that makes the city and the body that tries to escape it, and the process of mutual creation undertaken in that constant and constantly failed escape.

Architecture is a geometrical form, ready to be pasted over maps on which the World is now written, at the beginning of the modern city. Architecture allows the Empire of infinite expansion and accumulation to mark itself as the only knowledge that is allowed in the World. Divergence from Architecture's geometry equals divergence from reason, and that equals divergence from Man: to have no Architecture is to be *deformed*; to be *unhuman*. To inhabit a space that does not consist in the performance of bodies and buildings making each other is to be an empty space, a darkness in the bursting lights of the city of Man.

The New Columbus

Of the many new origin stories circling the galaxy of America, maybe the strongest orbital pull is enforced by the World's Columbian Exposition. The Exposition was a huge architectural fair, held in Chicago in 1893. It was organized by architect Daniel Burnham and revolved around the classical European aesthetics he had learned from his time studying at the École des Beaux-Arts in Paris.

The Columbian Exposition defined nineteenth century architecture, employing 10,000 people, welcoming 150,000 attendees per day and bringing together the world's top architects. It was set up to celebrate the 400th anniversary of Christopher Columbus's colonization of Turtle Island — or, in the polite euphemism used for the exposition, his *arrival in the New World.* The architectural fair was nicknamed "the white City"[22] because of the abundant Neoclassical buildings on display, all white, smooth, and clean, attending to the imperial aesthetics of Europe that sought the establishment of a racializing ethics of whiteness.

At the ideological and architectural center of the Exposition was the Court of Honor. The Court was an axis of Renaissance and Classical buildings, all white and rising out of a lake with fountains spraying into it. Here was the architectural court of reason, the unity of judgments and perceptions, the bringing-together of thinking and feeling as a pure aesthetic conditioned on the permanence of juridical, imperial reason. It was a court; an institution of the laws of Empire. And its code was the exemplary unity of whiteness, its cleanliness and its purity. No previous structure had so perfectly revealed the mutual construction of modern architecture and imperial reason. Kant's rational Subject and Louis Sullivan's *System of Architectural Ornament According with a Philosophy of Man's Powers* are here brought together in ideal unison, revealing how they always made each other. Man as the reason of Empire, and Architecture as the physical environment of Man.

At the Exposition, Modernist architecture was crawling into the white coat of scientific modernity, claiming to have achieved the higher secular principles of purity, shaking off the excess of spiritualism and belief in anything but profit. The highest abstraction, the purest eschatology: free exchange was the only belief of the Exposition and of Science.

While architecturally the Exposition was unique in its American dedication to imperial predecessors, the dedication to Empire and capitalism had occurred before, as well as the attempt by a capitalist power to assert global dominance.

In the sixteenth century, and fifty years or so either side of it, the Republic of Genoa, in what is now northern Italy, was the

---

22 Kenneth Frampton, *Modern Architecture: A Critical History* (London: Thames and Hudson, 2018), 56.

apex of a new capitalist class. Northern Italy was where Shakespeare set Othello and its noble cast of characters, as well as *Romeo and Juliette*, *The Merchant of Venice*, *The Taming of the Shrew*, and *The Two Gentlemen of Verona*. It was the hub of a new capitalist force, and the burgeoning society of new nobles was looking to the Republic of Genoa for its social codes.

Niccolò Machiavelli's *The Prince* focuses on the strange emergence of the "new prince," the ruler who did not inherit power. That is, *the capitalist*. This new capitalist prince must maintain not only power itself, and the population's conformance with the borders of power, but also justify *why* this new prince is in power. Since it is no longer inherited, anyone could supposedly be in power. A new pathology of justification is begun, and "the ends justify the means" is the maxim that rules this new obsession.[23]

In the seventeenth century the Netherlands took over as the trend-setter of capitalism, beginning the mass market of overseas trade. The British cycle of capitalism followed with the rise of industrial production and the global expansion of Empire. Then, as Britain's capitalist supremacy began to show signs of waning towards the turn of the twentieth century, the United States of America had begun its rise to universal domination.

Giovanni Arrighi, who wrote the classic text *The Long Twentieth Century* on the cycles of capitalism's history, sets the beginning of America's global domain as 1860.[24] The Columbian Exposition, one generation into this new expansive throne, was the firm establishment of America presenting itself *as World*. To affirm the continued nature of this new global center, an origin story was required. There was, of course, the great origin story of Columbus, to which the 1893 Exposition was in honor. The narrative pivoted on this curious gentlemen Christopher Columbus, born exactly where and when Arrighi says capitalism began: the Republic of Genoa, in 1451.

---

23 For more, see Niccolò Machiavelli, *The Prince* (New York: Dover Publications, 2000).

24 Giovanni Arrighi, *The Long Twentieth Century: Money, Power, and the Origins of Our Times* (London: Verso, 1994), 364.

Humbly, he sought new knowledge, but no one would give him access to it. Like the horny schoolboy in every Hollywood blockbuster, he went around prodding the hot girls/European monarchies and they laughed at him. *I'll show you,* he said like the schoolboy. He put posters of maps up in his room. His mum told him to take them down because the Blu Tack will stain the wall. His older brother laughed at him for not having posters of girls in bikinis.

He stuck to his *guns* anyway, and then *he showed 'em.* He sailed, all on his own with no crew at all, battling nature in individual supremacy, a true American hero, riding the waves as the schoolboy drives across the country, stopping at occasional motels to have sex with the receptionist who has incredibly huge breasts. She asks, every time, why he's so mysterious and beautiful and what wounded him because she can see that he is hurting but he keeps it all inside, under that beautiful mustache. He grunts. Says she wouldn't understand. Then zips up his flies and drives away, sails to the Americas.

The architects of the Columbian Exposition attempted to begin a new origin story, and that was Chicago, the white City itself. To have a good origin story, a divine act needs to immediately precede it. An act of erasure needs to clear away whatever was there before. God begins the world by flooding it, killing everyone and everything, except a few chosen heroes who become the origin narrative of a new time.

For the white City, that erasure of the past was the Great Chicago Fire of 1871, which burned for three days in October, covering almost nine square kilometers and bringing down 17,500 buildings. That was followed by the necessary divine test, in which the God of Empire and Capital sends a challenge that confirms the population's dedication. For America's new origin story, this came as the Panic of 1893 (after the Panic of 1873), an economic depression that caused huge losses to most Americans.

The scene had been cleared. All the previous characters were washed away and a new hero could emerge. The hero was Architecture and came in two styles: high, and white.

America had been cleared for a new story, a story led by the rules of Machiavelli's new prince: any ends are justified by any means. The new prince decides the ends, and he does whatever he wants to get them.

To make an entirely new narrative, a new origin for the global distribution and circulation of one particular form of money; *American* money, the story cannot simply be told *over* nature. It cannot be an addition to the world. It cannot maintain the foundations of something before it. God had to abolish everything in order to make Noah the origin.

When Christopher Columbus sets out to sea from Seville, as Sylvia Wynter writes in her essay "1492: A New World View," he does not ride the waves of existing forms of thought that have structured the geographic reason of Europe.[25] Up to that point, there had been two global zones: one was *temperate,* a habitable and warm place where *people* lived, and the other was *torrid,* an uninhabitable, extreme, and primordial inferno where, if anyone lived there at all, only *barbarians* could survive.

Arriving in the land later called the Americas, though, Columbus discovered that these lands were, evidently, inhabitable, since his ship was greeted by people. As Miguel León-Portilla has shown, Columbus and his sailors were impressed by the complex and well-functioning society in Central America.[26] This was, undeniably for Columbus, the *torrid* zone, and yet here life thrived. In the rationality of his contemporary, it was impossible that this land even existed. The earth was balanced by weights and measurements that kept the seas and lands in check. This area, "the nonexistent antipodes of the Western Hemisphere," as Wynter says,[27] should have been under water as far as Columbus understood. However, it was precisely his ability to believe contradictory theories, to convince himself of

---

25 Sylvia Wynter, "1492: A New World View," in *Race, Discourse and the Origin of the Americas: A New World View,* eds. Vera Lawrence Hyatt and Rex M. Nettleford (Washington, DC: Smithsonian Books, 1994), 5–57.
26 Miguel León-Portilla, cited in ibid., 14–15.
27 Ibid., 19.

the existence of this impossible land and the inferiority of these equal people, that made his project so successful.

Columbus rooted his thinking, symbolically, in the ocean. The oceanic movement was the condition for the undermining of his adherence to Christian ideology. He believed the Second Coming of Christ was imminent, and preparations had to be made. Strange things were happening in the waters. No synthesis could come of this. European thought had been anchored in a sea far beyond its own capacities of reason, and the hysterical waiting for the Lord allowed the expansion of Europe's second great religious principle — profit — at any cost and any amount of twisted ideologies.

Columbus's first imperial mission — necessarily, if not explicitly acknowledged — was to initiate a global idea of time. All of life had to be encapsulated into one progressive idea of a kind of time that gradually improved things in unequal measures. Some were more advanced than others, but everyone was on an ideal trajectory to advancement. Europe, it goes without saying, was written as the forefront of this advancement — European capitalist modernity and its Empire.

It was René Descartes who, in philosophy, began the consignment of Europe to the time that is, after John McTaggart, in physics called "A series time."[28] A series is the three-part configuration of time we know from the narratives of European modernity. Past, present, future, and time as a flow from beginning to end. This idea of time as an orderly movement, as Michelle M. Wright says, is "at least deeply problematic [...] and at the most illusory, a trick of the mind because experiments in particle physics seem to indicate that time does not flow and, therefore, tenses of time exist only in the linguistic and psychological register, not the physical world."[29] Or as the contemporary scholar

---

[28] John McTaggart, "The Unreality of Time", *Mind* 17, no. 68 (1908), 457–74.

[29] Michelle M. Wright, "Black in Time: Exploring New Ontologies, New Dimensions, New Epistemologies of the African Diaspora," in *Transforming Anthropology* 18, no. 1 (2010): 70–73, cited in Fred Moten, *Stolen Life* (Durham: Duke University Press, 2018), 205.

Ian Baucom writes in his book *Specters of the Atlantic,* time does not flow; it accumulates.[30]

Hegel places Africa in a stagnant zone where time does not pass.[31] Columbus, however, before Descartes and way before Hegel, had already demarcated the geographic zone of this linear time-flow. At the borders of the ocean, where land rises and the laws of property are in order, time flows according to what, a century and a half after Columbus, would become Cartesian law. That is, in Columbus's new world configuration, time flows according to the expansion of land. The past becomes the present as Europe arrives there. The European way of seeing illuminates the darkness of the barbaric past, and, with the united humanism of expansion, together they become the future. All is united into Europe's singular way of seeing.

The ideal narrative that colonization tells is that this flow of time and space is conducted equally, by the newly designated global human race, with Europeans and Indigenes cooperating to expand the proper logic of land laws, and turning all being into a form of property, properly abstracted like capital and its global flow. Time, capital, and land are all held at a distance that makes them look the same. The reality, of course, is nothing like the narrative. Indigenous cession of all their lands and subsumption within the laws of Europe is the condition for this progressive flow of spacetime.

These ideas were not presented as a thesis and antithesis, working together through reasoned and equal debate to reach a synthesis, which is the process of dialectics. This was the hyper-expansion of a European imperial command that subsumed everything into itself. It was not a thesis, but a command, the first command that begins the world, in a reenactment of Genesis. *In the beginning Columbus created the Empire and the racial-*

---

30 Ian Baucom, *Specters of the Atlantic: Finance Capital, Slavery, and the Philosophy of History* (Durham: Duke University Press, 2005).

31 G.W.F. Hegel, *The Philosophy of History,* trans. J. Sibree (Kitchener: Batoche Books, 2001). See also Ronald Kuykendall, "Hegel and Africa: An Evaluation of the Treatment of Africa in The Philosophy of History," *Journal of Black Studies* 23, no. 4 (June 1993): 571–81.

ized body. Now the body and land was formed and void, darkness was over the surface of the skin, and the Empire of Columbus was hovering over the waters.

Columbus said, "Let there be gold," and there was gold. Columbus saw that the gold was good, and he separated the gold from the darkness. Columbus called the gold "profit," and the darkness he called "slave." And there was murder, but there was not mourning—the first day.

The dialectical thinking that attempted to tie the bows of history and keep it all together only worked in the European rationality of geography, when land followed the codes of Christianity. Everything was justified by the geographic beliefs of early modernity. But the ocean stamped into modernity's emerging foundations a pathology that was called Blackness. The entire contents of the Americas was labelled as a pathology of Blackness. Those barbarians live in the torrid, uninhabitable nonland, but this binary signifier did not apply only to the ground on which people were born. Columbus's innovation was precisely to form an ontological coding from this geographical limit. Those who lived in the torrid land lived in torrid bodies, and their subjectivity was pathological because it survived its torrid cage. As Sylvia Wynter points out, this geographical narrative of race fit neatly over the now necessarily abolished pre-colonial system of torrid and temperate zones.[32] Previously, barbarians were those in the uninhabitable torrid areas, while civilization was life inside the idyll of temperate geography. Race was the category of a new kind of subjectivity and representation that signified an internal torrid zone. All of Earth post-Columbus was inhabitable and profitable. All land could be appropriated for use. The torrid zones continued, though, in the bodies of the newly racialized populations, who had now been geographically categorized as Natives and Africans.

Africa became a homogeneous mass of labor power, and Indigenous Americans allegorically became a unified group of ra-

---

32   Wynter, "1492," 19–20.

cialized semi-life, stuck in over-heated bodies, subject to the hot furies of a time before modernity.

Blackness is not the antithesis of modernity, and European capitalist modernity is not the thesis. It is the abusive command, the first blow of the prison guard's whistle, the click of a loading gun. The suspension of dialectical thinking is enacted as Blackness is marked in the ocean, which becomes *the Ocean* after Columbus, in his naming project as "Don and High Admirable of the Ocean Sea."[33] Blackness washes over the shores of Africa, over the skin of Africans, as it splashes at the bow of slave ships. Dialectical history was cut when Columbus barged the geographical rationality of whiteness into modernity's commanding orthodoxies.

The same process of reinventing nature in order to establish a new origin was attempted through the Columbian Exposition. The Exposition was designed by Daniel Burnham, who wanted to make is as Neoclassical as possible, exerting a fully European aesthetic onto the lake-front of Chicago. However, two of the most influential architects in Chicago at the time — Dankmar Adler and Louis Sullivan — argued that the Exposition should introduce an autochthonous American vernacular, a style that can unite Americans *as* Americans.

At the same time, another protest was being mounted against the Exposition and a different facet of its whiteness — that is, its whiteness. Frederick Douglass, Ida B. Wells, and other renowned abolitionists and writers composed a pamphlet denouncing the racist exclusion of American Blacks from the World's Fair, entitled *The Reason Why the Colored American is not in the World's Columbian Exposition: The Afro-American's Contribution to Columbian Literature,* which could be purchased for three cents directly from Wells, at her Chicago address.

The writers' contentions against the Exposition were numerous. The foremost, and most general, criticism is given by Wells in her preface. The legacy of Black Americans, she writes, is so

---

33 Christopher Columbus, *The Four Voyages* (London: Penguin, 1969), 38.

great that any representation of the USA without Black contribution, and a display of Black life, is necessarily untruthful. The World's Exposition, however, banned the involvement of Black Americans, and removed any sign of their presence, leaving visitors inevitably to ask, as Wells writes, "Why are not the colored people, who constitute so large an element of the American population, and who have contributed so large a share to American greatness, more visibly present and better represented in this World's Exposition?" She continues:

> The exhibit of the progress made by a race in 25 years of freedom as against 250 years of slavery, would have been the greatest tribute to the greatness and progressiveness of American institutions which could have been shown the world. The colored people of this great Republic number eight millions — more than one-tenth the whole population of the United States. They were among the earliest settlers of this continent, landing at Jamestown, Virginia in 1619 in a slave ship, before the Puritans, who landed at Plymouth in 1620. They have contributed a large share to American prosperity and civilization. The labor of one-half of this country has always been, and is still being done by them. The first crédit this country had in its commerce with foreign nations was created by productions resulting from their labor. The wealth created by their industry has afforded to the white people of this country the leisure essential to their great progress in education, art, science, industry and invention.[34]

It is not only that Black Americans have contributed greatly to the sum of what the USA is, but rather, more radically, that the luxury that allows white Americans to even consider the possibility of establishing an event celebrating the USA in which Black

---

34 Ida B. Wells et al., *The Reason Why the Colored American Is Not in the World's Columbian Exposition: The Afro-American's Contribution to Columbian Literature*, ed. Robert W. Rydell (Urbana: University of Illinois Press, 1999), 4–5.

Americans are not only not present but also forcibly absented, is precisely the luxury that has been constructed for them *by* Black Americans and their long history of enslavement. The privilege of being white inheres in not having to question why the Fair is exclusively white.

This logic of race is still very present in the US imaginary. As Moten says after a lecture, he is saddened by the fact that he is unable to read the scientific philosophy of Daniel Dennett, since Moten — in the requirements of his contractual obligation to New York University and its hefty workload, on top of being a father and everything else he is and does — simply cannot have enough time to read and know everything. However, what saddens and infuriates him even more is that Daniel Dennett, a white philosopher, does not even *think* he needs to read Frederick Douglass; he is blissfully unaware that there is any knowledge outside of his own tradition, which, in the codings of US epistemology, means his white tradition.[35]

Another contention of the writers of the 1893 pamphlet is the particular policies of the Exposition's management, such as the disqualification of any "colored man [from being] employed on the force of the Columbian Guards," leading contributor F.L. Barnett to conclude: "Theoretically open to all Americans, the Exposition practically is, literally and figuratively, a 'white City,' in the building of which the Colored American was allowed no helping hand, and in its glorious success he has no share."[36]

Barnett's and Wells's contributions to the pamphlet focus on the contemporary conditions of exclusion that were rendered into every space of both the American landscape and the American mind. Wells's is particularly concerned with the laws and national legislation that establish the permanent operation of

---

35 Fred Moten, "Manic Depression: A Poetics of Hesitant Sociology," 2017 Northrop Frye Professor Lecture, University of Toronto, April 4, 2017, available at https://www.youtube.com/watch?v=gQ2kodsmIJE&t=2794s.

36 Wells et al., *The Reason Why the Colored American Is Not in the World's Columbian Exposition*, 70.

racism throughout the USA, with many of her key points as true today as when she wrote them.[37]

Douglass's contribution, on the other hand, resolutely focuses on the past that allowed the conditions for white Americans to accept without question the fact of a fair celebrating their nation in the forced absence of Blackness. "What I have aimed to do, has not only been to show the moral depths, darkness, and destitution from which we are still emerging, but to explain the grounds of the prejudice, hate, and contempt in which we are still held by the people, who for more than two hundred years doomed us to this cruel and degrading condition. So when it is asked why we are excluded from the World's Columbian Exposition, the answer is Slavery."[38]

Neither Douglass and Well's protests concerning the constituting racism of the Exposition nor Adler and Sullivan's vernacular distain for Neoclassical white succeeded in convincing Burnham. The Exposition was built in the most rigorously Beaux-Arts style (except, as I write below, Sullivan's own contribution), entirely in white, and solely for the enjoyment of white people.

This style was taught at the École des Beaux-Arts in Paris throughout the nineteenth century. The teachings favored French Neoclassical architecture, but with now very recognizable adaptions. The Beaux-Arts style moved away from Classical materials in its Neoclassical design, making public buildings in a Roman style out of iron and glass. Also, elements of Gothic and Renaissance architecture were merged with the regular geometries of Classicism.

Both Burnham and Sullivan had studied at the Beaux-Arts school in Paris. Having returned to America, Sullivan took on a more American style, seeking architectural independence for

---

[37] In Chapter II, "Class Legislation," for example, Wells denounces the system of Electoral College votes that favors the states most heavily invested in slavery, a system that continues in the twenty-first century.

[38] Wells et al., *The Reason Why the Colored American Is Not in the World's Columbian Exposition*, 10.

the emerging Empire of American capitalism, while Burnham kept a closer dedication to the doctrine of Beaux-Arts.

The architect who implemented the autochthonous regime of America and its aesthetic separatism was one of Sullivan's students and worked between 1888 and 1893 in his firm. His name was Frank Lloyd Wright.

It was in 1893 that Wright set up his own architectural firm in the suburbs of Chicago. The following year Burnham became impressed with his work and offered to fund the twenty-seven-year-old Wright to study at the École des Beaux-Arts for four years, and then spend two years in Rome, but Wright refused. He had to stay American, in America.

This was the new prince; the hero of America's origin story as Empire of World. This was the new Columbus.

The end of this new American origin was always to bring together the aesthetic signs of height and light. The highest was the best, and the lightest was the best, and both were America. The skyscraper and Chicagoan Neoclassicism had to come together as a single autochthonous project that established the supremacy of the USA, as God's chosen land that emerged from the diluvian fire of 1871, pushed through the Father's divine test of 1893, and redeemed itself forever when the Holy Son Frank Lloyd Wright — miraculous son of no earthly architectural school — turned the white body into a building and a building into America.

The way Sullivan had tried and, ultimately, failed to do this was by interpreting height and light simply. He thought that the higher and the lighter a building grew, the better it necessarily became. He was famous for building skyscrapers. Steel was his metallurgic patron saint.

However, there was a profound aporia within highness that especially concerned American life. Highness was full of problems. For one thing, being a republic, rejecting the monarchical empires of Europe, was a crucially constituent part of the new American urban ethics. They were *independent, free, going solo.* They had no king or queen. Henry Ford was the new prince of America, not some feckless dandy born with a crown and painted for a palace wall every half hour.

Highness carried suggestions of monarchy, of a vertical structure of power that led from the proletarian mass to the dukes and all those intermediary titles and then to princes and princesses and kings and queens. America had to assert a new kind of superiority, not the European highness of the crown.

Another problem was the distance of living high up in a skyscraper. The blackness of distance, the disconnect from tangible power, the centrality in an urban surround; these were all anathema to what America wanted to define as its clean, smooth, and totally white new urban ethics.

After formal emancipation and the institution of Jim Crow laws, Black people began to move from the largely agrarian South to the more industrial North. White Northerners accordingly, in a landscape framed by racism, sought ways of moving themselves away from the Black people arriving in the industrial cities. Being high up in a tower as a mark of white success was not really enough separation. For one thing, from the top of a tower the people below look *dark,* and if they look up at the tower, the inhabitant also looks *dark.* Since the purpose of these architectural pursuits was the maintenance of America's foundational white supremacy, it was unfeasible for America's racist architecture that the privileged inhabitant of the top of the tower appeared to be Black from a distance.

Furthermore, the industrial cities were polluted, busy, and dirty, and the new urban ethics of whiteness were premised precisely on white cleanliness, *against* the dirt of industry, so white flight was already in preparation as a desire.

The steel skyscraper could not so simply help the racist architectural endeavors of the New American Empire. Neither could the World's Columbian Exposition. Both of them attempted to fit a previous nature. They accepted that there was something called "nature" that preceded their own architectures: that was their fatal flaw. Never could America truly exert a new origin story, a new principle of the built environment based on white supremacy and a global Empire of capital, if it accepted any previous nature.

Frank Lloyd Wright's architectural reinvention of nature is the most innovative because it was not based on any previous notion of nature. Wright did not try to build according to any natural principles, or to construct mimeses of natural or historical forms like those tiresomely predictable boat-like or wave-shaped buildings that architects in the blissful absence of imagination build whenever water is anywhere near. Instead, Wright built his own nature. His architecture assumed the form of modern American nature.

Wright gave a fittingly expansive American name to this new hybrid of mythical contributors called Nature and America. He called it the "Prairie Style." The style was moving outwards, rolling into American life and toppling any difference that lay in its way.

Wright's tutor, Sullivan, had been looking for such a style, a way of asserting absolute Americanness, away from the trite white European nostalgia of the Beaux-Arts style. He designed the only building in the white City Exposition that was not white. His Transportation Building was multi-colored and heavily ornamented, attempting to initiate a new civilization that arose to a hybrid unity of nature and structure, with ornament complementing the fundamental simplicity of form. It was also the only building applauded in architectural circles outside of America. But still, the American public, as Kenneth Frampton writes, "preferred the gratifying distractions of an imported Baroque, the 'white-City', East-Coast emblems of imperialistic fulfillment that were so seductively presented to them in Daniel Burnham's Columbian [Exposition] of 1893."[39]

Sullivan had argued with Burnham about this use of color and ornament. Sullivan thought that the fair was holding American architecture back by half a century, throwing it into early industrial Europe rather than letting it really free itself as America, as the American ideal of white freedom. After the international

---

39 Frampton, *Modern Architecture*, 56.

recognition for his Exposition building, though, Sullivan's architecture firm with Dankmar Adler collapsed, as did most things during the Panic of 1893. The economic depression caused massive losses, forcing even very well-paid architects to close.

However, Wright, like Columbus before him, was the object of no social flows of capital. Instead, he marched into unmarked territories, killed everyone there and claimed this freshly emptied World as his own. In the year of depression, and the year in which he did not take part in the most enormous architectural celebration in American history, Wright seemed to do the opposite of what everyone else was doing. He *set up* a new firm, rather than closing, and began a new architectural style. And it was very successful. As Charles L. Davis writes in his book about the racial politics of Modernist architectural style, "By the interwar and postwar periods the Prairie Style had proliferated beyond the geographical confines of the prairie, which transformed this regional style into a national sign for modern domestic life."[40]

The Prairie Style was formulated in retaliation to the European Classicism of the Columbian Exposition, and the Orientalized, Baroque ornament of Sullivan's cast-iron swirls and semi-circular arches. The Prairie Style, while never mimetic of nature, was built in the affect of the Midwestern prairie: long, flat, pastel-shaded and, most importantly, *American*.

It was a style explicitly organized to be *indigenous,* to be *native* to American aesthetics; the point was to begin a style that would, in turn, *begin America.*

The implicit suggestion, of course, was that America had no beginning before this moment. Wright and his Prairie School practitioners rejected both the Native American Indigenous origin and the imperial origin of Columbus. They wanted explicitly to free themselves from European influences and the Orientalism of European styles at the time, and, implicitly, to reject the notion that an autochthonous, native American style could be formulated in collaboration with actual Native Americans. In-

---

40 Charles L. Davis II, *Building Character: The Racial Politics of Modern Architectural Style* (Pittsburgh: University of Pittsburgh Press, 2019), 5.

stead, the style was for, of, and by the suburban bourgeoisie. It was for the economic and cultural elite on the outskirts of the city; for the families with huge plots of land marking their difference from the dense living of the inner-city.

This spatio-social mechanism racialized the inner-city as a dark and dangerous void within the new American nature that is the wide prairie, the open space, and the Wrightean house with its horizontal expansion. Nature has been folded into the outwards movements of the house. The domestic and always white dream of detached homeownership with a big plot of land assumes the form of nature, as any residual Indigenous notions of nature are subsumed in the totality of property logics. Everything has to be *owned* or it doesn't exist.

A notable feature of the houses designed by Frank Lloyd Wright, in opposition to the vertical structures of Sullivan and Adler and other early skyscraper architects, is that they expand horizontally. They move, like Columbus, outwards, away from the mass and the normative center of thinking. They define the mass, the horde, the inner circle as a homogeneous system of stagnant conformity by moving away from it, by highlighting the perseverance of the *individual hero* who seeks something else.

The narrative is never focused on the collective, on the group in the inner-city, in the place where things happen. Europe is the inner-city for America as Wright seeks a white Nativity for his country. Then the Black housing project becomes the inner-city for America as the Prairie Style seeks to assert the absolute superiority of open domestic expanses as safety and freedom, against the danger and darkness of the group. The focus for this New American Empire is always on the fleeing individual, who always flees to more oppression, remaining adamantly within the orbit of what created him (and he is always male!), rather than disappearing like a fugitive. This is the hero who runs in order to define the group that stayed as stagnant. This is the hero exemplified in the motto of the USA: *e pluribus unum* — out of many, one. It refers not just to nations, to the one American nation emerging from the left-behind world, but the *one* American hero, too.

The American hero, from Robert Frost's "The Road Not Taken" to Bruce Willis's thousand variations on the exact same white-man-hero-gun-escape-shoot drama scene, is always a lone rogue. He is troubled and burdened by an oppressive past, but he escapes from it by thinking differently, on his own. He does not speak about his problems. His gun speaks for him. And sometimes his dick.

The American Hero, eponymous murder-machine of the American Dream, is a lone wolf, braving it in the Badlands against the barbaric natives, shooting them up wherever then drinking that peculiarly American weak beer and driving someplace else in an automatic car because it's difficult to manage gears when you're holding a gun.

This architectural history of the USA is not an independent spatial development, occurring as an esoteric conversation among architects and urban designers. What I am trying to study throughout this book is the long historical interplay of architecture and philosophy, how a dominant society's presiding understanding of subjectivity and the self informs and constitutes the possibility of enacting self-understanding as the physical foundation of social space.

Kant never built anything, never traveled very far or saw much. Hegel was uninterested in practicing the arts and architectures he wrote about. By studying these monumental leaps in the violent constitution of an expansive, transcendental self with the manifold criticism that Black Studies opens, an understanding of thinking as space, of philosophy as architectural opening, can provide the groundwork for abolishing the racializing function of the city. In the final subsection of this chapter, I attempt to pursue reflections of the architectural history I study above to in the theory and philosophy that dialectically grounds the physical form of the city in the human understanding of ourselves.

The mirror stage in Lacanian psychoanalysis is the moment in which a baby recognizes herself in the mirror, noticing that she is borne within a physical form like other objects, however she does not yet recognize herself as an object with subjectivity that can be independently perceived by other subjects external to her. It is still inconceivable that Mummy has a separate life. For Michel Foucault, the mirror stage does not begin and end at the age of about six months, as it does for Jacques Lacan.[41] Mirrors are always repositories for an ethereal absence in which the subject marks herself, standing before her own absence as not so much an ontological challenge to confront her own death, but rather as a psychoanalytic challenge to be confronted with the hideous recognition of *what one really is*. Meaning that at some level, *she* — the subject — actually exists, but it also means, *what it is to be one*, what is contained in the unbearable proposition of being singular.

> The mirror is, after all, a utopia, since it is a placeless place. In the mirror, I see myself there where I am not, in an unreal, virtual space that opens up behind the surface; I am over there, there where I am not, a sort of shadow that gives my own visibility to myself, that enables me to see myself there where I am absent: such is the utopia of the mirror. But it is also a heterotopia in so far as the mirror does exist in reality, where it exerts a sort of counteraction on the position that I occupy. […] The mirror functions as a heterotopia in this respect: it makes this place that I occupy at the moment when I look at myself in the glass at once absolutely real, connected with all the space that surrounds it, and absolutely unreal, since in order to be perceived it has to pass through this virtual point which is over there.[42]

---

41 Jacques Lacan, *Écrits: The First Complete Edition in English*, trans. Bruce Fink (London: W.W. Norton & Company, 2006), 75–81.
42 Michel Foucault, "Of Other Spaces (1967), Heterotopias," trans. Jay Miskowiec, https://foucault.info/documents/heterotopia/foucault.heteroTopia.en/.

In the mirror I must recognize the unbearable fact of my necessary individuation within this scene: I cannot be other things, since I am in fact *not there*. The mirror is a machine of making me aware of how *not-there* I am. I arise into the awareness of myself as an illusion of thereness. In fact, I am absolutely stuck here, since I will never be materially two; only the placeless utopia of the mirror can make me momentarily believe so, and ultimately make me painfully aware of that possibility's impossibility.

Fred Moten takes this further and reveals that it is not the effect of the mirror that brings this awareness of one's unbearable oneness, but rather the *fact of seeing* itself that the mirror allows. Speaking of Black poetry, the we of Black sociality against the universalization of appropriation, Moten says:

> It is as if what sustains us in our trial is precisely that which is given to us as trial, a terrible capacity to come to know ourselves, which is not just about what it is to look at ourselves from *their* [the whites'] perspective, but is more fundamentally bound up with the ruminative inhabitation of a perspective as such. Manic depression is not what results from looking at oneself and discerning one's wretchedness; it *is* such looking, such discernment.[43]

The mirror, then, is not an elusive placelessness that only provides the ethereal *not-thereness* of the subject in a virtual externality; it is rather the very apparatus of the impossibility of being socially, being multiply, within the perspective of individuality's visuality.

What happens, then, when a double scene — spilt by four hundred years — contains the arrival of people burning with racial hatred and hooked resolutely on capital as the mechanism for making the World, and difference is encountered? In the first of these scenes, Indigenous difference is encountered on a continent named the Americas, peculiarly, after the fifteenth-century cartographer Amerigo Vespucci. In the second, the difference

---

43 Moten, "Manic Depression," 45'–46'.

encountered is Blackness after chattel slavery. The territorial formation and architectural scene of these encounters is different, but in both the mirror remains positioned in front of the arriving beholders of subjection.

When the first scene arrives, the European sailors look at Indigenous land to see themselves, but what they find is the unbearable fact of their absence; they feel the echo of the violence with which they see. The *way of looking* necessarily inheres in the impossibility of being *there,* in the mirror, in the other world. By the time of the second scene, the white City exposition, there is a necessary, constitutive mirror built within the architectural facades, painted mirrors designed for whites to see themselves everywhere, as literally as possible, in order to cover up the repeated scene of the possibility of difference.

The time gathered in these scenes occurs through a conflation of the abstraction that is subjectivity and the materiality that is land. The projective Kantian geographic model of European arrivals in the Americas builds a continent of mirrors, in which European white subjectivity can establish a novel foundation of whiteness and territorial whitening, claiming that the current Indigenous users of the land are not using the land *properly,* since they neither profit from it nor construct mirrors in it. This rule by which British colonizers in North America claimed dominion is *terra nullius*: unused, unowned land. The land was considered by British colonizers to be improperly used because the fundamental principle of capitalism was not practiced, which is the supremacy of property ownership. Property accumulation was not the defining measure of social success in Indigenous society. Indigenous land had *use value,* rather than *exchange value.* The accusation against Indigenous people was that they did not know how to use land to profit from it, which justified their removal from it.

The movement occurring in this appropriation of land into profit as the archetypal spatiality of modernity is the abstraction of property and race. As Brenna Bhandar writes, the material law of property is being concentrated into the abstract values of a racialized system of representation: the abstraction that is Black comes to equate with the material that is property, while the abstraction that is white comes to equate with the ownership of property. A Black person is a slave, while a white person is a slave-owner. The abstraction that is Native or Red comes to equate with the misuse of property, or the inability to properly conduct the exchange of land as a commodity. A Red person is land.[44] The abstract principles of social representation merge, although in complex and untidy ways that are difficult to trace, with the material laws of sovereign property.

As Cheryl Harris says in her canonical essay, "Whiteness as Property," the category white comes to constitute protection against slavery.[45] In the colonial transition from early to late modernity, the abstraction that is whiteness takes on the characteristics of material property: the right to use, enjoyment, reputation, and status, and the power to exclude. The feature that principally allows whiteness and its regime of racial codes to define the proper use of property is the promise of futurity. Property ownership in capitalism, unlike other social and economic formations, is based on an expectation. Capital is a promise. The basis of property ownership in capitalism is the expectation to be able to use property as the owner wants, regardless of who currently uses the land, and the expectation to make profit from it.[46]

Commodities are valuable in capitalism for their exchange value, which is the amount of money they can be traded for, rather than their use. Commodities and property are abstract notions of capital, but the seismic step in building an entire social way of being on racism is that those abstract values of property are manifested in the human body. To colonize land is to colonize bodies, and the ownership of property that is justified

---

44 Brenna Bhandar, *Colonial Lives of Property: Law, Land, and Racial Regimes of Ownership* (Durham: Duke University Press, 2018).

45 Cheryl I. Harris, "Whiteness as Property," *Harvard Law Review* 106, no. 8 (June 1993): 1708–91.

46 This is discussed throughout Harris's essay, but see esp. ibid., 1714–15.

by law regardless of who uses the property is transferrable to the ownership of people.

The land is necessarily entwined in these machinations that code everything in modernity. The laboring human, the property beneath and the commodities produced are all reliant on each other to maintain the structure of codes and violences that form a capitalist society. These mutually constitutive abstractions — human, property, nation — are the foundation of modernity.

Philosophers at the height of colonial empires described the capitalist way of running states as a brilliant development away from the savagery of communal life, with no property and therefore no law; no law and therefore no property. As Jeremy Bentham writes in his 1802 *Theory of Legislation,* "Property and law are born together, and die together. Before laws were made there was no property; take away laws, and property ceases."[47] "[T]he life of man" in nature, Thomas Hobbes writes, is "solitary, poor, nasty, brutish, and short."[48] Or in the distinction Kant makes, "civilized" societies that distinguish between art, religion, and labor *have* culture, while "uncivilized" societies that supposedly do not make such distinctions *are* culture.[49]

Later criticisms of the Enlightenment position, with the development of postmodern and anti-humanist thinking, present the idea that land has always had agency throughout these colonial shifts in abstractions and relations. The land, the sea, the air, the constitution of each, are not just arbitrary elements open to alchemy. They are an agential force that can collapse the organizing of humans in their pursuit of some universal elixir. These theories, which Zoe Todd locates precisely in Bruno Latour, focus on a global commons circulated by the climate, which

---

47 Jeremy Bentham, *Theory of Legislation* (London: Trübner & Co., 1871), 113.
48 Thomas Hobbes, *Leviathan, or the Matter, Forme, & Power of a Commonwealth, Ecclesiasticall and Civill* (New York: Touchstone, 1997), 78.
49 David Lloyd, *Under Representation: The Racial Regime of Aesthetics* (New York City: Fordham University Press, 2019), 46.

operates a superhuman agency.⁵⁰ However, as Todd writes, the climate in this European version of Indigenous theory — which never makes references to any Indigenous thinkers — becomes a "blank commons," an open dumping ground of "Euro-Western theories of resilience, the Anthropocene, Actor Network Theory and other ideas that dominate the anthropological and climate change arenas of the moment."⁵¹ The appropriation of Indigenous theory is molded into a European design that makes it sound like another set of funky findings led by Derrida, Foucault, and Deleuze, resting on the implicit groundwork of Bergson, Kant, Hegel, and Descartes.

Aileen Moreton-Robinson takes this argument further, noting the universalization of this imperial position in every social referent of settler colonies.

> We are no longer the sole possessors of our ancestral lands taken by conquest, cessation, or as terra nullius (land belonging to no one). These lands are appropriated in the name of the Crown, signifying the rule of the king and the masculine capacity to possess property and to bear arms. Furthermore, these masculine attributes are embodied in nation-states, as the representation of patriarchal white sovereignty, and displayed in bodily form as the police, the army, and the judiciary.⁵²

The fights against the imperial brutality of the police, against the appropriation of the city as a site of abstract and unlived investment, against the abstraction of race and its codes of material property, against the monarchy and the history of murderous

---

50 Zoe Todd, "An Indigenous Feminist Take on the Ontological Turn: 'Ontology' Is Just Another Word for Colonialism," *Journal of Historical Sociology* 29, no. 1 (March 2016): 4–5.
51 Ibid., 8.
52 Aileen Moreton-Robinson, *The White Possessive: Property, Power, and Indigenous Sovereignty* (Minneapolis: University of Minnesota Press, 2015), xx.

colonialism it stands as a singular sign towards — these fights are all fights of the land.

Land is the site of the colonial mirror, the heterotopia of white universalization and the smooth white modern world of the prairie, more than any Marxist sense of the land as the battleground of primitive accumulation.[53] Land is where the American Hero stands, and where Red and Black emerge in their antecedence as complex alternatives to this singular mode of territory and profit, and it is the formation of land in this sense that is so important to the notion of racialization in architecture in the British context, despite the general absence of Indigenous thinking about land in British theory. The pursuits of the land and the people, in this Indigenous model, are formed as a co-constituting resistance to the imperial mirror. In *Red Skin, White Masks,* Glen Coulthard makes this clear:

> [T]he theory and practice of Indigenous anticolonialism, including Indigenous anticapitalism, is best understood as a struggle primarily inspired by and oriented around *the question of land* — a struggle not only *for* land in the material sense, but also deeply *informed* by what the land *as system of reciprocal relations and obligations* can teach us about living our lives in relation to one another and the natural world in nondominating and nonexploitative terms — and less around our emergent status as "rightless proletarians."[54]

The land conceived as an agential force in the Indigenous model allows a critical position that does not simply re-dictate the laws of territory as the boundaries of the commune or the borders of another set of socially use-productive exchanges. Rather, it brings out the liberatory sound inhering already in the land and puts its ear to it.

---

53 Karl Marx, *Capital: A Critique of Political Economy,* Volume I, trans. Ben Fowkes (London: Penguin, 1990), chap. 26, 'The Secret of Primitive Accumulation', 873ff.

54 Glen Sean Coulthard, *Red Skin, White Masks: Rejecting the Colonial Politics of Recognition* (Minneapolis: University of Minnesota Press, 2014), 13.

While the city is constructed on a model of suburban bourgeois racism that facilitates the permanent positioning of the colonial mirror for white observation that hides the constitutive violence of the *way of seeing that is whiteness,* within that, beneath that, beyond that, there is land to live on, as long as there is a means to render its teleological History irrelevant. As long as there is a way for the seeing eye to be seen, to turn the eye in on itself and slice the Wrightean formative whiteness from inside our expansive subjectivity.

There is an opacity already marked within the epistemology of the city. The construction of an urban area is always, it seems, accompanied by this attendant logic of opacity and visibility, demarcating a grid of visuality in which the things that are *most seen* have to perform according to a certain racialized and gendered coding that changes as it enters the opaque and unseen areas. In his work on *Playboy* magazine, Paul B. Preciado comes to the realization that "pornography was not so much about unclothing the body but rather about the possibility of constructing a visual fiction that enabled the reader to eroticize everyday architecture: to see what was happening behind stranger's windows, to view through opaque walls, to peek into hidden interiors."[55] In *Playboy,* these configurations of visibility, secrecy, sexuality, and opacity are built around the "girl next door," the "Playmate," the "naughty housewife" and other tropes that reveal the co-constitution of the hypersexualized and mutely domesticated binaries of modernity's feminizing violence. In the architecture of the city generally, however, these codes are given in the boundaries between estates, shopping centers, roads, parks, Colombian Expositions, and whitening subjectivities.

The scene of subjectivation does not necessarily occur within the somatic boundary of an individual person; the economic, social, and historical force that forges the ontological form of life against the chattel-state of social death also envelopes within its movements the buildings, air, climate, geology, fauna, flora, and

---

55 Paul B. Preciado, *Pornotopia: An Essay on Playboy's Architecture and Biopolitics* (New York City: Zone Books, 2019), 59.

chemical composition of any designated site. As Neferti Tadiar writes, "[i]f the distinction between economic forms allows us to recognize that it is money as capital rather than simply 'the market' or 'enterprise' that serves as the key principle of subjectivation under neoliberalism, then it is important to recognize [...] that such subjects include states, corporations, emergent sectors of elite classes in developing countries, and not merely individuals."[56] Money as capital and all its attendant logics, from geological extraction to ferrovitreous construction, emerge ontologically only as features of capital's material coagulation. They precede the categorization of capital in another form, in a form unrecognizable by my own visuality built within the strict perspective of neoliberalism, but *ontologically* the physical urban forms I perceive are already subjected, individuated, molded into proxies of the subject-logic of Kantian modernity.

What studying Wright's World of white mirrors allows us to see is the violence of seeing, or what Elizabeth A. Povinelli calls the "cunning of recognition," which gathers these fragments of thinking geological extraction, architectural construction, and ontological individuation together into a conceivable ethics of (anti-)recognition. In *The Cunning of Recognition,* Povinelli suggests

> that before we can develop a "critical theory of recognition," or a politics of distribution and capabilities, we need to understand better the cunning of recognition; its intercalation of the politics of culture with the culture of capital. We need to puzzle over a simple question: What is the nation recognizing, capital commodifying, and the court trying to save from the breach of history when difference is recognized?[57]

---

56 Neferti X.M. Tadiar, "The Life-Times of Disposability within Global Neoliberalism," *Social Text* 31, no. 2 (Summer 2013): 23–24.

57 Elizabeth A. Povinelli, *The Cunning of Recognition: Indigenous Alterities and the Making of Australian Multiculturalism* (Durham: Duke University Press, 2002), 16–17.

Why, that is, do we live by the mirror? Why must the way of seeing — that Motenian discernment that ruminates on one's wretchedness or allows one to eternally be suspended above the recognition of wretchedness — be the only way of understanding land and earth? How, ultimately, do we see differently?

Ways of thinking that disestablish the protected "breach of history" and disallow difference are manifold in their methods. For Moreton-Robinson, "racialization is the process by which whiteness operates possessively to define and construct itself as the pinnacle of its own racial hierarchy,"[58] making it extremely difficult to resist, since every movement against this possessive definition is incorporated into the language of white liberal activism, subsuming Indigenous and Black pursuits into another face of the white expansive territory. As Todd brilliantly sums it up, "the revolution will be mediated."[59]

Moten's tradition of "black optimism" situates this project of liberation in a specific site, rather than in a strictly ontological mode. A physical space of collective thought exists within — and always with the possibility of being against — these abstract notions of property and race that inform the entirety of modern life and knowledge. Moten calls that physical space, with Stefano Harney, "the undercommons," and it is where planning happens, collective planning that is not dependent on the forms of ownership that keep the royal colonizers in their absolute denial.[60]

In the undercommons, a space of Blackness emerges that is both *before* and *against* modern being. Blackness is a space, unidolized, of becoming that dodges precise definition, existing *before,* in both its spatial and temporal meanings, the construction of the city and the social significance it maintains for the categories of race and property.

---

58 Moreton-Robinson, *The White Possessive,* xx.
59 Todd, "An Indigenous Feminist Take on the Ontological Turn," 11.
60 See Stefano Harney and Fred Moten, *The Undercommons: Fugitive Planning and Black Study* (New York: Minor Compositions, 2013).

Blackness does not emerge out of the subjectivity of racist modernity, Moten emphasizes. It is not a form imposed on life by colonial regimes. Blackness precedes colonialism and escapes its violent force, a gas that bursts out of police claws. Black life has been conditioned as the object of modernity, subjected to hundreds of years of enslavement and murder, tortured daily by the Empire's police regime. But Blackness is the form beyond, out from the outside. Blackness is "another agential mode — not the sovereignty of the state of exception and of the outlaw dimension internal to the law but the agency of an other outlaw, the one who is abandoned to the law even as she is abandoned by the law, [...] who is [...] out from the law's outside."[61]

The crucial point in this definition of Blackness is that it is not a specific and irreducible *African* mode of being. Blackness, for Moten, is unmappable in the cartographic logic of modernity;[62] it is an antecedent form that precedes the formation of the colonial chromopolitics of skin color, slavery, and territorial expansion. "Blackness, which is to say black social life, is an undiscovered country."[63] Here, the Indigenous conception of the land's agency and its co-constitution with sociality is not in opposition to Black Studies' notions of Black antecedence.

In the tradition of Afropessimism, which I have been thinking with throughout *Building Black*, it is African Blackness specifically that bears the ontological antagonism to modernity, differentiating it from the oppressions deployed against Indigenous, Asian, and other people who form the objects of white supremacist capitalist modernity. In Black optimism, these movements into land, against the extractive violence of coloniality, can be thought together.

The sharp divides that part the theories of Afropessimism and Black optimism are often formulated by outsiders, or at least not by those who claim affiliation to either tradition. In-

---

61 Fred Moten, *The Universal Machine* (Durham: Duke University Press, 2018), 50.
62 Ibid., 207.
63 Moten, *Stolen Life*, 202.

terestingly, the principal proponents of each tradition — Moten and Harney, heavily reliant on Denise Ferreira da Silva, for Black optimism, and Wilderson and Jared Sexton, following Saidiya Hartman, for Afropessimism — themselves rarely mention any antagonism between the two ways of thinking. Sexton writes about his deep affinity with Moten,[64] and Moten has written a long essay explaining how closely tied his own thinking is with that of Sexton and Wilderson. In the essay, "Chromatic Saturation," which forms a large part of his 2018 monograph *The Universal Machine*, Moten recognizes at length the principal difference between his thinking and that of Sexton and Wilderson:

> I have thought long and hard, in the wake of the remarkable work of Frank B. Wilderson III and Jared Sexton, in a kind of echo of Bob Marley's question, about whether blackness could be loved; there seems to be a growing consensus that analytic precision does not allow for such romance but I remain devoted to the impression that analytic precision is, in fact, a function of such romance. And this, perhaps, is where the tension comes, where it is and will remain, not in spite of the love but in it, embedded in its difficulty and violence, not in the impossibility of its performance or declaration but out of the evasion of, the evasion that is, its open natality. More precisely, if Afropessimism is the study of this impossibility, the thinking I have to offer moves not in that impossibility's transcendence but rather in its exhaustion. Moreover, I want to consider exhaustion as a mode or form or way of life, which is to say sociality, thereby marking a relation whose implications constitute, in my view, a fundamental theoretical reason not to believe, as it were, in social death. Like Curtis Mayfield, however, I do plan to stay a believer.

---

64 Jared Sexton, "The Curtain of the Sky: An Introduction," *Critical Sociology* 36, no. 1 (2010): 16, and throughout Jared Sexton, "The Social Life of Social Death: On Afro-Pessimism and Black Optimism," *InTensions Journal* 5 (2011): 1–47.

> This is to say, again like Mayfield, that I plan to stay a black motherfucker.[65]

In a 2020 interview with Harney and Moten on the Millennials Are Killing Capitalism podcast, Harney brings up another particular point of contention between the two traditions. This is focused on the notion of the "surround," which is "not another territory. It's not an opposing sovereignty. This is particularly important to try to learn from Indigenous scholars and Indigenous movements."[66] The surround is "not [about] the claiming or identifying of a territory in opposition to settlement; it's about the destruction of the notion of sovereignty itself; the notion of a land that would belong to you [...] The surround is constant insurgency against sovereignty, and everybody who participates in it."[67] He goes on,

> there's so much misunderstanding, especially in Afropessimism, about Indigenous sovereignty. That comes from putting things backwards — imagining that sovereignty precedes the rebellion, and that's just not right [...] The experience of Indigenous struggles is that one can find a home [in the land], a fugitive home. That land is not sovereign [...] there's not a fence; there's nothing permanent in that way about its ownership.[68]

The crucial temporal difference between Black optimism and Afropessimism is that, for Black optimists, the sociality of rebellion precedes the imposition of sovereignty; the life of Blackness

---

65 Moten, *The Universal Machine*, 193.
66 Fred Moten and Stefano Harney, "'Give Your House Away, Constantly': Fred Moten and Stefano Harney Revisit *The Undercommons* in a Time of Pandemic and Rebellion (Part 2)," *Millennials Are Killing Capitalism*, podcast, July 4, 2020, https:// https://millennialsarekillingcapitalism.libsyn.com/give-away-your-home-constantly-fred-moten-and-stefano-harney.
67 Ibid.
68 Ibid.

and the agential land is antecedent to the appropriation of land and people into the necropolitics of capital and coloniality.

Escape from this brutality of World, for Harney and Moten, is not rooted in the same World-ending social death as it is for Wilderson, Sexton, and Hartman. Instead, escape is a constant and social movement into the surround. In this sense, a fugitive movement out of the mirror, away from the white facades of the exposition, far from the ubiquity of whiteness's urban construction on and appropriation of land, is a movement *beneath* the way of looking of the sovereign eye. This movement is both Indigenous and Black, operating in the otherwise space beneath, beyond, and before the World that Frank Lloyd Wright, Christopher Columbus, Daniel Burnham, or Louis Sullivan could design in the white coordinates of territorial visibility and expansion.

3

Spaces

Ants, I

Westfield first opened in 2008 in an area of west London called white City. The shopping center was opened by a company called the Westfield Group, which in 2014 split into two separate companies, the Scentre Group for its shopping centers in Australia and New Zealand, and the Westfield Corporation for those in America and Europe. Westfield Group's first shopping center was opened in July 1959, in the City of Blacktown, a suburb of western Sydney, Australia.

My first job in London was in Westfield, in White City. I had just arrived to the capital. It was early spring 2011, and I moved into my girlfriend's room in Hammersmith. She was older and had been renting a room in a shared house there for a year or so. We had met in a cafe I worked at in Cambridge, where I'm from. She came and asked if we serve beer. I said "No" and simultaneously fell in love. Or that's how I remember it now, compacted into a single snapshot, compared to a few hundred other brief and faded scenes around that time.

The day before arriving, I had been working as a tour guide on the River Cam, punting up and down the river with frozen hands for cash-in-hand that was spent immediately on beer and fags. I thought when I arrived in London, somehow a different reality would open. I cycled from King's Cross to Hammersmith with a huge bag strapped to the seat beneath me. I remember stopping at Marble Arch for a cigarette and thinking conclusively, *Life has been achieved.*

The space of my adulthood had opened, at least an introductory room, and I believed in the structure so fervently. This was the house I would inhabit forever. The house of the city, of the population, of voting adults, of wages and taxes and food shopping and suits and cycling to work and repairing bikes. It began as a conclusion: *In this space, life is done.* It was a universal proposition that included me in its finality.

At the time, of course, I didn't feel like the immediate conclusion was limiting. I wanted it. I wanted life to be concluded for me. Not ended, not over, but set in a certain mode of adultness that I could comfortably disrupt. Feeling like a revolutionary for bringing a touch of childhood to this rigid structure in the adult city.

As soon as I arrived at the house in Hammersmith, I threw my bag down and opened a bottle of rum, offering it around to the housemates. One of them told me not to smoke inside. Another said it's too early to drink. My girlfriend said I should go and look for work — rent was due in a few days.

It now seems like a ridiculously obvious process of development into adulthood: I had thought that adult life was just adolescence but without my mum nearby. Disappointed, penniless, drinking alone in the shared kitchen and scorned by a house of older workers in their mid- or late-twenties — they seemed as mature as people could possibly be to me then, aged nineteen. I had my first insight into the realization that adulthood is the dismemberment and ridicule of the adolescent.

At some point I would have to laugh at my adolescence, otherwise I would never be an adult. Immaturity would have to become a fun sidekick if I wanted to enter but vaguely disrupt the house of the adult city, its architectural structure that covered me now.

I can't remember if it was that day or the next day, but soon I went looking for work. I had never been to west London before, and I just wandered. I went up the Shepherd's Bush Road, all its shabby hotels and dusty Victorian ex-glamor. I stopped at a little restaurant somewhere, and a huge old man came out to answer my question.

"Are you looking for any staff?"

He gauged me up and down, then sniffed, walking away. "I only hire young women."

I got up to Shepherd's Bush Green and saw, rising from behind a row of three-story Victorian or Edwardian buildings, the sprawl of glass and random metal toppings of Westfield, a mass of melted materials dribbled over a suburban plot of 150,000 square meters.

This endless enclosure — a paradox that makes perfect sense inside Westfield — did not feel miserable like the Lion Yard concrete shopping center in Cambridge, or the derelict Grafton Centre. The aesthetic of this shopping world that felt both Puritan and perverse, like its aesthetic emblem America itself was comfortable, somehow. As comfortable as anything in the glassy violence of American capitalism.

The comfort of the scene imposed itself on the outside world, too. The house I was living in, its dull humidity and lingering residue of smoky evenings, felt tedious and attached to some ancient world that now I wanted to get rid of. The clean, smooth whiteness of Westfield had set itself as the standard of space. Terraces are too clogged in the open cathedral of the shopping center.

The particularity of Westfield space is that it spreads like melting rubber. It doesn't just grow upwards, stout and firm like the obvious imperial roots of 1930s Chicago styles. From the top of those towers, as Adrienne Brown writes, people below look like ants, like anonymous black figures, and two things are revealed in that sight.[1] It means, for one thing, that the violence of sight is openly accessible to the viewer, which undermines the

---

[1] Adrienne Brown, *The Black Skyscraper: Architecture and the Perception of Race* (Baltimore: John Hopkins University Press, 2017). See esp. chap. 2, "Architecture and the Visual Fate of whiteness," 35–81.

project of modernity. The whole point of the ubiquitous racial scheme of capitalism is to cover its violence; to pretend that it is itself the warrior of justice, defending against barbarism and evil, never allowing its subjects to confront the violence of their own actions. Hipster neoliberalism now allows for an ironic self-confrontation with violence, but nothing is done about it because it's ironic and because it's only used to further the pursuit of profit, buying more guilty products to improve the self, and assuages any need to actually do anything, to stop investing in property, because the moment of pseudo-confrontation has happened.

Secondly, the revelation of this towered sight means inevitably that when the viewer goes down to the ground level, they will also be an ant. They cannot retain the illusion of constant somatic superiority, because they can't stay in the tower forever.

In the middle of the twentieth century, when the London County Council and later the Greater London Council moved away from their signature social housing blocks — five-story red-brick with external balcony access — council housing was built higher and higher, with London blocks regularly reaching twelve or fifteen stories. This teased the skyscraper into the complex violence of the British class system, linking high-rise with low-class, taking away the social and economic value of living in the sky. But then with the Thatcherite privatization of councils and the subsequent purge of socially-owned housing, and a return of the imperial desire to oversee the city in the renewed fanaticism of post-1980s hypercapitalism, views became valuable and ex-council flats were plastered with sleek white surfaces, making them look fancy and worth ten times as much on the market as when they were built.

Our attachment to living in the sky is always shifting according to the social and economic creeds of the moment. Societies' relationships with skyscrapers have hugely changed over the century and a half since they were first built, especially with what academic and architect Pooya Ghoddousi calls the "Dubaization" of architecture, in which the built environment seeks affectless smooth surfaces that grow only upwards, with nothing in between them and surrounding life aggressively unconsidered.[2] Now high-up living is generally desirable, although something of its self-assurance was rattled after the burning of Grenfell Tower.

Whatever the relation, though, the comparison between towers and ants remains. From high in the tower, in the regal and religious cosmos of social space, everything else looks like a horde of ants.

When the council approved a proposed monumental development in Ealing, west London, which would feature two enormous 55-story residential towers, a campaigner who wants — like most progressive contemporary architects — lower-rise and higher-density building, responded by affirming that "human beings don't appreciate being reduced to the scale of ants."[3]

In a community comment page of the now-closed Guardian "Cities" series, someone called RomulusX writes, "In Hong Kong I lived on the 42nd floor — people on the street below looked like ants, and it never got really dark."[4]

A children's book about skyscrapers by Seymour Simon, entitled Skyscrapers, begins with the first thing to note about these structures: "Skyscrapers are super-tall buildings that seem to scrape against the sky. When you look down from a high window, people on the street look like tiny ants."[5]

In *Swimming Across,* the autobiography of a Hungarian Silicon Valley pioneer, Andrew S. Grove writes about arriving in New York, and explains what feels like a familiar reaction to the American aesthetic. "The skyscrapers looked just like pictures

---

[2] From personal conversations between the author and Pooya Ghoddousi during his tours of London architecture with his students at the Bartlett.

[3] Robert Booth, "'Eyesore' London Tower Approved Despite Housing Concerns," *The Guardian,* February 28, 2020, https://www.theguardian.com/uk-news/2020/feb/28/eyesore-london-tower-approved-despite-housing-concerns.

[4] Francesca Perry, "'It's like being on an island in the sky': Your Stories of High-rise Living," *The Guardian,* February 24, 2017, https://www.theguardian.com/cities/2017/feb/24/stories-high-rise-living-tall-buildings-skyscrapers-island-sky.

[5] Seymour Simon, *Skyscrapers* (San Francisco: SeaStar Books, 2005).

Fig. 1. Westfield, White City.

of America. All of a sudden, I was gripped by the stunning realization that I was truly in America. Nothing had symbolized America more to me than skyscrapers; now I was standing on a street, craning my neck to look at them [...] The cacophony of the traffic filled my ears. Mobs of people brushed past me. The perspective made me feel like an ant in the bottom of a canyon. I suddenly felt very, very insignificant in my new surroundings."[6]

Now the ant itself is speaking, but he remains an ant. Antness is not only a condition imposed by those high in the tower on those below, who might seem to themselves a regular human size. Rather, the skyscraper redefines the entire city and the population as ants, or at least always at risk of becoming an ant.

Many years after arriving in America, when he was a renowned businessman and millionaire, while writing his autobiography, surely Grove associated more with the top of the tower than the bottom in that paradigm of American aesthetics. Or possibly his residence in Silicon Valley and its remythologized vernacular architecture — those quaint gentrified terraces so

---

6   Andrew S. Grove, *Swimming Across* (London: Hachette UK, 2008).

renowned of San Francisco — was a kind of resistance to the binary hierarchy of the skyscraper city and its synonymy with industrial society.

What seems clear across the literature on cities and the cultural imaginary is that the world is turned into an ant-world when steel pillars hold up floating walls and they scrape the sky. Little black animals scatter over spread pavements once humanity is familiar with living a hundred meters high.

But Westfield is a white blob, not a steel frame holding its inhabitants at a great height. It does not carry those inside it above the city to look down from a distance on the rest. Westfield has no views of anything. It *is* a view. Its internal balconies only open out to reflections of themselves, to new solid layers of their exact replicas.

One important change this seems to make is an openness to the person inside the building. Going up a skyscraper, you become the *person-in-a-skyscraper*. Looking out from a high window, you are part of the building. You are conditioned in the ethics of a skyscraping way of seeing. You become an ant precisely because the experience of being in a tower has such a profound impact on the construction of your body.

In Westfield, however, the body does not become part of the building. There are doors everywhere, and no passage really leads to anywhere different. In a skyscraper, the higher you go, the further you are from the exit and entrance. In Westfield's amorphous blob, you are always next to a door. You never really get inside the building; you never enter its workings.

How do I describe the feeling of being lost in something that allows me easy access to an exit? What words are there to describe the feeling of being trapped by an open, accessible space?

Attempting this aporetic description requires a reformulation of the question of architecture. To adapt a question Denise Ferreira da Silva asks of humanity, Westfield is not really an ontological problem. Maybe, instead, Westfield is a methodologi-

Fig. 2. Westfield, White City, interior.

cal problem. In the trappedness of its openness, Westfield has collapsed any familiar methodology and a new one is needed.[7]

What language suffices to explain the feeling of existence within a blob that prophesizes only perpetual consumption? How is it possible to even connect with something called "feeling" while existing in a colorless void of ultra-bright lights and infinite products to be consumed and reconsumed? I have no a priori method for thinking this bizarre space.

In this methodological problem, when I'm inside Westfield I really discover the limitations of Kant. Kant cannot explain how this space is co-existent with other space, existing outside of a temporal chain but simultaneously with all other spaces. He provides no method for understanding how the projections of a pure capitalist reason can initiate a space that is unthinkable to

---

[7] Denise Ferreira da Silva, "Before Man: Sylvia Wynter's Rewriting of the Modern Episteme," in *Sylvia Wynter: On Being Human as Praxis*, ed. Katherine McKittrick, (Durham: Duke University Press, 2015), 104. Da Silva asks, "What will help us to open up the path? I think it should begin with asking different questions, methodological rather than ontological ones: instead of the question of who and what we are, we need to go deeper into the investigation of how we come up with answers to the questions."

the mind. How could Kant explain the object here? The object in Westfield — the thing that is not the Human mind — is controlling the mind. The architecture of Westfield is the agential force in the scene, undoubtedly. The white walls and shiny infinity convince everyone inside it that they *need more things,* and suddenly the ideality of the mind is collapsed. The rational thinking being cannot think away this scene.

I arrive, instead, at a methodological question that architects have to contend with. The low-rise sprawl of Westfield gives ample access and subverts the vertical hierarchy of the skyscraper, but its oppressive entrapment of its inhabitants is just as acute.

What Does Space Say? Part II

To spell broad narratives out for the purposes of this narrow book (and its narrow author), England spent the eighteenth and nineteenth centuries trying to expand the Kantian category of Architecture onto the world, in order to assert itself as the universal referent: all things are England, are trying to become England, or are sub-England — which is only semi-life. To do that, it had to continue the expansion of Architecture while hiding the unity of buildings and bodies, and meanwhile to make a massive profit from it all.

England's expansion of the bourgeois category Architecture functioned in a similar way to the Copernican turn. Nicolaus Copernicus changed the astronomic focus from geocentrism (Earth is at the center of the universe) to heliocentrism (the Sun is at the center), first in a short, anonymous, and untitled pamphlet in 1514, then fully in his magnum opus *On the Revolutions of the Heavenly Spheres,* in the year of his death, 1543. This theory is generally taken to mean that humans, from Copernicus onwards, were decentered and devalorized; humanity's value as the central point of the universe was undermined. However, as Sylvia Wynter says, this is seen from a biological point of view. The removal of an animal from the center of the universe and its placement among the general order is biologically a demotion from semi-divinity to normality. However, the Copernican shift in his own age would have been seen theocentrically — based on the logics of God and the Christian cosmos. Theocentrically, Earth was fixed in the center of the universe as the site of the Fall, where God punished humanity with the Flood after the original sin in Eden. Earth was the postdiluvian site of endless suffering, not a privileged place in the universe. As Wynter says, *"to be at the center was to be at the dregs of the universe. The center was the most degraded place to be!"*[8]

The Copernican turn placed humanity in a more privileged position by removing Earth from its central place as a condition of God's condemnation. Instead, Earth was just another planet, revolving just another star. The privilege of that position is to be within the orbit of life, rather than the object of divine punishment. England had the same problem as the Earth in pre-Copernican Christianity. It was condemned to always be seen for its sins. It was the figurehead of global Empire, having taken this bloody crown from the Netherlands.

As England expanded Architecture across the world, the hyper-visible impediment of exceptionalism was removed. It hid the colonial frameworks of power with which English overlords controlled Caribbean plantations, the trade of Africans as slaves, and the global trade of commodities.

With England in the limelight, as the country proudly beating its chest as the first industrial empire, every act of violence had an obvious source. Every feeling had an Oedipal origin, a fucked-up father to blame and eventually to sacrifice. It was obvious who was doing all this, and the many, many great slavery abolitionists, freedom fighters, and revolutionaries who struggled, in ways both small and monumental, against the imperial nation had a very specific target. Architecture became the solution to the problem of being the obvious source of Empire.

The expansion of the privileged category Architecture to the whole World was an expansion of the logic of the factory into

---

[8] Sylvia Wynter and Kathrine McKittrick, "Unparalleled Catastrophe for Our Species? Or, to Give Humanness a Different Future: Conversations," 9–89, in *Sylvia Wynter*, ed. McKittrick, 14. Original emphasis.

places without factories. And in this expansion, there is a manifold of forces at play. In this section, I study Architecture's creation of the contemporary spatial logics of race and gender.

I propose the industrial use of iron as the moment when traditional gendered spaces of the built environment are modernized and turned to the pursuits of Empire. Iron was, from its eighteenth-century beginning, a refusal of ornament. Its simple aesthetics and rigid form make room for a new concept of simplicity, of smoothness and universality.

Once iron construction has smoothened the ideology of building, the use of ornament is a feminizing and racializing act. Orientalized ornament, as I will explore more below in a discussion of Westfield and Anne Cheng, was extremely popular in European artistic circles at the times of the First and Second Industrial Revolutions. Ornament was treated as an exotic, inferior toy to be used for sexual and aesthetic fantasies of distant semi-life. Meanwhile, to be smooth, iron, and modern is the architectural constitution of the ideal human: white, male, and a constitutive part of Empire. This narrative is intertwined with every other part of Modernism and its liberal ideology. Scientific development, biological evolution, iron and steel architecture, high-rise living, critical philosophy, fascism and communism, free market economics, and the fundamental proposition of modernity that is the individual — all stamped into the city's steel tombstones and the cast iron memories of our mythical origin story. As the architect Alfred Loos sums it up, *"The evolution of culture is synonymous with the removal of ornament from utilitarian objects."*[9] Man is one of those utilitarian objects.

Man as utilitarian iron not only functions to literally build cities. The emblem of modern white Man and the physical manifestation of his properties in iron construction did not only allow high-rise blocks to hold themselves up. As is so key to the thinking of hugely influential French architect Eugène Em-

---

9 Alfred Loos, "Ornament and Crime (1908)," in *Programs and Manifestoes on 20th Century Architecture*, ed. Ulrich Conrads (Cambridge: MIT Press, 1971), 20. Original emphasis.

manuelle Viollet-le-Duc, iron and Man — as a singular global referent — constructed each other. For Viollet-le-Duc there is a direct continuation from medieval soldiers in iron armor to modern European men in iron boudoirs, and that continuation inheres in the fact that, in both scenes, iron and Man merge as one. Iron becomes humanity and humanity becomes iron, and at the end of the process, neither humanity nor iron is left as it was before. The technological alchemy of body and appendage eradicates the previous singularity of their forms. There is no more body and no more appendage. There is a merged interaction of both. And precisely what that alchemy creates is *the individual*. The individual body is now the marker of Enlightenment humanity, a being created within the social, economic, and historical frameworks of Europe's profit-seeking cult and the global network of enslavement it relies on. It is an alchemy that emerges from the production of iron.[10]

The sign for iron is the sign of Mars: the circle with an arrow pointing up and right — the sign for masculinity, too. Named after the God of War. The surface of Mars is red because of iron ore. Men are red because they are iron arcades, public marketplaces of changeable aesthetic surfaces premised on the European-History-narrative of a solid iron core. The public realm had always been the stage of performing masculinity; where men met and gathered, as the *civis,* as the *socius,* as collective power that sets its definition against the internal privacy of feminized domestic space.

Iron, however, opened the interior of rooms as a performance space for the individual. Iron buildings allowed for open interiors that had the same function as the outside. With an iron structure upholding the building, fewer weight-bearing walls are needed, and interiors can open up, allowing expansive rooms and more windows. Moving resolutely away from the candle-lit, heavily curtained interiors of the *Ancien Régime,* the new nineteenth-century iron interior in Europe brought bare,

---

10 Martin Bressani, "Prosthetic Fantasies of the First Machine Age: Viollet-le-Duc's Iron Architecture," *AA Files* 68 (2014): 43–49.

white classical openness back, again merging the aesthetics of Ancient Greece with the height of Europe's Empire as the new industrial ethics of the city. The public space of masculinity was taken inside by the openness of iron arches. The interior of a room became the signifier of the aesthetic principles of the person who designed it.

In his massive collection of notes and unfinished musings, *The Arcades Project*, Walter Benjamin discusses this new form of interior space. For Benjamin, capitalism in the age of iron is a phantasmagorical force. It opens a space set around the glorification of the exchange value of the commodity. The space of iron is a space in which a person enters as a subject of commodity-exchange; the main — or only — act possible in this iron universe is the trading of commodities, by private individuals, to accumulate a personal profit.

In this iron world of exchange, where no one feels or does anything and the only law is to trade, the world exhibition is the height of all action. The festivals that were so popular in the nineteenth century, beginning with London's Great Exhibition of 1851 in Hyde Park that displayed the Crystal Palace, brought in millions of viewers. All the famous faces of the 1850s world attended: Dickens, Darwin, Marx, Brontë, Tennyson.

"World exhibitions glorify the exchange value of the commodity. They create a framework in which its use value recedes into the background. They open a phantasmagoria which a person enters in order to be distracted. The entertainment industry makes this easier by elevating the person to the level of the commodity."[11] Here Benjamin reveals, again, the tangled signifiers that construct each other. These iron arcades are not only built by Man and men: they create Man; they make iron out of men. The human is the commodity in the privatized interior of iron arcades, as the racialized body is the ornament that must be refused by Modernist architects in order for modernity to progress.

---

11 Walter Benjamin, *The Arcades Project*, trans. Howard Eiland and Kevin McLaughlin (Cambridge: Harvard University Press, 2002), 7.

The iron interiors of high industrial modernity provided a setting for a performance of masculinity that was not only focused on labor. It was, until this historical moment, which Benjamin sets exactly in the fifteen years following 1822,[12] labor that had exerted the fullest force of gender divisions. Gender was a cohesive referent only in that it referred to different types of labor, however historically inaccurate the designation might have been: *Women* performed the labor of reproduction, cooking food, and keeping people alive. *Men* performed the value-productive labor of making products, constructing commodities for sale, fashioning things that have value on the public market. The referent that is *female* refers to a kind of labor conducted in the private space of a home, while the referent that is *male* refers to labor conducted in public space: on a farm, in a factory, on the roads or the markets.

As Angela Davis emphasizes throughout her 1981 classic *Women, Race & Class,* the historical reality is far more complex than the binary system of gender suggests. She writes, "woman's place had always been in the home, but during the pre-industrial era, the economy itself had been centered in the home and its surrounding farmland. While men had tilled the land (often aided by their wives), the women had been manufacturers, producing fabric, clothing, soap, and practically all the other family necessities."[13]

The interior individuality of iron construction in the nineteenth century allowed the imposition of its own space and time over all others. All time before industrial modernity was overwritten, and now the economy was solely external: it was the public marketplace, where men were. And the internal was the possibility of the private expression of the individual. Interior space was where men went to be *themselves*. As Benjamin says,

> For the private individual, the place of dwelling is for the first time opposed to the place of work. The former constitutes

---

12 Ibid., 3, 15.
13 Angela Y. Davis, *Women, Race & Class* (London: Penguin, 2019), 28.

itself as the interior. Its complement is the office. The private individual, who in the office has to deal with reality, needs the domestic interior to sustain him in his illusions. This necessity is all the more pressing since he has no intention of allowing his commercial considerations to impinge on social ones. In the formation of his private environment, both are kept out. From this arise the phantasmagorias of the interior — which, for the private man, represents the universe. In the interior, he brings together the far away and the long ago. His living room is a box in the theater of the world.[14]

As the interior is defined by an iron masculinity that performs its own individual privacy away from public surveillance, the public is also redefined as the eternal theatre where men conduct their socially productive labor. Iron simultaneously constructs the private masculine space of the interior and the possibility of its adornment in the expressions of self, and, through a retroactive binary that turns the other into its opposite, the public masculine space of the marketplace. At the moment of the iron arcade, masculinity becomes a principle that transcends space. It grows beyond the limits of spatial difference. Masculinity takes over the feminized domain of interior space.

In the 1950s, further developments in technology produced another significant shift in the architectural semantics of masculinity. In *Pornotopia,* Paul Preciado notes that the crucial movement of mid-twentieth-century masculinity is a pornographic gendering of internal domestic space, beyond its dominant but binary position in the external public sphere.

The spatial importance of *Playboy* centered on the question, "What of the bachelor and his need for a place to call his own?"[15] This was an explicit rejection of the green-lawn, suburban domesticity of wife-and-two-kids quotidian life. "*Playboy* rejected a naturalist view of masculinity in favor of a constructed masculinity that emerged as a result of the use of image and informa-

---
14 Benjamin, *The Arcades Project,* 8–9.
15 Preciado, *Pornotopia,* 36.

tion technologies. [...] The penthouse is a center of operations that enabled the soldier/husband to become the spy/lover."[16]

The technological shift initiating this newly rendered masculinity was the pornographic film, which was emerging widely in the 1950s. This novel mode of cinema made the masculine collective formation of a certain kind of visuality possible by projecting the spectral absence of women into the room designed for the gathering of men, all united by a sexual pursuit of women, but simultaneously bound by the emergent pleasure of being with men, *heterosexually*.

> The transformation of pornography within the twentieth century came with the appearance of photography and cinema as technical apparatuses for *intensifying sight*. [...] A pleasure even more intense than sexual pleasure, based on the exclusion of women and the homoerotic consumption of female images, seemed to define the visual economy of pornography: the gender-pleasure arising from the *production of masculinity*. [...] Moving-image pornography operated as a virtual, external and mobile masturbatory prosthesis of subject production.[17]

The creation of an architectural designation of neo-masculinity is simultaneously the construction of that subjectivity. A conceptual formulation of the *new man,* as bachelor, as divorced and expert at mixing cocktails and fantasizing over women's sexualized absences, did not precede the architecture of men separated from women. The suburban 1950s home, as Dianne Harris writes, was designed specifically to materialize the ideology of the "everyday life of white domesticity."[18]

---

16 Ibid., 35.
17 Ibid., 41.
18 Dianne Harris, "Modeling Race and Class: Architectural Photography and the U.S. Gypsum Research Village, 1952–1955," in *Race and Modern Architecture: A Critical History from the Enlightenment to the Present,* eds. Irene Cheng, Charles L. Davis II, and Mabel O. Wilson (Pittsburgh: University of Pittsburgh Press, 2020), 229.

The rise of a white suburban architecture as the material form of an ideally heteropatriarchal and racist society began in the 1950s through an establishment of the built signifiers of gender and race, positing these movements of white flight against the standard designation of "blight" and a need for "renewal" of a "neighborhood's 'complexion' [...] used to describe work performed in black, inner-city neighborhoods."[19] The photographable home of white families constitutes physical and semiotic protection against the still-emergent form of racialized space.

The home becomes homely, safe, valuable, only if it is both representable in the visual logics of architecture's gendering codes and definable by being placed into the racializing categories of architecture's history. White suburban architecture in the USA, its pornographic rejection in the bachelor pad, and the technologies of seeing and capturing that accompany them create a coherent designation for the social referents of race and gender. What all the essays in *Race and Modern Architecture: A Critical History from the Enlightenment to the Present* show, including Harris's, cited above, is that architecture has formative agency in the complex signifiers of post-Enlightenment urban spaces, in which the regime of capitalist modernity is enforced and performed. As the editors, Irene Cheng, Charles L. Davis II, and Mabel O. Wilson, write, the book

> insists upon seeing race in every context, not just in the typical sites examined by architectural historians. In practical terms, this means countering the expectation that race is only operative in nonwhite or subaltern spaces. Instead, we hold that race operates in the construction of both the statehouse and the outhouse. *Race and Modern Architecture* contends that architectural historians must take account of the whiteness central to the universal mythologies of Enlightenment discourses and how these have relied on the suppression of particularity and difference.

---

19 Ibid., 232.

Now, bringing this to the Kantian mind and the ampliative World of Empire that achieves its most successful growth between the lifetimes of Kant and Benjamin, some complex and uncanny continuations between race, gender, iron, and architecture are to be found.

Kant had internalized the organization of the building in the Human: the mind was a building, with rooms for different kinds of thinking, floors with a hierarchy of importance, and windows to absorb the light of the world. Transposing that logic back onto architecture, the internal becomes privileged. The internal room was a place for men to make themselves special and individual, to design according to the latest fashion. This is the privileged internal architecture unique to industrial modernity.

The inside was where Man's reason could thrive. The outside was where labor took place. The factory is an external architecture, created to a stock form rather than designed and decorated according to individual taste. The factory is where many people gather, all dressed for the outdoors, and labor to produce tradable commodities on a global market that is the definition of externality: it is the outside of the whole World; the external market that connects the internal spaces of the entire global population.

In other places, however, this spatial distinction did not exist. Imposed in the colonial Caribbean, the internal place of domesticity was privileged like in the houses of the factory capitalists in Liverpool, Bristol, or London, but where was the underprivileged place of the factory? The enslaved people in the Caribbean worked on plantations, which were outdoors. They were in fields, on farms, not covered by the anti-architectural signifier of the oppressive factory. They had the *internal* architecture where men designed themselves; but the *external* architecture of industry did not fit their context. The internal is a referent to the aesthetics of whiteness, the place from which white male managers run plantations. The external, meanwhile, in this emergent global space, is unfixable in a particular architectural aesthetic.

A social category of space was extracted from the particularities of English industrial production and embossed as a foundational framework on other places. But it did not fit there. A heliocentric model was pushed onto places with a wholly different cosmos. The Copernican turn is really a geometrical turn; it affirms that the universe can be charted according to a universal geometrical model. It mathematizes reality, turning it into a series of digital codes and calculations.[20]

This mathematical framework (heliocentrism or the Manchester factory production line), though, is produced in a particular time and space, and according to a certain logic. It does not fit universally, but it is imposed universally anyway.

The result of these complex movements in Architecture and History is to mark a scientific distinction between human geographies. The logic of a heliocentric model of categorization suggests that all that can be mathematized is *full life* and all that cannot be mathematized is *semi- or non-life*. Meaning, *all the things that fit in the mathematics of modernity are logical and all the things that do not fit in the mathematics of modernity are illogical.*

The industrial production machine of England consumes the plantations of its global Empire and then blames that consumption on the irrationality of those who inhabit the outside, the non-geometrical plantation.

The irony of this view, among the many painful ironies, is that the geometrical model was initially conceived in Ancient Greece precisely in order to mark the limits of fields and farms. The massive risk taken by classical astronomers was to place the universe in an essentially agricultural logic. Geometry was designed to mark the boundaries of planting, crops, seasons, and growth, but it was projected onto the cosmos, and it worked for them.

When, two thousand years later, the same geometrical model was then imposed back on agriculture in the plantations of industrial Empire, it was done explicitly to eradicate the reality of those plantations. It was done to deem them unfeasible, unreal,

---

20 Hubert Krivine, *The Earth*, trans. David Fernbach (London: Verso, 2015), 48.

partial, broken, and formed of people who were also only half-formed.

Ants, II

I walked into Westfield and found a Spanish bar in the middle of an open plaza staggered by overlapping balconies, suspended between the horizon of a cinema and the infinite glass door of a sports clothing shop. I asked if they needed any staff. The manager, a tall and thin Spanish man with the few long hairs left on his head gelled tightly to his scalp, shrugged. I asked the same question in Spanish. He lifted up the bar-door and walked towards me. "You're English?" he asked.

I nodded.

"And you speak Spanish?"

I nodded.

He gave me an apron and I started work.

Staff lunch was solid white stuff inside liquid red stuff. Color was the only sense available to the diner. Nothing tasted of anything. The tapas available for customers was heated in a microwave, having been cooked hours or days earlier in a kitchen somewhere else, since they weren't allowed to cook in the open amphitheater of shopping's central atrium.

Like in any restaurant, the managers were formed of a pure and primordial evil, an evil so intense and spiteful it was often hard to remember that they were Human. The only time they allowed themselves the faintest suggestion of pleasure was when the "head chef" appeared.

The uniform of the head chef was spotless: white, tailored, and ironed. We all suspected he had bought the chef's kit from a costume shop. How could a chef not have a single stain on his uniform?

He walked in, up the escalator and across the enormous open pitch of white squeaky floor and white walls, as if he expected a cheering crowd to greet him and carry him to the kitchen that he'd never been in. What exactly made him the head chef was unclear, as he only appeared once every few weeks, and had obviously never done a day's work in his life.

We looked him up online and it turns out that his dad is a millionaire who owns many restaurants in Spain. He was given the money to invest in these mini Westfield empires by his father. Maybe he also gave him the money for the little chef's hat he wore so proudly.

Since then, this illusive trust-fund head chef has written cookbooks which, in a moment of almost-shock dampened by miserable predictability, I found in a bookshop once. His smiling face, glazed by the idiotically happy stability of the permanent millionaire, the cross-generational accumulator, stamped onto the cover, bordered by the same sparkling pastiche of a cook's clothes as always.

I walked from Hammersmith to Westfield most days, about two miles away. Sometimes I would cycle, but the bike interfered with my alcoholism. Walking, I could drink a few cans of beer on the way, then sit in Shepherd's Bush Green and smoke until my shift started, then run panting up the stairs.

I could syphon spirits from the bottles on the bar for a while, but almost no one ever bought them and, once I'd been there for a few weeks, the manager with the odd bald-but-long-hair look leant across the bar. He was twiddling the desolate ends of his two or three strands. His eyes landed on the bottles.

"Ayba! Was there a party here?"

He spoke no English and never ate anything, at least not at work, which lasted for twelve hours a day.

There had been no party, and people rarely drank at this bar. It distracted from the laborious pursuits of the shopping center.

After that I had to find new ways of stealing, of feeding myself.

I offered to do more of the manual work when it was quiet at the bar, which involved hauling the boxes of beer up from the delivery slot in the basement to the storeroom somewhere up in the cranium of Westfield's interior skeleton.

With a wheelie trolley, I could carry five boxes at a time, each with twenty-four bottles of beer. No one ever counted them — as long as there remained enough to fill the fridges in the bar.

I'd drink two or three quickly, then begin to make my way down the stairs, but if no one came I'd turn around and drink a few more.

I carried chewing gum with me constantly for years. And cigarettes, which cover the boozy smell with something more acceptable in the middle of the day.

We finished work around 10 pm. I'd stop by the off license on Shepherd's Bush Green, buy four cans of lager and a bottle of wine. If it was cold, I drank standing up, shifting from side to side. On the rare warmer nights, I sat on the grass. Then I got home, creeping into the room where my girlfriend slept, and told her, again, that the restaurant closed at midnight and I'd only just finished.

Ants, III

I was an ant, but unspatially, I was an ant, anxiously. I drank and drank, antily. Tinily, my tiny, worthless drunken me. I drank and drank, pre-spatially. Dodging out of form, away from models that move on forth, compounding spatial dioceses into inward measurements. How far can a bottle go inside me, how long how long is an evening and all the booze. I was drunk for a decade. I stumbled out of atria and into closed holes, zipped, and sealed wind traps where no one ever called my name, and I'd forgotten it. I drank and drank for a decade without stopping. I lost every friend, punished every proximity with my hatred, poisoned every moment of nearness with a steaming spout of anger. Choo choo, the snort is keeping him awake again. I bought speed every weekend and never slept, I drank the longest bottles of rum I've ever known, and the cigarettes and the holes in my clothes. I got fired from Westfield and found a job in a pub in South Kensington, serving bourgeois arseholes. I started nicking the booze and the clothes the customers left in the pub as they shuffled back to mansion comforts and I walked for an hour into ten cans of lager. When the pub in South Kensington fired me for stealing money, I moved to a pub in Covent Garden. When the pub in Covent Garden fired me for stealing wine, I moved to France. I got a job cleaning houses in some un-heard-of town and I drank and drank and drank. I woke up in the sea one day and a Polish woman was asking if I'm OK. No, obviously.

I returned to London after several months and I got a job in a restaurant in Marylebone. I had a fight with the manager, a tiny Italian who always told me I was *"a fucking iiiiiiidiot"* and that my girlfriend was a boy which I never understood, or never got why he was always saying it to me, but he was always saying it to me. I drank. I also drank. I broke everything. Nothing ever gets fixed in the blobs of antiverticality or the spread that's so unthought.

Black Space in Gaston's Basement

Philosophy, like Architecture, has to contend with the weird manifestations of Empire that sometimes make it aggressively present, then sometimes it's an absolute totality and cannot be distinguished from anything else, then sometimes it's even worse than ever because it seems to have gone, to be subsumed in an ocean.

One particular twentieth-century thinker spent his life sorting through these problems. His life assortments have been very influential for architects, artists, and other thinkers. His name is Gaston Bachelard.

Bachelard was born in the Champagne hills in 1884 and died in Paris in 1962. His work centered on the philosophy of science, approaching themes of physics, space, psychoanalysis, chemistry, and epistemology with a philosophical demeanor that seems very out of place among his contemporary French thinkers. The trends in phenomenology, Marxist structuralism, and existentialism involved deeply working through the signs and signifiers of capitalism, or unearthing linguistic artifacts that reveal the plural condition of humanity, or any number of other philosophical tasks that claimed universal validity and strict rationality.

Bachelard, meanwhile, meanders through his books as if he's still writing the notes, in preparation to begin. In his final work, he notes the feeling of inner immensity, the private communication between his ears and his eyes, the hundred-year-old memories he has in his seventies, the logics of stealing eggs, the pain of finding empty nests in his garden, and a million other glittering poetries that make for wondrous reading but are as full of philosophical problems as a press release from the government.

In *The Poetics of Space,* Bachelard is consciously closing his lifelong experience in the sciences. He is trying to distract himself from decades of scientific study, and instead engaging with "the problems posed by the poetic imagination."[21] He wants to think *within* the structure of a house; to *be* a part of the house, which is "the human being's first world. Before he is 'cast into the world,' as claimed by certain hasty metaphysics, man is laid in the cradle of a house. […] Life begins well, it begins enclosed, protected, all warm in the bosom of the house."[22] He wants to be, as he later puts it, "a psychologist of houses."[23]

Why is the house presumed to precede the person? The house, for Bachelard, exists already once the person is born. It is the place into which the human being is first welcomed, setting this spatial life on a linear timescale, like Giedion theorizes for architecture in general.

For Kant, this slow revelation could only occur through the Human mind. Any process of ideal development, in which the essence of a structure is exposed through thought, requires the rational judgement of a Human being or, more precisely, of *Man*. For Hegel, this process requires a dialectic of moral principles, with aesthetic, and therefore moral, attributes of phenomena gradually becoming perfected through History's *Geist*.

But for Bachelard, somehow, this temporal process of space occurs *before* the Human is aware of it. The house is already a warm and comforting womb by the time the baby arrives. There

---

21 Gaston Bachelard, *The Poetics of Space,* trans. Maria Jolas (London: Penguin, 2014), 1.
22 Ibid., 29.
23 Ibid., 93.

is no mention of the parents' or carers' preparation of the home, or of the architects and builders and contractors and city planners and factory workers and truck drivers who allowed the materials coalesced as this house to coalesce as this house. There is, moreover, a striking absence of any mention of people *not* born into this warm and comfortable home. Like many European philosophers, although he doesn't mention it, Bachelard is focused only on modern Europe, and even more specifically on twentieth-century bourgeois France. There is only the baby, arriving warm and new, into an urban ontology that makes life out of life-space.

So how is this human born into the protection of a house? It is near the beginning of the book that Bachelard begins to reveal this striking novelty in his thinking.

The simple house, he laments, has been dismissed by philosophers. No one really thinks of the primitive space of a house, a simple dwelling, a patch of ground and materials and the comfort it provides, alongside the opportunity to control the pathologies of comfort — to protect ourselves, to scare ourselves.

If we "are willing to dream," the "humble home" can become a universe in itself, a universe that, indeed, *creates* the possibility of humanity. But these philosophers nowadays "know the universe before they know the house, the far horizon before the resting-place."[24] The investigation of the resting-place is so important that Bachelard has put down all his tools; he has given up his philosophy of science and he is standing here, naked in a humble home, just looking around.[25]

The Poetics of Space is a phenomenological study of houses. It is a study of the consciousness made possible within the lived space of a house. And it is conducted in Bachelard's signature method of merging rationalism and empiricism: the house can both be known through the human mind — through what the mind experiences and what the inherent reason of the Human being neurologically contains — and meanwhile through the ac-

---

24 Ibid., 27.
25 Ibid.

tual objects themselves, the specific knowledge of the objects and what they allow the thinking subject to think.

Bachelard is concerned with these other philosophers — the ones who know the universe before they know the house — giving the absence of Human reason away to the cosmos. The non-I is an abstract concept for them, and a World-consciousness exists on this planet and it stretches among populations. For Bachelard, however, the non-I is right here, at home.

The I inhabits a space, and if it *properly* inhabits that space then it constructs around itself the possibility of the non-I. It makes for itself its other. Otherness, in this theorization, becomes architectural. It is the imagination itself, resident in a physical structure, that constructs the borders of its own possibility. The I exists inside a space prepared for it, and projects the non-I onto the edges of what it defines as inhabited space. "In short, in the most interminable of dialectics, the sheltered being gives perceptible limits to his shelter."[26]

Importantly, these "perceptible limits" are imposed not architecturally but imaginatively. The inhabitant of inhabited space brings an entire past to the house he inhabits, and, uniting dreams and memories with inhabited space and these constructed borders of thought, the dream then stretches *beyond* the memory of the inhabitant. The house is an extender of dreams. It pushes the dreams and memories past the beginning of life. The memory elongates into the pre-past, before the dreamer was born.

The house has temporal tentacles that inhabit eras before it was even constructed. The poetics of the house is a time-shifting space that expands as the inhabitant "willing to dream" inhabits it.

The inhabitant dreams of other fantasies of protection, of being protected from the outside, that are not limited to the physical surroundings of this house. The dreams are exactly *not bordered,* but they are also the force that constructs their own borders. The dreamer, that is, dreams of protection by summon-

---

26 Ibid.

ing the memory of previous houses, of the womb, of safe places against the fearsome terror of the outside, and, simultaneously, the dreamer undermines this protective house by projecting onto it the fantasies of break-in, of danger, of darkness. "Memories of the outside world will never have the same tonality as those of home and, by recalling these memories, we add to our store of dreams; we are never real historians, but always near poets, and our emotion is perhaps nothing but an expression of a poetry that was lost."[27]

This is the universe created by Gaston Bachelard. This is his anthropocosmology of the house. A universe made by Humans and houses.

This universe has a very particular geometry, defined by both time and space. In some ways the ideas in *The Poetics of Space* relate to what philosophers had conceived of as the space of thinking, the time of being, but in many other ways Bachelard is completely unique. Or, if his ideas in the book seem classical at best, mired thickly in a time many millennia before them, at least his style of saying it is new and exciting. As he says throughout *The Poetics,* precise geometries and sciences do not account for this experience of houses. Only poetry can make the leap.

The first chapter of the book, after its long introduction, is titled "The House. *From* Cellar to Garret. The Significance of the Hut." From cellar to garret is a crucial movement for Bachelard's poetics. Also crucial is that, within the narrative structure of the book, the garret seemingly precedes the cellar. The title of the chapter says *from cellar to garret* but while reading, the first thing we explicitly encounter is the garret.

This first mention of the garret is of its imagined absence. It is a place of promises, of a future held in the security of the past. Here lie the memories of a bizarrely perfect place, "at once small and large, warm and cool, always comforting."[28] Even though we recognize the fallacy of these dreams, we still cling to the perfec-

---

27 Ibid., 28.
28 Ibid., 32.

tion of the attic's comforting past, the "shell" it forms around us in the "repose that is pre-human."[29]

Before this there is no mention of the cellar. There is, however, a discussion of the outside, of the fearsome place "outside the being of the house, a circumstance in which the hostility of men and of the universe accumulates."[30]

The garret — the top of the house — is a clear and redeeming pinnacle, holding inside it the memories of safety, even beyond its own existence. It might be gone; it might have never existed. But the memory is stored above the being who experiences it. Meanwhile, there is another place that is cast out, that is thrown beyond the boundaries set up by the dreaming inhabitant. That place is where hostility resides. Implicitly, according to the logic of the title that rises through the house, that place is the cellar, the bottom of the house — the basement.

Later in the chapter this cosmos becomes clearer. The protection earlier described as a projection of the dreamer onto the house is given more nuance. Bachelard uses an allegory from Carl Jung to describe the terror of the cellar. If a man hears a noise in his house, he rushes to the attic to see what it was. He finds nothing there because he knows that the noise came from the cellar, but he dares not go there. He is comfortable establishing his empire in the attic, pointing his finger around the property he owns, where his maternal memories are stored, but he cannot access the tremendous horror of the unknowable basement.

There is, throughout the book, a property-logic to the house. Implicitly, it is only through the logics of ownership that a person (who in the book is always male) can access these memories and poetics (or possibly politics) of verticality. This logic of property ownership allows the man in his house to be comfortable in the parts he can own, and he can own them because they are separable from the commons. That is, he is comfortable in the parts of his property that are intangible to other people. He knows the attic well, and that is where he goes when he hears a

---
29 Ibid.
30 Ibid., 29.

scary noise, because no one can access the attic. The attic is the least accessible part of the house to other people.

The most accessible? The basement, of course. The "*dark entity* of the house, the one that partakes of subterranean forces."[31]

The basement is outside of the logics of property ownership because it is accessible to other people. It is inherently connected to others — to the commons, to unownable land, to *nec plus ultra,* torrid zones, and no man's land — in the imagination of the owner. The cellar is connected to the outside. That is why the owner cannot think of it, cannot run to it when he hears a noise. The basement is in the connected ground, not the free, untouched, and individual protection of the higher air. It is too distant from his comfort in property-possession.

However, connectedness to the commons does allow the fantasy of domination. It allows the owner to imagine his global reach, to dream of colonizing the basements that are all connected. The underground is at once the fearsome impossibility and the illustrious dream of total domination.

> If the dreamer's house is in a city it is not unusual that the dream is one of dominating in depth the surrounding cellars. His abode wants the undergrounds of legendary fortified castles, where mysterious passages that run under the enclosing walls, the ramparts and the moat put the heart of the castle into communication with the distant forest.[32]

The basement connects both spatially and temporally to the outside, the beyond-outside. It is in the time of castles and moats, the distant past when men were coated in iron, when they fought bloody battles to conquer terrain. And it is spatially outside, in the forest.

The forest, etymologically, means *outside,* coming from the Latin *foris* — the same root word as *foreign* in English, although not in French (*étrangère/étranger*), the language in which Ba-

---

31 Ibid., 39.
32 Ibid., 41–42.

chelard writes. *Foris* in Latin is in opposition to *civis*, meaning a *citizen*, a *civilized* inhabitant of the rational center of society, *the civic* hub where everything is proper and in order, unlike the *foreign foris* outside, beyond the limits.

The forest is not only a collection of trees but the linguistic referent of outsideness.

Much later in the book, Bachelard gives more details about the position of the forest. Its position in time has a huge impact on his original claim that when the inhabitant enters the house, everything is already set, as he sees it. The forest is in the basement, and the house is the city above. And "in the vast world of the non-I, the non-I of fields is not the same as the non-I of forests. The forest is a before-me, before-us[:] forests reign in the past."[33] The forest is long before Man, and exists as a temporal precedent to the city. It is there already; a witness to its own creation.

But what really separates the comfortable upstairs of the house, where the logics of property ownership reign, and the basement, where the commons is accessible to anyone and the only dream is imperial domination of the unpossessable mass?

The answer given by Bachelard is reason. Ideal Kantian reason. Ideal smooth white Sullivan-and-Wright Modernist Kantian perfection in the rationally judging subject. "When we dream there [in the cellar], we are in harmony with the irrationality of the depths."[34] "And, as I said before, when we dream of the heights we are in the rational zone of intellectualized projects."[35]

The house is an active agent in the social fears of the property owner. The man in his house, running upstairs towards his space of rational comfort every time he hears a noise, avoiding the irrational darkness of the basement, is formed in a cosmos centered on himself. Bachelard, at the beginning of the book,

---

33 Ibid., 206.
34 Ibid., 39.
35 Ibid.

confirms it as the anthropocosmos. The universe of Man: neither heliocentric nor geocentric, but anthropocentric.

In that universe, the house does not precede the invention of Man. Neither Man as the general universalizing referent of white European imperial men in modernity, nor man as a singular being. It would seem that the house *does* precede Man as Bachelard describes the temporal process. But, what he unwittingly reveals in the rest of the book is that the universe itself is the invention of Man, and it begins when he owns a property. Once the house becomes *his,* his universe is universalized. There is only *one* universe now, and it is the universe of My House. It is the logic of my own property ownership.

The command that brings the Universe of Man into being is his purchase of a property.

The basement is so terrifying because it also bears the suggestion of not being owned, of being accessed by anyone. Its borders can be transgressed by barbarian outsiders. And the outside, and the below, and the basement — these signifiers are *darkness.* They are Black, and that is where the logics of property ownership do not quite reach because there is always this beautiful connection to the forest, through the moat, under the city, beyond the rationality of the civilization: beyond the *civis,* into the *foris.*

This underground beneath the city sings to me like Fred Moten and Stefano Harney in the *undercommons.* I recognize the song from an album of theirs I nicked from a record shop back when there was free nickin in the city, back in record shops. The tune is in my head, but it hits so differently to my own arrhythmic movements. It is an oceanic space that removes itself constantly from entrapment in the racializing logics of property ownership. And even Bachelard, maybe without knowing it, knows this: "We all know that the big city is a clamorous sea, and it has been said countless times that, in the heart of night in Paris, one hears the ceaseless murmur of flood and tide."[36]

---

36 Ibid., 48–49.

What he is hearing, out the window in his insomnia, is the ocean, and the ocean is the beyond that he fears so much, but in that fear also resides the possibility of escape. In the undercommons is the hope of the end of modernity. Beyond the Blackness of the basement, beyond the building that crushes it further and further into the ground, is "a region that is beyond human images, […] like an animal in its hole."[37]

In the basement, there is the irrationality of *beyond-reason,* thrown further than the Kantian universe can account for, outside the American modernity of Sullivan and Wright, beyond the nocturnal wanderings of Bachelard. That is where the hope is, the hope of antiracism in an undercurrent that carries all the fears of white modernity above it. Bachelard keeps saying it before me, jumping in: "It possesses the felicity of intense poverty; indeed, it is one of the glories of poverty; as destitution increases it gives us access to absolute refuge."[38]

The happiness of ontological poverty; the ecstasy of living beyond the idiotic limitations of property-possessive logics. I would not idolize that state as readily as Bachelard, who does it without realizing it, but I point out that Bachelard and Fred Moten have similar claims, both pursuing escape in the otherspace of the basement:

> Certain experiences of being tracked, managed, cornered in seemingly open space are inextricably bound to an aesthetically and politically dangerous supplementarity, an internal exteriority waiting to get out, as if the prodigal's return were to leaving itself. Black studies' concern with what it is to own one's dispossession, to mine what is held in having been possessed, makes it more possible to embrace the underprivilege of being-sentenced to the gift of constant escape.[39]

---

[37] Ibid., 50.
[38] Ibid., 52.
[39] Moten, *Stolen Life*, 158.

The Black place is an inescapable connection to the (under)privilege of constantly escaping, escaping the constant entrapment enacted by the house of modernity, by its nation-as-house, by its Man-as-house, by the hook that descends from the attic and calls the basement irrational and dark. But the darkness allows a cover for escape, constantly.

This constant escape provides, Moten writes in another book, an "understanding of blackness as exterior to civil society and, moreover, as unmappable within the cosmological grid of the transcendental subject."[40] The basement cannot be traced by the property-logic of the house, because the house thinks that it was built at the same time as the basement. The inhabitant arrives, newly clad in life, seeking comfort and a store for extensive memories of security, and believes that the house, the inhabitant, and the city were all built together.

---

40 Moten, *The Universal Machine*, 195.

4

Fantasies

The Black Witness

What I have been arguing in the previous three chapters is that Architecture is a part of the global technological development of the seeing Subject; the Human as an apparatus of seeing. The Human who sees the building is an apparatus of seeing, and together the building and the Human make a technology of *the witness*. This technology has a racializing function in the epistemology of contemporary cities. The way cities can be known in modernity is through the racializing constitution of the Subject, as formulated in the ontological and aesthetic theories of Kant and Hegel.

In this chapter, I begin by proposing a theory of the witness in relation to the racializing space of modernity discussed in previous chapters. I then use this formulation of the witness to study more deeply the political, social, and ontological meaning of Westfield, the London shopping centers that I discussed in Chapter Three. The study of Westfield here is conducted through Anne Anlin Cheng's theory of ornamentalism. I then bring this all back to the Kantian foundations with which this book began.

In his essay "'A Self-Unsealing Poetic Text': Poetics and Politics of Witnessing," Jacques Derrida explains the three Latin derivatives of the witness which in French, Derrida's language, is *témoin*. The first is *testari*, which is the act of witness-bearing. The second is *testis*, meaning someone who is present. The third is *terstis*, meaning the third; someone who is present as a third person, as an extra presence to the subject and object involved in the event being witnessed.[1]

The witness is the bearer of a third position that sees an event and survives it. This is the additional definition that Derrida gives. The witness is *superstes*, "'witness' in the sense of survivor: someone who, having been present then having survived, plays the role of witness."[2] To be a witness is to have survived. As Ian Baucom says in *Specters of the Atlantic*, "To speak of witnessing, of the work of testament, is thus to speak of the witness as either/or and both 'terstis/superstes,' as third or survivor or third and survivor at once."[3]

As the survivor, as the lingering third after the event involving the subject and object, the problem of the witness is that their testament is always in question. Hannah Arendt's report on the trial of Adolf Eichmann, published as *Eichmann in Jerusalem: A Report on the Banality of Evil* in 1963, is the propagator of exactly this paradox of witnessing.

The witness is, by definition, the one who was there; the present third person, the survivor. And yet, the witness is questioned. The witness is disbelieved. The title of Derrida's essay, which is taken from Arendt, emphasizes the problem: the poetics and politics of witnessing. It is always an act both poetic and political. Arendt rejects outright the testimony of witnessing on precisely these grounds. Witnesses, she observes, always have a political and an aesthetic agenda.

---

[1] Jacques Derrida, "'A Self-Unsealing Poetic Text': Poetics and Politics of Witnessing," in *Revenge of the Aesthetic: The Place of Literature in Theory Today*, ed. Michael P. Clark (Berkeley: University of California Press, 2000), 186.

[2] Ibid., 187.

[3] Ian Baucom, *Specters of the Atlantic: Finance Capital, Slavery, and the Philosophy of History* (Durham: Duke University Press, 2005), 176.

A true witness, she writes in her signature conservative language and approach, should be a "righteous" man, a man who knows how to deal with the "poetics and politics" of witnessing. He should have "the rare capacity for distinguishing between things that had happened to the storyteller more than sixteen, and sometimes twenty years ago, and what he had read and heard and imagined in the meantime."[4] The witness is not to believed precisely because of his distance from the events he survived.

The witness is untrustworthy *because he is a witness* — because he survived. But he did not only survive. The witness also, by being a witness, by having survived the event and having *become its witness,* is exactly the person who does *not survive* the event. The witness is the person most tied to the event, because he is the one who must *bear witness* to it. He has not survived it, because he is its witness, which means that the event lives on in him, continuing to constitute him. The event remains, and he remains in the event, never having survived its finite moment.

Giorgio Agamben also contends with these paradoxes of the witness. In the third volume of his *Homo Sacer* series, *Remnants of Auschwitz: The Witness and the Archive,* he traces the two Latin origins of the witness: *terstis* which is to be a third party in a legal dispute between two contending claimants; and *superstes* which is someone who has lived through something, and can therefore bear witness to it. At the beginning of the book, Agamben complicates the ethics of the witness. He notes that not only is the witness a survivor, but often the possibility of becoming a witness is the very reason for surviving. "In the camp [Auschwitz], one of the reasons that can drive a prisoner to survive is the idea of becoming a witness."[5] To take revenge on their oppressors, to feel the glory of having lived through it

---

[4] Hannah Arendt, *Eichmann in Jerusalem: A Report on the Banality of Evil* (New York: Penguin Books, 1994), 223–24.

[5] Giorgio Agamben, *Remnants of Auschwitz: The Witness and the Archive,* trans. Daniel Heller-Roazen (New York: Zone Books, 1999), 15.

and coming out the other side. But, "to justify one's survival is not easy — least of all in the camp."⁶

The witness, then, is a figure who simultaneously inhabits two times. The witness exists in the event's future, while being simultaneously bound to the contemporary of the event. The witness is both able to bring the event to life as its speaker in a future in which the event necessarily no longer exists, and the witness is the bearer of the historical truth of the event as the person who was there at the time.

The witness is the figure that allows the continuation of social time. The illusion of a social flow — what Kant calls "progress perpetually toward the better"⁷ — is allowed by the contemporary witness *bearing* the events of the past. The process happening, though, is not so much a *flow,* as it is often perceived, but rather an *accumulation*. The witness is gathering within them the load of history, bearing its truth and thus inventing the authentic truth of now; they create the nowness of now by accumulating past time within them as the paradoxically truth-bearing but always-in-question witness.

Derrida points out, in *Specters of Marx,* the links between witnessing and the inheritance of history. This is how time is passed on. Bearing witness is the inheritance of an impossible death, an incomplete death of pasts for which we are forever in mourning. We are, meanwhile, forever trying to understand the impossibility of our mourning. "All the questions on the subject of being or of what is to be (or not to be) are questions of inheritance." He goes on,

> That we are *heirs* does not mean that we receive this or that, some inheritance that enriches us one day with this or that, but that the *being* of what we are *is* first of all inheritance, whether we like it or know it or not. And that [...] we can

---

6   Ibid.
7   Immanuel Kant, "An Old Question Raised Again: Is the Human Race Constantly Progressing?" in *Religion and Rational Theory,* ed. and trans. Allen W. Wood and George Di Giovanni (Cambridge: Cambridge University Press, 1996), 308.

> only *bear witness* to it. To bear witness would be to bear witness to what we are insofar as we *inherit,* and that — here is the circle, here is the chance, or the finitude — we inherit the very thing that allows us to bear witness to it.[8]

The circular logic about the witness is revealed perfectly here. What we inherit is the ability to bear witness to our inheritance, and our inheritance is what we bear witness to. Culture is continued by the constant inheritance of its constant loss.

In this sense, the witness is a creator of the present. The witness is the figure who conditions the possibility of society contemporarily defining itself — of having a culture that is distinct. It does this only by mourning the loss of a previous culture, either merrily or dejectedly, and that mourning initiates the possibility of another culture now, born by, and accumulated within the testimony of the witness.

In this formulation, taken to this degree of circularity, the witness becomes more than a singular survivor of a single event. The witness becomes the creator of cultural contemporaneity, the accumulator of time, and the bearer of now.

On May 25, 2020, George Floyd, a 46-year-old security guard who had spent most of his life in Houston and moved to the Twin Cities in 2014, bought cigarettes from Cup Foods, a shop on the corner of Chicago Avenue and East 38th Street in Minneapolis, Minnesota. The person working in the shop thought that Floyd had used a fake $20 note and called the police. Four police officers responded. They arrived and forced him onto the ground in the middle of the road. Derek Chauvin, a 44-year-old officer with eighteen complaints on his official record and who had been previously involved in multiple shootings, in which he was the shooter, pushed his knee into Floyd's neck for almost nine minutes, while Floyd proclaimed that he could not breathe.

---

8   Jacques Derrida, *Specters of Marx: The State of the Debt, the Work of Mourning and the New International,* trans. Peggy Kamuf (London: Routledge, 2006), 67–68.

Derek Chauvin, J. Alexander Kueng, Tou Thao, and Thomas Lane murdered George Floyd between 8.17 and 8.27pm.

On May 26, protests began in Minneapolis, involving a variety of participants with political demands ranging from liberal to radical. Some demanded, and continue to demand, reform of legal institutions, including a reduction in police funding. Other, more radical, demands included the total abolition of the police, which has long been a pursuit of anarchists and other radical anticapitalists.

In the following weeks, protests emerged across the country, and then around the world. The political commentary quickly turned to the violence of the protest. Conservative commentators from ITV news hosts to Priti Patel, the British secretary of state, condemned the protests with familiar dismissals, calling it "thuggery" and "criminal."[9]

The hundreds of thousands of protestors may have seemed, initially, to have eclipsed the origin of the protests, which was the murder of George Floyd. The spectacle had become the protests themselves, rather than the event that triggered this wave of their manifestation or the demands around which they were based. The witnesses had accumulated history inside themselves, inheriting the lost time of that to which they bore witness: the murder of a Black person by a white police officer.

However, there is a power that attempts to break the accumulation of history within a radical subject who demands change. There is conservative power; there is the force of government, of the nation, of Empire and Capital, that is inherently opposed to the accumulation of history within radical subjects. It is impossible for the power of Empire and Capital to accept the radical mourning of the witnesses, of those who demand to be able to mourn the loss of a history that they inherited.

---

9 Imogen Braddick, "Priti Patel Condemns 'Thuggery' of Black Lives Matter and Extinction Rebellion Protests in Tory Speech," *Evening Standard*, October 4, 2020, https://www.standard.co.uk/news/uk/priti-patel-black-lives-matter-extinction-rebellion-protests-tory-speech-a4563016.html.

The narrative changed accordingly. As government ministers in the UK began to be repeatedly questioned about the importance of these massive protests, they could not posit the entire meaning of the event in the "thuggery" of the protestors, because, once the protestors include hundreds of thousands of people, the implicit revelation is that an entire city's-worth of people in this country are thugs who want violent change. Once they become aware of that and it is ordained by the official narrative that their radical demands are of a size that is itself history, and they are capable of accumulating themselves as history, of being witnesses of themselves — they no longer suffer the inevitable misery of the heir: that the past cannot be mourned because the witness is always in the paradoxical third position, unbelieved, unreal, just an accumulator of pasts. Becoming a witness of oneself means that the witness then inhabits the first and third positions. They become both subject and witness; they are the event and the survivor of the event.

The powers of Empire at this point move the narrative back to the original event. They say that they are appalled by the murder of George Floyd, but that all of these protests are only concerned with the USA and the minor instances of police brutality that sometimes erupt out of the generally smooth fabric of American policing. What is hidden here is that the police and police brutality are not separate things. There is no distinguishable manifestation between them. The police are brutal and the act of policing is one of brutality. The police, as an institution, as a social proposition, is the violent imperial force charged with the task of defending bourgeois property, and providing the ontological protection bound up with the somatic and social referent of property ownership, i.e., whiteness. Police officers occupy protests not to protect protestors, as the most obvious example for anyone who has ever attended a protest: they are there to protect the property of the people who are not protesting. The protestors have renounced their status as proper possessors of property by involving themselves in the protest, and instead they have become threats to property, so they are policed.

The narrative is refocused on the original event. The original event, however, has been accumulated inside the protestors as those who bore witness to history.

But, of course, the protestors did not witness the murder. The witnesses were not there when it happened. Instead, the protestors were the witnesses of their own absence in the original event: what they bore witness to was their own absence. The inheritance the protestors received, and that they had to mourn, was the fact of their own absence in history. *We were not there when he was murdered. We failed to stop another murder.* Their own absence in history is the mournful inheritance they have to confront as they protest, as they demand the eradication of the force that enforces their absence.

The police exist to expel the presence of the witness, in order for the police's enforcement of History to be not only unwitnessed but unmourned. The police refuse the process of mourning, of mourning every absence in the history that accumulates within Black protestors now as they enact the time of now — as they initiate contemporaneity — by speaking that past to which they did not bear witness.

I feel that I have reached another point in the finitude of Derridean circularity. The witness is the creator of history, because the witness speaks now, saying that she was not there, and by that process she brings history to herself, accumulating it inside herself. The event occurs when it is later spoken by the witness. The death of George Floyd as history, as an event, did not only occur while Chauvin was murdering him on East 38th Street in Minneapolis. It occurred, again and again, while the protesters enacted the culture of now by accumulating their own absence at the scene of the event inside themselves, inside the contemporary, and by doing so they created the contemporary.

The event is a ghost haunting the moment of the witness. The witness is the initiator of the spectral re-emergence of the event as history. Ian Baucom says, reading Derrida, "the event, like the specter, is an untimely apparition: untimely in the sense that it first appears as the reapparition of itself, emerges into visibility (as an event) not at the moment of its happening but only within the retrospective purview of [...] its subjects."[10] It is the absence of a witness of the event — of a survivor who bears the event's testimony — that itself bears witness to the original event as now. The contemporary means to bear witness to a past accumulated within the contemporary subjects who were absent for history, who are mourning their inheritance.

So what is being described in the testimony of the witness? What is included in the Black Lives Matter protests after the murder of George Floyd?

It is clearly impossible that the protests serve to demand the life of George Floyd. Within a liberal argument, it can demand legal retribution for his murder, demanding that the murderers are arrested and punished for the crime they committed. A radical argument would not demand this, because the law is itself what killed George Floyd, so demanding retribution from the law is never going to change anything. That is only asking for a temporary catharsis, to momentarily patch up a social wound to distract the polity possibly until the time of the next racist murder committed by the police. The law cannot protect against the law. The police are not the force who can limit the violence of the police.

Revealed in this aporia is the fact of protesting as a mode of sociality that conducts what the Afropessimist tradition calls "the general antagonism,"[11] which states that, as Stefano Harney says, "there is a constant and ongoing rebellion and insurgency against identity, which is primary. [...] [The] institution [or the state then] steps in to try to quell an insurgency, to try to [...] get what it wants from this general antagonism, but it breaks out again and again all the time." Ultimately, "we don't rebel against [...] the police because there's police. The police come after us

---

10 Baucom, *Specters of the Atlantic*, 121.
11 See, for example, Jared Sexton, "Afro-pessimism: The Unclear World," *Rhizomes* 29 (2016), http://www.rhizomes.net/issue29/sexton.html.

if we show ourselves as that primary antagonism."[12] The protest, then, is not the act of calling out the police, or an attempt to cancel the police's presence at the protest, allowing instead a segregated and individual parade in which the police allow their own absence for the staging of the event. Instead, the fact of the protest is itself the constant and ongoing justification of the power of the police. The protest functions as a means of revealing again what the originary conditions of the police are: the maintenance of property, in its abstract forms, like race and gender, as much as material forms, like houses and civic buildings.

Having revealed the fact that the police functions only to protect the property of property owners — and their property includes their whiteness, their ontological status, their position as urban referents of property ownership — the demand for police reform or justice from the courts and the law become futile. Witness, then, in these protests inheres in the fact of the protest itself. Protestors bear witness to the fact that protest is an ongoing act, that the form of sociality that is rebellion is an ongoing and permanent antagonism in the mechanism of state violence. The regulation of this rebellion is the function of the state, at which it always fails, since protest continues, and since Black life still exists.

Ian Baucom presents another question and answer to add to our questions above. "To what does the witness bear witness? To bare life, abandoned."[13] The witness sees the lost pasts that constitute the excluded life of society. The witness watches the rejection of certain forms of being from the accumulation of History. Some subjects are thrown overboard, and those subjects no longer roll into the coagulation of History, stuck inside the body

---

12 Fred Moten and Stefano Harney, "'Wildcat the Totality': Fred Moten and Stefano Harney Revisit *The Undercommons* in a Time of Pandemic and Rebellion (Part 1)", *Millennials Are Killing Capitalism,* podcast, July 4, 2020, https://millennialsarekillingcapitalism.libsyn.com/wildcat-the-totality-fred-moten-and-stefano-harney-revisit-the-undercommons-in-a-time-of-pandemic-and-rebellion-part-1.

13 Baucom, *Specters of the Atlantic,* 189.

of the witness, the disappearing spectacle, waiting to become another case of impossible mourning, another death untold.

The protestors in 2020 and the years since bear witness to their own ability to feel the loss of George Floyd, to feel the recurring possibility of the institutional murder of Black people; the protestors bear witness to their own absence in history, and the possibility of the endless repetition of that absence. The protestors bear witness to their own melancholy, to their liberal feelings of compassion for a historical absence. Through their own absence, the event was accumulated inside them as an inherited mourning, as the grief of a past absorbed into the performance of contemporary melancholy, and by that performance this moment is defined.

The testament of witnesses is to themselves and their own contemporary production of a history that ends in themselves.

Frantz Fanon is on a train. A white boy sees him. The boy turns to his white mother.

> "Look, a Negro!" It was true. It amused me.
>
> "Look, a Negro!" The circle was drawing a bit tighter. I made no secret of my amusement.
>
> "Mama, see the Negro! I'm frightened!" [...]
>
> I could no longer laugh, because I already knew that there were legends, stories, history, and above all *historicity* [...] Then, assailed at various points, the corporeal schema crumbled, its place taken by a racial epidermal schema. In the train it was no longer a question of being aware of my body in the third person but in a triple person. In the train I was given not one but two, three places. I had already stopped being amused. It was not that I was finding febrile coordinates in the world. I existed triply: I occupied space. I moved toward the other ... and the evanescent other, hostile but not opaque, transparent, not there, disappeared. Nausea....
>
> I was responsible at the same time for my body, for my race, for my ancestors. I subjected myself to an objective examination, I discovered my blackness, my ethnic character-

istics; and I was battered down by tom-toms, cannibalism, intellectual deficiency, fetishism, racial defects, slave-ships, and above all else, above all: "Sho' good eatin'."[14]

The moment the boy points out Fanon's Blackness, Fanon is separated from himself. The corporeal schema crumbles. The subjectivity of existing within a body, in the history of the socius and its myth of progressive time, is collapsed upon recognition of immediate difference.

Suddenly, as the full subjectivity of the boy is proclaimed by an assertion of his own whiteness, the removal of the Black body is enacted: the Black body cannot exist in the schema conducted within a frame of white normativity. The boy is saying, *look, there is a thing that is impossible to recognize as the same as me.* The thing in front of the boy cannot possibly be recognized within the white supremacist schema of modernity, of progressive time and motion. Something is stopping the whole scene, and it is Blackness — it is the recognition of Blackness that initiates a break in the scene that then redefines the problem as Blackness.

Fanon is not, importantly, turned into an object of the scene. He is removed from binary opposition to the white boy, because he is excluded from expressing shock at the whiteness of the boy. The scene is premised on only one moment of shock, one break in the being of the scene's progressive time. The boy is shocked at the Blackness in front of him, but Fanon cannot be shocked at the boy. He can only be shocked at the fact of the boy's shock, and that can only happen later, when he has become a witness of the event.

The boy is the Subject of the scene. The boy's mind — in the World of Kant's transcendental ideality of space — is the condition for the spatialization of the scene. The scene's geometry is figured according to the centrality of the white boy. He is the figure who decides the positioning, who positions himself as the body from which observation happens, whether or not he is

---

14 Frantz Fanon, *Black Skin, white Masks*, trans. Charles Lam Markmann (London: Pluto Press, 2008), 84–85.

in the center. This is precisely how Kant formulates the ideality of space, according to the Copernican revolution. He proposes that Copernicus could not discover anything a priori, by thinking, not by observation, about the celestial bodies by working on their own framework of space. Instead, Copernicus had to set Earth in motion and leave the stars stagnant in order for them to conform to his movements in space. The subject had to become the geometrical decider; the human mind projects onto space its own formulations of thinking, and that is how the World is ordered. As it is for astronomy after Copernicus, so it is for Kant's transcendental ideality of space.[15]

The white boy positions Fanon, but not as his object. On the train he is not still in space, stuck there for the boy to observe him. The boy, after all, is shocked that Fanon is there, and Fanon is triply there. The Subject is not shocked by the presence of an object in Kantian geometry because the Subject is the one who decides the stagnant position of objects.

Moreover, Fanon *occupies space*. He is an intruder, a bizarre apparition from another time. He is a ghostly presence haunting from the battered-down past, from a forgotten scene already thrown overboard.

Fanon is outside the schema. He is beyond the possibility of being ordered in the astronomy of ideal white space. He occupies a third space, an impossible specter of witnessing, while remaining in bodily form on the train, but only witnessing his absence. He is the re-emergence of a spectral form that speaks this event into being despite and because of his own impossible absence in the scene. He was there, he saw it happen, and yet the scene is necessarily premised on his absence. How could he be more absent than a Negro in the racist ideality of Kantian space? How could anything mark his absence more than the pointing white finger of the boy and racist ontology snapping a hole in the scene, erasing a dark face from the photograph?

---

15 Immanuel Kant, *Critique of Pure Reason,* trans. Paul Guyer and Allen W. Wood (Cambridge: Cambridge University Press, 1998), Bxvi.

Fanon is forced to see himself from outside himself in this scene. He is projected away from his own body in the geometry of the boy. His body may remain a simple object in the scene of some other witness on the train, but in this scene, in this testament borne in the specter accumulating history in his impossibility, his testimony always in question, always disbelievable, always and necessarily forever absent — here he is a witness only to his own absence. He inhabits, always, the third position.

The third position is occupied already by the Black subject in Kantian modernity. The Black subject is the meaning of the witness. The absent historical figure who is coded in the contemporary as absence, as the impossible non-presence always haunting the cuts and breaks of the past, is what we refer to when we say Black.

So what is the Black witness? The witness-as-Black-(non)subject is not the same as the Black witness.

In *The Black Atlantic,* Paul Gilroy provides the possibility of thinking further into a figure called *the Black witness.*

Gilroy looks at a scene in Frederick Douglass's *Narrative of the Life of Frederick Douglass, an American Slave.* The autobiography, published in 1845, follows Douglass's life in slavery, and his eventual escape. He then became the most renowned Black abolitionist in American history.

Gilroy emphasizes the "simultaneous self-creation and self-emancipation" of "slave narratives."[16] The slave is the witness who cannot bear testimony. As so many eighteenth and nineteenth century paintings and photographs show, depicting the white bourgeois family and then, in a smudged corner, the Black boy attending to them, the slave is always there, but has no right to carry this testimony into the future; the slave is the figure who exists only in the original past of the event, rather than in the future in which the event is hauntologically, spectrally, ghostly, activated and brought to social being by the testimony of the wit-

---

16 Paul Gilroy, *The Black Atlantic: Modernity and Double Consciousness* (London: Verso, 1993), 69.

ness. The slave is the one who is there, but, being in a third position even to himself, unable to attend to himself as a Subject and only able to see himself from outside ("Look, a Negro!" says the slave even of himself), cannot later speak this event into being.

For the slave, to speak of his own emancipation, of his own history and to summon the accumulated past as a retrospectively activated event, is a monumental act that warps the racism of time. The slave is pulling himself into the contemporary, initiating a contemporary moment that can be spoken into being by the slave, and thus eradicating his definition as slave.

When Douglass speaks of his emancipation, his escape from his enslaving owners, he is becoming the witness: he is speaking a past event into being by bearing its testimony, by speaking from the third position as the one who survived, who accumulated the lost time of the past. That is exactly what the witness is, and it is exactly what the slave is barred from in the temporality of slavery's Empire, which is also called modernity.

Douglass emphasizes this act in his narrative by confronting the reader's suspicions of the narrative's veracity. Douglass knows already that his readers will be suspicious because the Black witness occupies an inherently paradoxical position and is defined by the fact that he cannot inherit history, opposed to the witness who bears the testimony of their own spectral presence in the inherited past. He is a possession of those lost in history, only allowed to exist in the past, and never to inherit it or survive. The Black witness's paradox is this: he is the one who is bearing testimony, and what his testimony bears witness to is the fact that he is disallowed the status of witness. Gilroy quotes him as writing:

> I may be deemed superstitious, and even egotistical, in regarding this event as a special interposition of divine providence in my favor. But I should be false to the earliest sentiments of my soul if I suppressed the opinion. I prefer to be true to myself even at the hazard of incurring the ridicule

of others, rather than to be false and incur my own abhorrence.[17]

The reader may disbelieve Douglass, but Douglass must take pains to believe himself. He dismisses the reader's drive towards suppression, exerting instead the risk of his own self-suppression, which he then rises out of.

The suppression imposed on him by the white reader has been replaced, narratively and literally, by the suppression he bears within him and the capacity for suppression that he has accumulated through the testimony he bears. It is not his status as witness that frees him from the category of witness initially. So agonistic to his own status, he has reinvented the witness and carried himself away from even that new paradigm. He is free of a new notion of freedom.

His own narrative is here advertised as a form of self-initiation. He is enacting the process of bringing himself into being in a World that adamantly tries to remove him from being.

Gilroy says that self-initiation is the philosophical style of the *Black Atlantic* and the way in which the "vernacular components of black expressive culture" have brought themselves into being. This style is autopoietic: it creates itself out of itself.[18]

The Black witness is making himself. He is formulating a Black possibility of witnessing out of the being of the Black witness. Meanwhile, he is also eradicating the possibility of the prior status of witness.

Fanon writes away the possibility of the boy's hegemonic view of the scene, not repositioning the geometry of the memory but rather abolishing the codes of geometry. Douglass elicits the fears of the white reader who cannot bear the possibility of this slave giving testimony to the end of his own enslavement. He writes away that form of witnessing, pushing out the discourse

---

17 Ibid., 69, citing Frederick Douglass, *Narrative of the Life of Frederick Douglass, an American Slave, Written by Himself* (Cambridge: Harvard University Press, 1960), 56.

18 Gilroy, *The Black Atlantic*, 70.

of the witness and bringing in the purview of his own self-suppression, out of which he then breaks. In both of these scenes, we find the mutual forces of the Black witness: both destructive and constructive. At once, the Black witness destructs the foundation that initiated her own status as non-witness, and then she constructs an alternative status out of a different ground.

The Black witness is the bearer of a testimony that is disallowed in the language of modernity. The Black witness accumulates a past that has already been thrown overboard. The Black witness brings the submerged past to the surface of the water, and then, rather than simply revealing it into the same light as the previous testimony, uses eyes that work underwater to see the Black testimony as something entirely different. The third position slips out of the frame of seeing itself as an outsider, and reconstructs a frame elsewhere, accumulating an alternative past. Freedom from freedom is the revolutionary act of the Black witness. The Black witness does not free herself by claiming the right to bear witness. Instead, she frees herself from that freedom, constructing a new foundation of the witness.

To gain freedom from freedom, to achieve a different kind of testimony that initiates the being of the slave, that brings the object into being and allows it to see itself with its own politics of witnessing, with a testament accurate to itself, no reform or withdrawal of funds will suffice. To ask the police to reform themselves, or for the government whose property the police serve to protect to begin debating changes, is to ask only that the slave bear witness to himself as slave. Instead, to fight for freedom from freedom, to initiate the autonomous and otherwise-being of the slave, to destruct the foundations of slavery and construct a world free from the chains of the freedom to bear witness to an impossible object, only abolition will work.

The abolition of the police is the only way to gain freedom from freedom, to bear (Black) witness to a past thrown overboard and construct a politics of seeing in the ocean, out of the slave ship.[19]

Ornamental Fantasies

In her 2019 book *Ornamentalism,* Anne Anlin Cheng wants to make a feminist and antiracist study of East Asian women. Black feminism and white feminism are important areas of study, though small in comparison to subjects more conducive to capital, but movements that critically think the position of east Asian women are so unthought that she is even precluded from the emancipatory gesture of appropriating the label of racist color politics. "We accept black and brown, these brutish categories of color, as denominating categories of injury, but *yellowness* feels too ugly and crude to use."[20]

It feels to Cheng like the volume of the protest determines how acceptable the racial category in political struggles becomes. Any form of protest that is not in direct opposition, as a binary reaction to, the norms of white, European and North American, Protestant modernity are not considered sufficiently present to be accounted for. As she writes, "racial identity […] seems to garner recognition only when it can marshal sufficient indignation."[21]

Ornamentalism is a brilliant repost that emphatically pushes critical thinking of, for, and by Yellow women. I have capitalized Yellow, in the same way I do with Black, to emphasize their difference from the arbitrariness of colors — the skin is not paintable like a wall, not subject to fashion like the color of clothes;

---

19 The language of ships and the ocean in this section refers to the principal subject matter of Ian Baucom's *Specters of the Atlantic,* from which I draw my argument here: the mass murder of 133 enslaved Africans on the Zong slave ship in September 1781. For more on this event, see M. NourbeSe Philip, *Zong!* (Middletown: Wesleyan University Press, 2011), and Katherine McKittrick, *Demonic Grounds: Black Women and the Cartographies of Struggle* (Minneapolis: University of Minnesota Press, 2006).
20 Anne Anlin Cheng, *Ornamentalism* (Oxford: Oxford University Press, 2019), xi.
21 Ibid.

it is the determined result of the history of slavery and capitalism, and so I think the category of race should be grammatically noted as constructed, as a physical realm from which violent ideologies are drawn, like other proper nouns: the British Empire, Ancient Greece, the United States of America; and unlike changeable and natural categories.

One intriguing point she brings up at the beginning of *Ornamentalism* is that, in the history of race, people have not only been turned into things, but things also have been turned into people, and the relationship between person and thing is complex. The first example she gives of this is how the "yellow woman's history is entwined with the production and fates of silk, ceramics, celluloid, machinery, and other forms of animated objectness."[22]

For Cheng, these things are not simply nonhuman objects, arbitrarily associated with a certain racialized category of Human. Mutually, in their history of being used, appropriated by power and subsumed in the dominant narrative of History, racialized people and things become features imposed with the stamp of objectness in various stages of animation. Sianne Ngai calls this force of imposed animation, of being conditioned into a certain form of performance that justifies objectness, "animatedness."[23]

The things that are entwined in the being of Yellow women become prime commodities in contemporary capitalism, as the European basis of capitalist white supremacy stops looking towards North America as the bastion of industrial production and instead looks to China, Japan, and South Korea as the next stage into data-led digital production. Throughout this, Europe maintains its imperialist position as immovable sage, able to command who leads the next contortion of global capitalism.

The very basis of a commodity is fetishization, which in Karl Marx's terms means to forget the labor that went into the product. A fetishized sandwich just looks like a sandwich when you

---

22 Ibid., xi–xii.
23 Sianne Ngai, *Ugly Feelings* (Cambridge: Harvard University Press, 2005), 89–125.

laboriously unearth it from the brightly lit and cooled shelves of Sainsbury's supermarket. But behind that is a truck, and all the petrol that runs the truck and the copious materials that went into making it, that brought the sandwich to this shop. The labor of the driver, too. And at the factory, hundreds of low-paid employees work on endless repeat, bored out of their minds with sore necks from looking down at massive pots of egg mayo and stuffing it into bread slices. Then there's the chickens laying those eggs, the builders who built the cramped barn they're imprisoned in, and the farmer who collects and stamps those eggs. And so on. But it just feels like a sandwich, and that's Marx's fetishization.

So, when the Yellow thing is brought into mutually constitutive animatedness with the Yellow person, together making a commodity and an animated companion (and purchaser) of commodities, the sweat, blood, and tears behind the products is not only forgotten, but completely inaccessible. Westfield in Stratford is the ideal site of this — Yellow fetishism perfected to a T.

The Yellow woman, as Cheng makes clear, is a "ghost in Euro-American culture;"[24] just an imagined and abstract figure conscripted into the service of profit-production, and entirely dismissed as a real, living being from Asia.

In Westfield, it certainly feels like the subject has no distinction from the object. The object is an agential force that spatializes the possibility of a Subject's entrance. Those clothes call me in, and I'm useless at resisting. First, I just wanted all the drinks they had, when I was trapped inside Westfield in west London in exchange for wages. But now I want everything, when I am trapped inside Westfield in east London in exchange for the loss of my unbearable subjectivity. Inside, in that framework, I no longer have to decide. I am objectified, and my future is cancelled because this space is the absence of events; there will be, necessarily, no witness to this non-event.

---

24 Cheng, *Ornamentalism*, xii.

All that Westfield asks of me is that I don't ask. That I just let the object lure me into objectivity, into a glistening post-chromatic future when all the capital is accumulated already in the objects I purchase and I become.

The point of explicit imperialism, of the subsumption and trade of others by a global capitalist hegemony, or what Cheng calls, after Edward W. Said, "Orientalism," is to turn "persons into things that can be possessed and dominated."[25] The point is to profit from the reduction of a certain group of people to the same status as any inanimate commodity. In this scene, however, in the non-event of ornamentalism, the point is far more internal. The point is borne within the way of being of everything present. It cannot be protested against or refused, because it forms the foundation of existence in Westfield, and by proxy in the entirety of neoliberal architecture and the economic models it refers to.

Ornamentalism "is about a fantasy of turning things into persons through the conduit of racial meaning in order, paradoxically, to allow the human to escape his or her own humanness."[26] To be Human in Westfield is unbearable because the objects have control. The commodities are the witnesses of an event that is only themselves: their beckoning of Human addiction, their withdrawal of accumulated Human History and their theft of Human subjectivity. Humans lose their binary statuses, no longer Subjects and Objects. Everything is in pursuit of thingliness, attempting to escape.

The point of Westfield is to turn things into people, creating the racialized fantasy that things are people, too, and allowing Humans to temporarily escape their unbearable Humanness. The city is only formed of Humanity's endless attempt to escape it, to withdraw itself from the mutual construction of body and building. And the shopping center, in its white orbital blob, is nothing but the practice of escaping Humanness.

---

25 Ibid., 98.
26 Ibid.

To achieve a hybrid form of commodity-Humanity that is both body and product, architecture and flesh, as a single uniform of racializing space, Westfield has to conduct the fundamental principle of biological life, while also disallowing the realization of that principle. There is a simultaneous reproduction of the spatial conditions of orientalism and the impulse to reproduction itself. The space, this massive shopping center, must ground itself in the impulse to its own reproduction. That reproduction, however, is not architectural, but is based instead in the subjectivity of its users, in the life of its commodities. It expands through the machines that reproduce its way of seeing, just like Kantian subjectivity. For this purpose it uses both an aesthetic and an ethical principle. The principle is sex. Westfield has to be a site that is sexual, always suggestive of sex and reproduction and tangible proximity, but meanwhile always cutting contact before the possibility of actually doing anything.

The Yellow woman, for Cheng, is "persistently sexualized yet barred from sexuality, simultaneously made and unmade by the aesthetic project."[27] She has to be Puritan and pornographic. She has to be available for any eye, an insentient object that can be scanned for a moment's pleasure, and meanwhile exist as a temporal referent of the future, as a relic from a shiny post-commodity age when people are toys and toys are people. The requirements that merge the sexual fetishization of Orientalism with the economic logic of ornamentalism result in a being that is bizarrely stale in its pornographic performativity. It is a space that is neither inviting nor exclusionary, just a blob of sexual need that enforces sexual impossibility on everything. Westfield and the Yellow woman: zones of hypersexualized abstinence, where everything is wanted but nothing can be had.

The sexuality of the Westfield commodity also strains the tidy binaries of the Yellow woman, enfolding into itself the absolution of the American aesthetic ideal: hyper-capitalist and individually free and gun-wielding-dangerous and rock-and-roll, but Puritan and dedicated to the protection and preservation

---

[27] Ibid., 4–5.

of family. The Yellow woman's body, as Cheng writes, is a proxy for her material adornments, for the ornamental productions of her mythologized homeland. She is silk. She is gunpowder. She is celluloid. Smooth, deadly, plastically rejuvenating.[28]

The Yellow woman's body is then adaptable into physical surroundings. The city can become Yellow because Yellowness is a racist premise constructed by a unity of object and person that excludes both from the central conditions of other racialized subject positions: (white) Master, (Black) Slave, (Red) Land. Yellow is neither, inhabiting that site so terrifying to Fox News or ITV pundits and the rulers of the economy: communist capitalism; capitalist communism — an imagined place that is disciplined and ascetic, but loaded and ready to constantly shop.

A commercial building that replicates the racial coding of the Yellow woman finds itself in an ideal place in the cultural mind of the population by being neither too imposing, like incessant adverts puncturing through screens every second, nor too absent, like the moments of longing when all the shops are closed and there is nothing to consume.

The culmination, architecturally and culturally, of these intertwined aesthetics is the appearance of friendly innocence over a core of solid racist violence. Westfield presents itself as a neutral, silent site. It invested in the 2012 Olympics, by building a shopping center that dominates the entire sporting landscape of Stratford, so every single moment of action is prepared for and concluded by the ravages of a brightly-lit John Lewis underground furniture section.

It wears the smooth, white architecture of the very whitest Modernism. It sits above you, in the trading zones of east London's most egregious conflations of social housing and commercial vortexes, set in an endless circle in which each building only suggests the next: the debt of the mortgage, of the ever-rising rent; the debt of the credit card and another pair of shoes on offer; the debt of social value in the absence of the newest products.

---

28 Ibid., xi–xii.

Fig. 3. Carl Van Vechten, "Portrait of Anna May Wong," 1935.

The smooth whiteness of Westfield's surfaces always calls something towards it. It has a sneaky plan beneath the imperial surface of its apparently timeless architecture. Unlike the Human body adorned in jewelry and clothing, more like the fantasy of Yellowness in the neoimperial economy; Westfield's body is its own ornament — it only suggests itself. Just like the paradigm of a neoliberal racializing urge that Cheng calls the Yellow woman.

Westfield is a racialized site, an architecture marked in imperial codes of color and race. Its architectural presence is the ornament of itself—it exists only as an addition, an extra, an excess. As the Yellow woman, described by Cheng, and taken from nineteenth century arch-racist portraits of Chinese girls on display at theaters and fashionable galleries, is indistinguishable from the Oriental ornaments by which she is surrounded, Westfield's racializing force is carried in its suggestion that the bodies inside it can take its own ornament as theirs. The Yellow woman in Euro-American culture is seen as a commodity to have. Oscar Wilde's Oriental ornaments and millions of young British men on their way to Thailand for a taste. Yellowness is humanity-as-commodity and it serves in the imperial mind of Euro-American culture as a body to be bought, displayed, and treated as an ornament itself.

Westfield is the architectural equivalent, a building that seems to have no building, to be only the suggestion of more ornament, so when you walk around it you cannot help but get turned on by this empty hole at the core of the shopping center's logic. The Modernist rejection of Oriental ornament always carries within it the secret hope for more ornament—the sexualized side of the Puritan fantasy; the lust for ornamental crime underpinning the white progress of imperial design.

Positioning the Ornament

Anne Cheng uses the example of Anna May Wong to describe this ornamenting process. Wong was born and died in California, living from 1905 to 1961. Already by 1924, at the age of nineteen, she had gained international fame, becoming the first Chinese American movie star. Throughout her career, she played the role of the "Dragon Lady," an obviously racialized and mysterious figure who represents a merged architecture of Chinese body and Chinese ornament.

In addition to the many films and plays she acted in, the clearest illustration of her ornamental racialization is a series of photographs taken of her by the writer of an infamously racist novel, Carl Van Vechten. Vechten took up photography in the 1930s and photographed an enormous cast of celebrities over the next thirty years, including Salvador Dalí, Harry Belafonte, Marlon Brando, Billie Holiday, and Gertrude Stein, with whom he was good friends.

His photographs of Wong place her among ornaments that seem to accumulate through her body. In a photo taken in 1935, Wong's hair is held closely to her head and tied back, creating a solid black outline around her head against the white wall behind her. Sprouting from her simple white dress are artificial flowers. The flowers are solid and obviously plastic, not attempting to bear any resemblance to living plants. In the greyscale of the photo, the flowers take on the same tone as Wong's skin.

The solid shape of Wong's head, with its tightly-tied hair, alongside her largely unshaded grey skin, creates a scene in which the flowers and the woman are merged as a united form. They are neither subject nor object. Wong is not looking at the flowers; she does not even seem to notice that they are there. Like the flowers, she just exists, an ornamental frill in the lens of a photographer to gaze and appreciate her still and frozen beauty. She has become a flower, and the flowers have become her, a unified plastic force whose color is merged — they are one grey thing, in pursuit of thingliness.

In another photograph from the same shoot, Wong is looking into the camera lens. This time, the largest of the flowers — which is so shiny and solid, it looks like it's made of iron — is positioned right beside her head and angled with its center towards the camera. Just like Wong. Her grey head with its black outline, beside the grey flower with its black outline.

Wong is paradigmatically portrayed here as the ornamental thing, as the repository of a society's desire to claim itself as the bastion of progressive time. She is the witness of Enlightenment, holding inside her movements the cultural progression of a society. But in that status as enlightened thing, she loses her subjectivity. She cannot decide to be there or not. The one choice she is permanently barred from making is the decision not to be ornament. The decision, that is, to *not be Chinese.*

Anne Cheng brings out the complexity of Wong's status in *Ornamentalism,* writing:

Wong's relationship to fame and cinema is complicated. At once internationally renowned yet still relatively unknown in American cultural memory, alternately praised and denigrated as the great "Oriental Beauty" of the twentieth century, fluctuating between the proverbial Dragon Lady and the Lotus Blossom, and always the go-to It girl when it comes time to name an Asian American woman, Anna May Wong is, above all, a study in the tension between racialized corporeality and aesthetic thingness.[29]

She goes on to say that Walter Benjamin referred to Wong as a "moon" and a "porcelain bowl."[30] Wong is presented as an architectural site of culture. She is the space where the time of being accumulates.

This architectural thingness of Wong conditions her as a space between objectivity and subjectivity, a third space that cannot see itself. She is never allowed to hold the camera, never allowed to decide if she is ornament or not: even if she can decide to end her career or to end her life, she cannot stop being seen, and cannot stop being seen as Chinese ornament. Ultimately, Wong's status as a culturally enlightened site accumulating the time of society means that she is initiated by the people who have seen her. Her life is begun by those who have born witness to her absence. She is looked at as a thing that can never be now, that can only exist as a ghostly absence lingering in the future, accumulating pasts that society sees now. And I recognize this figure; I saw this figure in Fanon's train scene, in Gilroy's Atlantic, in Douglass's escape from slavery, in Bachelard's terrifying basement, in the inner-city buildings that Lloyd Wright steered architecture away from, in the undercurrent of Burnham's Exposition, and in the lustful objects of Westfield's endless windows.

Wong is another steppingstone in the infinite age of Enlightenment, the age that can necessarily never be complete because

---

29 Ibid., 62.
30 Ibid.

then the object and the Subject would have fully merged and there would be no one left to witness, to initiate the present being of the seen by syphoning through accumulated pasts and choosing which ones to keep, and which to throw overboard.

"If it is now asked whether we at present live in an *enlightened* age, the answer is: No, but we do live in an age of *enlightenment*."[31] So says Kant. But what he does not say is that enlightenment can never arrive because then there would be no distinction at all between Architecture and buildings, between universal forms and particular beings, between buildings and bodies, between ornaments and people, or between objects and subjects.

In the age of modernity, the museum and the body transfer their meanings between each other. The racializing force of Empire animates certain bodies as sites to be witnessed, to stand tall and glassy, while other bodies hold the capacity to see, to judge reasonably and to think in their architectural minds from the rational summit of their internal attics. Westfield spreads itself out, eradicating the attic and the basement. There is no vertical Empire in the architecture of Westfield. But there doesn't need to be. Empire is already worn within us. We are witnesses to our own disappearance. Architecture is our bodies now, with the help of Westfield's collapse of the obvious signs of imperial building.

How is it possible to think of a kind of art or architecture that negates these spaces? How do you remove the category Architecture from architectural practice? How do you build a building that does not hide its violence, that does not bear witness to a history that is nothing but itself?

Architecture has already built the city as History. The monuments of the city are the physical sites that accumulate chosen testimonies of History. The building is built *as* History. But how can an architecture arise that is *for* history? How can a practice be initiated that allows the histories thrown overboard to inhabit the spaces left empty in their absence? How to create a space

---

31 Immanuel Kant, "An Answer to the Question: 'What is Enlightenment?'" (1784), in *Kant: Political Writings,* ed. H.S. Reiss (Cambridge: Cambridge University Press, 1991), 58. Original emphasis.

in which Wong is not a glassy ornament but an agential subject who bears witness to her own presence?

How do we build *for* history, rather than *as* history?

The Transcendental Ideality of Westfield

Immanuel Kant is always concerned with perspective. Rational, aesthetic judgement is a way of seeing, a way of organizing space and projecting geometry onto the world. Geometry, as his theory of space fundamentally asserts, is only knowable through the Human mind, a priori. So, when there is a spatial problem, when space is opening aporias and dark holes of confusion that we cannot think about, there is no use in changing the object, according to Kant, since we cannot ever really know the object anyway. The problem stems from our own perception of space, not space itself. "If the course of human affairs seems so senseless to us, perhaps it lies in a poor choice of position from which we regard it."[32]

In this Kantian formula, a repositioning of the subject eradicates the caught lines of signification projected by the subject's spatial perspective. The logical grids of space are set out by the projections of subjectivity accurately, Kant maintains, but the positioning of the subject must be adapted in order for the proper kind of judgement to be universalized as aesthetic — and therefore moral — reason. The object of this judgement, positioned on the cartographic mechanisms of subjective space, is unknowable.

> But we should consider that bodies are not objects in themselves that are present to us, but rather a mere appearance of who knows what unknown object; that motion is not the effect of this unknown cause, but merely the appearance of its influence on our senses; that consequently neither of these is something outside us, but both are merely representations in us, hence that it is not the motion of matter that causes repre-

---

32 Kant, "An Old Question Raised Again," 300.

sentations in us, but that motion itself (hence also the matter that makes itself knowable through it) is a mere representation; and finally that the whole self-made difficulty comes to this: How and through what cause do the representations of our sensibility stand in combination with one another, so that those representations that we call outer intuitions can be represented according to empirical laws as objects outside us?[33]

For Kant, the outside is a false premise; it is a relation to the spatial projections of subjectivity. The appearance of an outside is the establishment of the universality of the subject who can see. It is the visuality of the seeing Subject who projects perspective, perspectival lines that lead to the Subject, and in that space, that universe of the Subject, reason becomes pure. In the movement of these appearances, it is difficult to distinguish between the ontological formation of the Subject as a subject, and the external constitution of the World. At what point does the internal constitution of the Subject give way to the unknown object that inheres in these moving appearances? Is there such a point?

The principal epistemological frame here is the ordered regime of sight that divides the World — and, indeed, creates the World, as Kant has it — according to the political and ontological mechanisms of subjectivity. In this bordered grid, how is it possible to think of the temporal form of this projective space that preconditions all of life into representations of the failed attempt to attain subjectivity? How to imagine a precedent and a continuation of the ethics of seeing that judge everything in the World as a competitive border against which the Subject must define itself, and a border that is unknown, unknowable, and so must be escaped from, in the constant failed flight of the Subject's unbearable subjectivity?

When I go to Westfield, there are ordering eyes in blue uniforms everywhere. There is a form of subjectivity that allows the public spectacle of subjective universalization to happen with

---

33 Kant, *Critique of Pure Reason*, A387.

the explicit aid of cartographic mechanisms and data-accumulative technologies. Some certain bodies, that see in a certain way, are allowed to reveal the machinic accumulation of moving objects as the ground of their own mythical constitution. Some bodies are allowed to claim the status of Subject based on their projection of a way of seeing, a way of judging Kantianly, which is called subjectivity. They do not look, they do not only see; they establish their own internal universe as the summit of universal phenomena, ordering space into a grid of perspective in which the most distant objects are smallest, the largest are closest, and everything results in the projecting eye of the subject.

Frank B. Wilderson III calls this self-constitution through the accumulation of violence *phobogenesis*.[34] These creatures are *made by fear*. All that shit outside there is unknowable and is scattered all over the spatial grids they project; and by that unbearable judgement they build themselves as Subjects. The political and ontological proposition that is subjectivity assumes a presupposed impossibility in the object-world. The only way a Subject can emerge, the only way a living being can assume the properties of subjectivity, is by constructing a defensive border at the limits of its body, defining itself as the magnificent achievement of not being outside itself, and then retroactively claiming self-constitution. The Subject is convinced of his own constitution-as-self, claiming to have made himself out of himself, an autopoietic universe in himself, by the fact that the objects that are not himself are unknowable to himself.

What Kant neglects is the temporal retrogression of projective subjectivity. For Kant, the Subject establishes the World outside of himself. His question, again, is: "How and through what cause do the representations of our sensibility stand in combination with one another, so that those representations that we call outer intuitions can be represented according to empirical laws as objects outside us?" Which is to say, how does the World or-

---

34 Frank B. Wilderson III, *Afropessimism* (New York: Liveright Publishing, 2020), 162. Wilderson writes that a Black person is *phobogenic*, which he defines as "Something that is induced or caused by fear."

ganize itself according to the empirical laws that I already know inside me? What is missed out in this temporal coding of the subjective grids of cartographic space is the retrospective assertion of the Subject's self-constitution after having emerged out of the World. The Subject, that is, against the Kantian scheme, emerges out of the World, constructed and constituted by all that is the World, and then, in the continuous rhythm of that project, the Subject slashes this constantly reconstituting symbiosis and claims to have made himself, claims to be absolutely external to all that is not him.

When I go to Westfield, again and again, there is a force that is constituted by Westfield and yet severs itself from the universe of the white blob. It separates itself and cuts the temporality of sharing that passes back and forth, in and out, between the buildings and the bodies. Once appropriated and absorbed into the coded mechanisms of profit-production, Westfield establishes what we know as the city, and then it claims self-constitution. It claims to be absolutely external and to have made itself outside the constitutive relations of the city.

That force, of course, is the police.

The police are always there, tracking every movement, claiming their own constitution of themselves as police-subjects because the world to them is unknowable. If it was knowable, there would be no crime, since crime is only the disjunctive perspective of an unknowable object when caught in the gridlines of the police.

The Kantian projection of space as subjectivity is constitutive of the moral and aesthetic claims of both the modern Subject, as Kant knew very well, and the police, which Kant was oblivious to. Something in modernity trips through the projections of space to merge the subjectivity of the full Subject and the police; something, rather, about subjectivity is constitutive of the violent enforcement of both racial and spatial distinctions in our peculiar economy that could be called modernity, capitalism, or Architecture.

Frank B. Wilderson III and his wife, Alice Wilson, are at a conference called Race Rave at the University of Santa Cruz, California, in 2001.[35] As an experiment to induce deeper thinking about race and its lived dynamics, the organizers split the attendees into different groups according to race. There are five rooms into which the main group must split itself: one for whites, one for Blacks, one for Reds or Natives, one for Browns, and one for Yellows. The crude categorization by color is part of the point of the exercise.

After some disagreement over those people who seem to slip between the categorical borders of race — Are Jews white? Are mixed-race people with one Black parent and one white parent really Black? What about Latinxs? — everyone found a space. The prompt was to discuss that particular group's experiences with the police.

Wilderson was in the Black group, and — once they had torn up and thrown away the planning sheet made by the organizers — he recounts a joyous and profound engagement with ever other person in the room.

> Once we had liberated ourselves from the constraints of having to make our suffering analogous to the suffering of the people of color, something truly profound occurred. For me, someone who was beginning to move from Marxism to what would a year later be called Afropessimism, the session was instructive because I was able to see and feel how comforting it was for a room full of Black people to move between the spectacle of police violence, to the banality of microaggressions at work and in the classroom, to the experiences of chattel slavery as if the time and intensity of all three were the same.[36]

Wilson was in the white group. Later she tells her husband of the stupidity in the group. The whites first, for some pointless rea-

---
35 Ibid., 201ff.
36 Ibid., 205.

son, started to list the states they each came from and how they ended up in California. Wilson tried to get them back to the question of the police, but they refused. Ultimately, they spent 90 minutes trying to evade any engaged discussion and study of the police. Why were the whites so resistant to talking about the police?

"Alice was shut down because the exercise threatened the most constitutive element of whiteness: white people are the police. This includes those white people who, like Alice, at the level of consciousness, do not want this birthright deputation. At a deep unconscious level they all intuited the fact that the police were not out there but in here, that policing was woven into the fabric of their subjectivity."[37] whiteness is the police that judges — and through that judgement claims the constitution of — the boundary between Human and Black; the border, that is, between subjectivity and social death; between the tower and the basement; between the Subject and the unknowable third position that lingers in the dark depths of the moving object. The police are an architecture of whiteness, holding the city in the rigid form of its racialized perspective, the lines of expansive spatial modernity written already into its city plan, into the floor on which everyone walks; and those lines already demarcate the boundary of life and nothingness.

The building, the city, cannot exist without this cosmic ontology that presents a knowable lightness and an unknowable darkness upon which everything rests. It is only through this way of being that the city as we know the city can exist, and it is all based on antiBlackness. In Westfield objects come to life as people, we the white and nonBlack consumers are the objects who have assumed the form of movement, of exchange. The Subject projecting its perspectival eye as the grids of universal space is Westfield, the corporation itself, the self-constituting and universal generative force.

---

[37] Ibid., 208.

It would be too Neoclassical to put a statue of Kant in the middle of Westfield Stratford, but there should at least be a window with his name etched into it. *Kant waz ere, forever.*

Thinking Back/Westfield Echo

If I am the rational animal, thinking my way — underway — into the knowledge of the impossibility of thinking, Westfield is pounding back in every thought. "Thought has the gift of thinking back, a gift given because we incline toward it. Only when we are so inclined toward what in itself is to be thought about, only then are we capable of thinking," Heidegger says.[38] I think in Westfield, inclining towards its white surfaces, the massive facades of shops, and it inclines back to me. But in the moment of this inclination, I realize with abject horror that I am looking at myself. Inside the shop window, in the shiny glass, I see a thing that is not myself as a commodity, that is not a commodity as me, but is rather an animated commodity that speaks me into being. I am only alive as I incline towards the walls of Westfield, as I incline to what in itself is to be thought about, expecting the gift of thinking back. Heidegger never went to Westfield. He didn't change his clothes very often, and he lived in a forest. A forest is the outside, by definition. Westfield also sounds like an outside, the fields out west, where the sun sets; the long expanse of open plains, the roaming flora, spread horizontally.

What way is there of speaking about this? The violence is totalizing, and the synthesis is a totality. Everything Moten says consumes the form of everything Kant says, and yet the murmur of Kant remains in every movement. I chew down and ruminate on the endlessness of this Kantian modernity. Everything happens at once, in a single moment, and History is so long, so melted into the crevices of experience.

I unincline. I lean back. Unlike philosophers. Unlike Kant who's always sitting with his legs spread on the carriage that

---

38 Martin Heidegger, *What Is Called Thinking?*, trans. J. Glenn Gray (London: Perennial, 2004), 4.

circles Königsberg, trotting round and round and round. I lean back and I watch TV. The same problems emerge, indubitably. The architecture of Architecture surrounds me.

In the Israeli series *Shtisel*, the main character Akiva's father, Shulem, gets up on stage at the first event to finally reward the artistic talents of Akiva.[39] Akiva has given a small speech and, despite their earlier argument, thanked his father, who then takes his place, unwelcomed, at the microphone. He is grateful to the rich Americans, seated in front of him, who have given their money to this prize. The gallery manager translates this from Hebrew into English for the rich American couple. The father then adds, to everyone's horrified embarrassment, that if they really want to help Israel then they should fund the school of which he is the head teacher.

There's this name on stage, Shtisel, constructed for the artist, the event for the artist [Akiva] Shtisel, but the absurdity of surnames is that the deictic reference to the surnamed being is a universalized referent. The command to notice Shtisel is not a command towards a specific entity, that initiates the linguistic (and, for Heidegger, therefore ontic) being of this thing, bringing it into the light and positioning it (that is, problematizing it) as a specific, singular referent in the world.

Naming something, speaking it into being, is the initiation of the cult of the individual of modernity. The process of naming is the process of bringing into the self; of forming the ideology of self out of the heterogeneity of forms of life. "One does not position oneself in the world; one is born into a name that's been chosen."[40] "Similarly, the racial and racist conceptualization and, therefore, regulation of blackness is inseparable from its naming."[41] To name a being as singular is to speak that being into the ontological singularity of capitalist modernity; to reduce the being to its smallest point, to its simplest nodal form.

---

39 Alon Zingman, dir., *Shtisel*, Season 2, Episode 5, "Love Pains," written by Yehonatan Indursky and Ori Elon, first aired November 28, 2015 on *Yes Oh*, https://www.yesstudios.tv/shtisel.
40 Wilderson, *Afropessimism*, 305.
41 Fred Moten, *Stolen Life* (Durham: Duke University Press, 2018), 2.

But crucially — and this is all in Kant's mind, in his architectural brain, his building-body — to reduce something is also to amplify it. The simplest form of being is the most universal, which is what Marx will later spend three thousand pages criticizing in his own beautiful way. The universalizable category is the presentation of heterogeneous life as an appropriable form. The universal category can be appropriated, copied, stamped, and reformulated, accumulated, reproduced. To name is to universalize. So the fact of bearing a surname is always the brutality of being universalized, of being subsumed into a Kantian category, a universal ontological imperative forced to refer always to the greater nodal point within.

Akiva Shtisel means his father, and Shulem is a word that ultimately means his own father. Shulem comes on stage, perfectly Kantian in his ampliative reduction of the ontological singularity of the naming ceremony of modernity, and folds the fact of seeing Akiva into its antecedent condition: seeing the father.

The Americans could point at Shulem and say, *I thought I saw you today*. I saw someone who looks just like you. And what does that mean? As Fred Moten says, it means that you are not you. You can be anyone, and anyone can be you.[42] Perception is not a fact to be relied upon. What you see is not what you see, and when you see you, it is certainly not always or necessarily you. Anything can be you; in fact, Moten goes so far as to say that *everything is you*. The only thing that is not you is *you*, because the perception of you is precisely what is wrong.[43] Akiva was/is/will have been in front of the room, watched like some fetishized token of the philanthropic justification for the wealth of the Americans, covering their violent imperial gestures of self-exertion in the commonplace illusion of the beneficence of wealth.

---

42 Fred Moten and Sondra Perry, "Fred Moten in Conversation with Sondra Perry," *Frieze*, podcast, December 10, 2018, https://player.fm/series/frieze/fred-moten-in-conversation-with-sondra-perry.

43 Ibid.

The great contemporary myth of the friendly billionaire is sickeningly everywhere, and we are all beaten black and blue [and *blur*] with the neo-colonial parade of rich people popping the canons removed from their slave ships in other centuries, other contortions of this regime. Every time they hand a penny down to the corpses that hold their flags up straight. Akiva has been or was or will be standing in front of the room, doing his thing, while all these people look on and, like Moten, he's like, *What the fuck am I doing here?* He is caught, like everyone who performs, who produces, who turns themselves into a plug-in machine of artistic production into which people offload all their shit in the therapeutic interior space of art, in the paradox of having no other way to speak than through the institution and yet only being able to speak in the language of the institution, being jaw-snapped and tongue-tied by the institution that invents language and then collapses all of life into its own institutional linguistic framework that, like Heidegger, speaks everything into being as the condition of modern possibility: emergence into life is the precise border of the institution. Like any artist, Akiva is on the impossible boundary between being unable to be silent (since that would preclude his status as artist, annihilating the being of the being) and only being able to speak in the oppressive and assimilatory language of the institution. Annihilation or assimilation. The same choice, in the end. Now, when in Westfield you realize that the wall is you, the object you desire is you and it is not an object at all, in fact it is you, then you realize that the only thing around here that is not you is *you*: and that is because you are a thing. Not to be confused with an object. You realize that the border that exists is a border between life and lives, all of which is eclipsed by antiBlackness. *Does it? Does it? Does it?* people ask when the claw of antiBlackness drums spiritually, immensely, revelationarily, the claw piercing and pumping the choral beauty of Black sociality, into the strict liberal atheist credence regime of Euro-American capitalism. They ask if it's really happening. *They* are not *themselves. They are anything but themselves.* Westfield obviously can't help you. It obviously can't do anything for us. It is a name for the father, a referent to a nodal point that enforces the conduct of all forms of life into the singularity of self, into Kantian categories, universalities. Westfield can swallow the critique of itself. It can consume the presence of the son, referring again to the father. How to criticize a power that is perfectly adapted to take the criticism of itself "like medicine," as Moten says, to build again on someone's critique of it?[44] How to depict an institution that produces the language of depiction? How to represent the horror of a regime that awards you a prize for your representation of it, and without that award you can't pay the rent, you can't eat, you can't live? How the fuck do we get a little bit of land that we can just talk on? There's no code for that. No plan.

Closing Questions for a Westfield World

Why does Westfield offer its user so little horizontality when its architectural form is the reduction of vertical Bachelardian highness? Westfield seems like a republican proposition: get rid of the high and create for the horizontal. A refusal of the divine right of the attic; a proposition that sweeps away the weird phenomenology of Bachelard. But then the problem of the object. Obviously, the object has agency in Westfield — it is a space that also refuses Kant, that abolishes the possibility of a transcendental ideality of space. But it turns the object into a person — it creates people out of commodities, and then the ontological distinction between purchaser and purchased is also written away. In Westfield there is no difference between the subject and the object; everything is concentrated into a hybrid third position. And in that totality of the third position, there is nothing left to witness. No event ever occurs, since there is no subject to witness it, to geometrically code the spatiality of the scene. Nothing ever happens, literally, because the initiation of the event in its future by the testimony of the witness is impossible since everyone and everything present already inhabits the third position. But there is nothing for that position to witness. It cannot see

---

44 Ibid.

itself in the politics of the white witness (as opposed to the Black witness, but Westfield is not the space to initiate a politics of the Black witness, that's as clear as can be). That is what the politics of the white witness is: the inability of the third position to see itself; its ability only to see the object. But here the object does not exist. It has merged with the Subject and been disbanded.

How do we understand the racialization occurring in Westfield's eradication of the distinction between subject and object? How do we think about space in the tight philosophy of modernity when Kant has been cast out? What is there left to say when all the thinking of modernity is collapsed by a massive shopping center in a place with the same name as the colonial fair that celebrates Columbus? How can buildings be built that contend with the collapse of witnesses, of Subjects, and the creation of animated objects who racialize the bodies of the ex-Subjects concentrated into third positions as impossible witnesses? How can a space be made that does not universalize itself as a new history but rather builds *for* history, not *as* history?

I abolished my own history inside Westfield. I wrote away the beginnings of a possible adulthood by drinking, by doing a job I hated, and spending all my money on booze. Westfield carries a destroying force in its blobby nothingness. Architects pull down the verticality of obvious imperialism, smothering the snarl of Louis Sullivan and patching up the subtle aggressions of Gaston Bachelard, and the other option, they quickly decide, is a massive blob that spreads horizontally and eases off the edges of sharp modernity, but nothing is improved. The Subject has no autonomous agency to refuse the event it is creating; the event is entirely cancelled and the only possible performance is the endless reproduction of abstract capital for investors. There is no other game to be played, and no other life to live in Westfield and its antimonumental white spaces. The spatial relations among the witness, the event, and philosophies and architectures of chromatics and of space, of geometry, and of subjectivity, are always racializing, always a racial force. How to build for history instead of as history?

Blackitecture

W.E.B. Du Bois points out the peculiar ontological condition of Blackness. It is not that Blacks *have* a problem in the colonial regime of modernity. Blacks, rather, *are* a problem.[45] Focusing this problem through the Kantian spatial lens that I have focused on in this book — the same Kantian lens that all being is focused through in the irreducible Kantianness of modernity — a scene opens up in which Black space is a problem, and in that scene — maybe only in that scene — a plan can be formulated for building escape.

I am not confronting, in this scene, the problem of Black space. Rather, I enter the scene with the proposition that Black space is a problem. As a problem, Black space contains the possibility of signifying otherwise; it contains a rupture in the signifying language of Architecture that projects its perspective judgement onto space, thus creating universal space.

Universal space is established by the police regime that is subjectivity. The principal universality establishes a building practice that is the city, and that principal universality then attempts to escape the conditions of the city because the city necessitates a basement to hold it up, to posit itself against. *At least the city is not and never will be the basement.* The maintenance of the ontological primacy of the city, just like whiteness, is constructed on the necessity of the basement's impossibility; the city is reliant on the antithesis of the basement. Just like Blackness. However, throughout this book I have referred to this antithesis incorrectly. I have called it "non-existence," or a "non-space," or the "non-subject." What Jared Sexton informs us is that Blackness/the basement is not a space of binary negativity, but a third and outside position that is the necessary impossibility of life. Rather, it is anti-existence; anti-space; the anti-subject.[46]

The horror of this binary construction forces the principal universality to try to escape, but it is the city itself that provides

---

45 Wilderson, *Afropessimism*, 168.
46 Cited in ibid., 214.

the spatial conditions for the principal universality to call himself a principal universality. If he left, he would be just a single point of being, anywhere, anything.

The principal universality is the ἀρχι, the *arkhi,* the chief, the arch of architecture. The city established by the principal universality and arch-being is the τέκτων, the *tektōn,* the carpenter, the builder: the producer, the maker, from the Proto-Indo-European root *tek̑* "to beget, bring forth." The architect is the leader of creation, the establisher of production. But it is only through the produced product, the creation of the city, that the architect can claim the ontological title of The Architect and thus speak himself into being as a named individual, a nodal point of ampliative individuation; it is only in the city that he can become a designated space of creation.

What is called Blackness in modernity is the opposite of what is called *arkhi,* the chief and the arch. Black is the destroyer of modernity, its necessary antithesis. *Blackitecture is a building otherwise.*

The interesting thing that Agamben points out about the etymology of *archē* — the *arkhi* of architecture — is that it

> means both "origin" and "command." To this double meaning of the term there corresponds the fact that, in our philosophical and religious traditions alike, origin [(]what gives a beginning and brings into being[)] is not only a preamble, which disappears and ceases to act in that to which it has given life, but it is also what commands and governs its growth, development, circulation, and transmission — in a word, history.[47]

The command of architecture, the command to build, is the origin of the history of architecture. The command carried in the power of that archetypal figure, The Architect, is borne continuously as the practice of building. There is no building, or meth-

---

47 Giorgio Agamben, *The Use of Bodies,* trans. Adam Kotsko (Stanford: Stanford University Press, 2016), 275.

od of building, that can exist outside and entirely external to the logics of architecture, since the language, ontology, and ethics of building is itself merely a continuing residue of the origin that is the Architect's command to Architecture.

The original command to build is the act of submerging Blackness as the basement; and that act is the retroactive constitution of the city: this is, and has always been, a city because it has ridden itself of Blackness by Architecture. The very language of architecture is the constant revelation of this originary movement: building only means architecture, and always means Architecture, when it is a continuation of the heroic command of The Architect pushing Blackness down into the basement and claiming the flag-waving glory of the sparkly white attic space, the divine and privatized openness that the commons can never reach from its lowly, submerged position in the underworld.

How could there be an architecture without the command of the chief? Without the chief/*arkhi* of the building commanding the structure into being as an object seen by a Subject, as an unknowable external object subsumed into the knowing grids of subjective perspective?

When the *arkhi* constructs a building, it is plotted on the projective gridlines of ampliative subjectivity. The world is fallen into these lines, collapsed into a grid plan that the subject extends as the primary movement and proof of his subjectivity — and that is always also to say, of his whiteness, of his masculinity, of his able body, of his marriage and property ownership. And marriage, of course, is a form of property ownership. The building exists as an object emerging into the dialogic ontology of the city — passing back and forth between subjects and objects, a dialogue through which they create each other — because the commanding subject has witnessed this act of creation and can carry it into the future; the illusion of a progressive time flow can be upheld by the existence of the Subject, who continues to re-command the building into being as he looks at it, as he speaks of it.

However, the Black witness is a mode of being that is not there for the event, that is silent and invisible. Black is an absence in the gridlines of time. Black is a break in the smoothness of Subjects' space. So what is a building that is not commanded into being by the *arkhi,* by the chief Subject, but is rather raised/razed by the Black witness? How can that be?

The Black witness affirms the previous existence of something that did not seem to exist in its time. Frederick Douglass does not assert himself as existing now by writing his autobiography; he says that he existed then. *I was in fact there. There was another part of that scene that you did not see.* Which also means, *in the World there is always a third position that cannot be seen by the Subject. The third position holds up the other two, though it is not seen or noticed. It is only whipped, only shot, only incarcerated.* And that also means, *between the present and the past there is a spectral presence, a thing that is always there but that you cannot see; in fact, your entire ideology of sight is based on your inability to see this thing, and your entire regime of time is based on the non-existence of this thing between the present and the past.*

The building that is built as Blackitecture is a basement. It is a basement that is not seen. When was the basement built? I don't know; there are no archives to answer such a question. The archival epistemology of this basement is resistant to the spatial questions of a City-Subject. Who was it built by, when, for what cost and purpose? These are questions that do not register in the archives of the basement.

A long time later, a Black anti-space and subject speaks her past into now as a material narrative, as a story that is being now. She speaks, and what she speaks of happened in the past:

There is a basement that exists in the past. It was there. It is here.

As she speaks of that past, its material existence is not commanded into being in the past or in the present, nor as the past or as the present. She speaks of it for the time it has lost. She speaks of it, and it runs under, a charge in the basement, a force beneath; where anyone can reach it and where it has always been.

There is a basement that runs, running on, and it runs in the city without singularity. It is a being that is anywhere, and it was always what the city is, and what the city isn't.

For Édouard Glissant, thinking is a "risk" that "becomes realized" in "the imaginary of peoples, their varied poetics."[48] Thinking moves into space, embracing people, re-realizing the reality of thinking space and spacing thought. It is a risk to think otherwise, and that risk realizes itself in the life of people. And so it is for the Black witness, too, who is the ongoing and unending collaborator of Blackitecture. The Black witnesses realizes a risk in time, not initiating a new mode, or commanding a new form into being. Rather, the Black witness opens up the lid of the basement, and what is revealed is the constancy of the risk beneath. It was always there, happening, going on. It didn't stop in the basement, and it was never just the past or the present. Never a subject or an object. It's a thing, and it has been here-but-not-here forever.

The basement is open to everyone, all the time, but the Subject and his City are based on the refusal of this knowledge, of this otherwise awareness. And in the openness of this Black building, the already-opened openness hidden in the people of the City is realized; the risk that is their ethics of sharing is slipped from the molded form of the City, and something starts to fizzle, to burn.

For Agamben,

Thought is form-of-life, life unsegregatable from its form, and wherever there appears the intimacy of this inseparable

---

48 Édouard Glissant, *Poetics of Relation*, trans. Betsy Wing (Ann Arbor: University of Michigan Press, 1997), 1.

> life, in the materiality of corporeal processes and habitual modes of life not less than in theory, there and there alone is there thought. And it is this thought, this form-of-life that, abandoning bare life to "man" and the "citizen," who provisionally served as clothing for it and represented it with their "rights," must become the guiding concept and the unitary center of coming politics.[49]

The performative facades of the social body are given away to the city, to its tombstones of violence stamped into the ground of subject-production. The social of the body is taken away, removed into an ontology of its own, a modal ontology that shifts away from shifty grounds. The risk of thinking is realized as it is removed from the oppressive borders of Man, Architecture, and the dialogic discourses of rights, alliances, and exchange. As that risk is realized, thinking emerges in a third position that is neither now nor then; neither thinking nor having thought. It is thought that Agamben holds, that he moves away from the light. *Pensiero*, in Italian: not *pensare* or *avere pensato*. It is a position removed from operation in the present. It is a potentiality to think, to be thought, and to have removed the thinking act (as a verb) from the acting subject, stipulating its external borders instead as a noun. It is only the possibility of thinking, the potentiality to think, removed from the subject's obligation to operate every potentiality as an act. The subject's unbearable duty is the obligation to act upon every potentiality: every possible moment is employed as an operative duty. Such is the burden of being Human. But Agamben removes the potentiality without the act, as Roberto Fai writes: *"Il pensiero, ogni pensiero, ha una particolare natura: venendo oferto agli altri."*[50] The thought, every thought, has a particular nature: coming offered to others. Or, arriving offered to others. Being offered to others is insufficient

---

49 Agamben, *The Use of Bodies*, 213.
50 Roberto Fai, "Giorgio Agamben e l'uso dei corpi," *Kasparhauser*, April 2017, http://www.kasparhauser.net/Ateliers/Filosofia%20italiana/Fai-Agamben.html. Emphasis added.

as a translation because the crucial meaning held in the verb *venire* (*venendo oferto*) is that it has already happened; it arrives in the state of being offered. It is not offered once it arrives; it was always already given away. The thought, the genuine thought, is not an act, or a potentiality that can be operated into use for the Subject. It arrives, already having been offered to others; having been already used. It arrives as a relation of use between the Subject and the Subject themself.

> *The structural form of Blackitecture is the building's use of itself. The building offers no operative service to its user. It creates no transcendental subjectivities between the perceived and its perceiver, or the building and its resident. The building arrives already given to itself, already offered to itself as a relation of use. It really has no other use. It is a form, a form of forms, a form that is always given away. Never will the door have a separate use, or the window be employed for anyone else, or the desk be operated into someone's individual pursuits. The form of Blackitecture is an integral form, dense on the inside, refusing the refusal of common space.*

And what if a building was not commanded into being by a chief of production? What if a building—instead of asserting itself as History, as the bearer of time and the tower over the basement—opened up the possibility of knowing what was already there? What if a building was only form, if it had no other form than form itself, and that form was the containment of all the refused refusals, the release of absence?

> *Blackitecture refuses the refusal of the Subject and the City. Blackitecture is not high or low, dense or sparse, full or empty. It is a form that opens up the internal meaning of formalism. It is Blackness and the absence at its core that references always the history that it is and that made it. It is a mode that sings the rhythmic eternity of modalities that cannot be presupposed by the gridlines of the Subject's City universalizing the cartographic logics of space's transcendental ideality.*

Hegemonic architectural forms, like those included in the ampliative logic that is Architecture, are based around the privatization of space. The building encloses open space and claims it as its own. It embraces a nodal absence and turns it into loss; what was the always openness of absence becomes the loss of a possibility of being otherwise. It becomes the private zone of internalized logics. It becomes an eye making grids of ownership. Every empty space in the city is within the heavily policed border of the regime of private property. Inside the tower there is empty space, but the emptiness is foreclosed by its privatization within the tower. It was absence, unknown and otherwise, and it became loss. It is just a lost possibility of profit-production.

> *Until Blackitecture is all over the City, rendering the City all over, hegemonic architectural forms like Architecture will never understand that Blackitecture is the antecedence of Blackitecture. It is always presumed by Architecture that Architecture is the original form. First, it claims, there was the City — a hegemonic form. There was City-as-capital; City-as-profit-production-machine; City as Subject. And then came the radical alternatives and divergent modes of thinking otherwise. But Architecture misunderstands two things. (1) Blackness does not exist as resistance in response to the hegemonic Architectural form that is whiteness. Rather, Blackness outlives, precedes, and exceeds whiteness. Blackness inhabits an antagonistic position because Blackness is before whiteness, because Blackness is the condition of being already shared* (venendo oferto agli altri: *arriving given to others), of already being given away by sharing ("Home," as Moten says, "is where you give home away:" "homelessness is the condition in which you share your house";[51] and that home is Blackness), and that is stolen by the imposing regime of whiteness that cuts and severs the constancy and (otherwise) survival of Blackness. (2) Blackness's antecedence is meant — as well as in a disjunctive temporal sense of arriving prior to another thing, existing before it — in the*

---

51 Moten and Harney, "'Give Away Your Home, Constantly.'"

> *Kantian a priori sense of antecedence, in which one thing being antecedent to another is not necessarily a temporal position, but rather a semantic position: the meaning, the Being, of Blackness comes before the meaning, or the Being, of whiteness because the totalizing ontology of whiteness relies on the subjugation of Blackness and the refusal of Black (anti-)subjectivity: the regime of whiteness is based on the premise of the white subject's pregiven subjectivity and right to refusal, which is built on the refusal of the Black's (or the anti-subject's) right: the white is allowed to diverge from the strict borders of the ontological totality, while the Black is necessarily disallowed that divergence, and indeed the entire regime is constructed by and upon that disavowal, that refusal of the right to refuse.*

Sharing comes before its extraction into the logics of profit. Meaning that Blackness comes before whiteness. And that, finally, means that Blackitecture is before Architecture. We discover the thing that was always there anyway, that residual openness. The ethics of Blackitecture is not so much a practice of building, but rather of opening.

5

Bodies

Throughout this book, I and my collaborators — both those internal to my body and our unwilling external participants, those in the galactic noumena of a Duke University Press three-book publishing contract — have stated a host of principles that we have later broken. We have repeated the same citations, drawing from them each time a new meaning, as if we were unaware of our former selves.

At this point of abandon, all I want to propose is some tangible use, an experimental theory readers can do something with. I have broadly attempted to insert an emotive sensation into each chapter as a noumenal object, hoping that this primordial feeling will emerge in the receiving imagination of the reader. The first, "Cities," is excitement, hope, and joy. It is Moten all over, the baritone laughter of Black study, his incredible optimism that literally charges my body with ecstatic energy — fully and resolutely *ek statis,* out of myself, standing apart from me. The second, "Sights," is the pose of philosophy, the supposedly unfeeling praxis of metaphysics. It is the performance of a performance, the restaging of a show in which all the Kantian characters cross Königsberg bridges and set their watches, pointing to paintings of Hegel, Kant, Nietzsche, all their foes and pets, and then standing very still with an icy glass at the hour of vermouth and pretend not to feel the wind. Like your granny says, your lovely granny: you don't need gloves when it's cold, just drink a little brandy. The ridiculous and beautiful intricacy of that moment, passing eternal notes between grandparents and grandchildren, is the unfeeling feeling of Chapter Two. The third, "Spaces," is anger. It is the loss, and the fury that rises, a green mist in the distant fields, a mist elopes — how sad to think, how furious — in nocturnal rhythms of love, betrayal, out the bamboo cage of Ono no Komachi. It is Robert Johnson glowing at the crossroads, Tracy Chapman snapping the cushion of a throne, Nina Simone turning back from the camera, upper lip hooked on a cigarette. *He was not a violent man,* her voice rustles in the wet electricity of violence. The fourth, "Fantasies," is mourning, kneeling over the dug-out earth, peering in. It is the sense of the coming politics, its happy sadness, its bloated loss. Everything comes together at the moment when everything falls apart. Narrative is a mnemonic mechanism of putting back together what is torn asunder, all tore up like Lee Moses. The fifth, "Bodies," is sadness. It is the perverse and ubiquitous sadness of the white man lamenting the heavy head that wears a crown, its unbearable lightness. It is the friends departed into folds of previous chapters, the unknown and unending emancipation of fugitive collaborators who never signed the only form of sociality my racist hegemony has access to — the contractual obligation. Fund me, friends, in the sadness of my final chapter and its rain, its MTV 1990s music video *thin man walks in rainy streets, Glasgowy, something edgy.* Ah, I grew up on sad white men, Dylan/Cohen/Reed/Morrissey/Cave. I wanted to be them, never knowing, in the idiocy of my already finished retrospective, that I was born as them, and the only pursuit beyond the naming ceremony, the only life in ethics, is to escape my designation as the men I loved, the men I never met, the father who left before I was born. Symbolically, architecturally, and literally.

My predecessors were overcome by the allure of dramatic bursts of emotion spilling into the beige space between Kant and Black Studies. I want to sit quite silently with the reader, facing each other, and just think about what we've become. We could be a scene in a Mississippi John Hurt song. *Some say we went to Memphis.* Others see that we're still here, so they don't mention it.

In this chapter, I begin by using a term from Saidiya Hartman, "opacity," to summarize my argument so far in this book about subjectivity. I then bring this back to Kant through Fred Moten and the latter's centering of the former as the first figure to open Black radicalism through his explicit foreclosure of Black radicalism. Moving into Denise Ferreira da Silva's difficult critique of normative spacetime, I attempt to propose an experimental theory of building in the absence of the World-forming institution of Architecture, which I have been criticizing throughout this book. Building without Architecture is a movement between objects that rejects the mode of relation, instead founding itself on constant adaption to every participant's reaction. The building and the body of the inhabitant become mechanisms of heat and light redistribution in response to each other's needs, giving architecture an ethics of sharedness as a replacement for its universalizing modern function, which I have compared to Kantian morality and aesthetic judgement. This movement in the ethics of building without Architecture is, I claim, a dance. While complicating this proposition further through Fred Moten and Stefano Harney's poetic theory of dance in the space they call *the undercommons,* I bring *Building Black* finally to a general architectural proposition for the city, employing Pier Vittorio Aureli's theory of islands as the basis for antiracist building after Architecture as love-of-dance.[1]

*

What has to be understood in order to understand the position of the subject — and the necessity of the Subject always meaning the white Subject — is that slavery does not only refer to people

---

[1] My theory of the ethics of the island and its non-relational refusal of universalization is fully developed in Elliot C. Mason, *The Instagram Archipelago: Race, Gender, and the Lives of Dead Fish* (Winchester: Zero Books, 2022).

being in chains; it does not only refer to a mode of labor that is unpaid, or of ownership that seizes the autonomous movements of the body, and specifically of bodies from Africa. Slavery refers to the ontological condition of being the anti-subject, of existing as a necessary antagonism to the rules of subjectivity and the World-making project of Subjects. This does not mean that Blackness is a referent of a social nothing, but rather of the anti-subject, the structural antithesis of the progressive Spirit of Hegelian time and Kantian space. That is the primary ontological layer of the significance of Blackness. The secondary layer that must also be understood is that modernity is the condition of genocide in which Black anti-subjectivity is blamed on the inherent non-existence of Black people. The reason this genocidal project called modernity gives for the antagonism that is the Black body is that the Black body is too opaque for the politics of seeing on which modernity's regime is constructed. In her World-collapsing 1997 book *Scenes of Subjection,* Saidiya Hartman affirms the deadly and difficult position of this problem.

> If the black body is the vehicle of the other's power, pleasure, and profit, then it is no less true that it is the white or near-white body that makes the captive's suffering visible and discernible. Indeed, the elusiveness of black suffering can be attributed to a racist optics in which black flesh is itself identified as the source of opacity, the denial of black humanity, and the effacement of sentience integral to the wanton use of the captive body.[2]

A source of opacity is opened, excavated for the power, pleasure, and profit of the white totality that is modernity. That source, that well of natural Blackness, keeps everyone alive. It is the necessary underside of the genocide's stabilizing ground. I think it is impossible to read Hartman's work without collapsing back-

---

2   Saidiya V. Hartman, *Scenes of Subjection: Terror, Slavery, and Self-Making in Nineteenth-Century America* (Oxford: Oxford University Press, 1997), 20.

wards off your chair and realizing that your life depends on being able to drink at will from the well of pain, suffering, and murder that is that condition of permanent enslavement, that is the immovable sign of anti-subjectivity, the source of opacity.

Being located in and as a source of opacity has the effect of opening the Black(ened) body to the projections of white genocidal fantasies, from the nineteenth century plantation in which Hartman places the immediate critique of *Scenes of Subjection,* as much as in 21st-century London or New York.

*

Fred Moten is interested in pursuing the Kantian project because its most radical disavowal is the disavowal of Blackness, screwing it tightly into a logic that accesses the depths of that study, which is Black radicalism. For Moten, Kant builds a city in which the city's own constitutive skeleton is revealed to everyone except the archetypal Architect himself, the figurehead in the attic. Kant makes a city-as-a-body with eyes that look only outwards, while every other constitutive element of the city and body can see in. Indeed, we are deeply convinced by the philosophy of Kant that tells us to look outwards, but nonetheless we see in. Moten trains our eyes, in a little-known training center beneath the ruins.

It is only Kant who cannot see what he is revealing, and yet it is only Kant who could reveal it.

> In order not to fly off the handle, not to have his hand or head fly off in some anti- and ante-analytic traversal and retraversal of every Königsberg bridge, Kant pulls back from the general impropriety, the general expropriation, that he also gestures toward or opens onto — the dark time or black time of the enlightenment's commonunderground, the double edge of the fact that modern times have only ever been dark. This *longtemps* of darkness and its black light, its open

and general obscurity, is seen by everybody but the overseer in his blindness.[3]

There is an ampliative logic of spacetime written over the earth of the city, I say as I dig my feet into the ground in preparation for the leap of abandon. This gridded logic of spacetime designates the emotive semantics of color, of light, and sound and rhythm, and what emerges is the proposition that the night pierces through at moments of rational collapse. When the wrong party is voted in, darkness dawns. When the wrong regime grabs hold of power, darkness unfolds. When the wrong moral commands are spoken universally, darkness is everywhere.

What is going on outside that spatiotemporal logic is the totality of darkness. It is not that the overseer, whose name is Immanuel, cannot see the darkness, or tries to look away from it. It is that the politics of observation that projects the ampliative logics of spacetime onto and as the city is a politics explicitly formulated to hinder the emotive reception of totalities and of darkness. Darkness, in the politics of urban observation, in Kant's architectonic apperception, is a threat posed by the improper application of categorical truths. Darkness is the result of a faulty synthesis in the causality of sensations and understanding. Darkness has always been everywhere, and it is in that darkness that radical construction takes place, a construction so radical that all it does is fall apart.

*

Through contemporary artistic practice, Denise Ferreira da Silva looks for a means of signifying without spacetime. Spacetime is a form of meaning that eludes the presuppositions of Kantian forms that pre-inscribe the semantic direction of signifying codes. In conducting experiments towards this radical practice, Ferreira da Silva attempts to move away from readings

---

3   Fred Moten, *The Universal Machine* (Durham: Duke University Press, 2018), xi.

and ways of thinking that are "critical (formal and analytical)," and instead engage in a study that is "poethical (material and decompositional)."[4]

A "black feminist poethics" is "the task of unthinking the world, of releasing it from the grips of the abstract forms of modern representation and the violent juridic and economic architectures they support."[5] The temporal step that cuts into the global scripture of selfhood, full architectonic and white Subjectivity in poethics is the resolute severance of the value form of modernity. Poethics removes from the spatiotemporal logic of Human understanding the coordinates of value that ascribe full spatial being to whiteness and a permanent ontological exile to Blackness. Ferreira da Silva seeks a "return of the total value expropriated from conquered lands and enslaved bodies."[6] This task of undermining the World constructed on signifiers of spacetime in the forms of the Human mind is practiced by finding instead the constitution of meaning in "the matter of the work and not in the forms in the artist's mind."[7]

Ferreira da Silva shifts into a radical movement in which judgement is given from the object and its material signifiers to the machine of perceptions regarding it, in disjunctive divergence from the standard Kantian schema in which all meaning is given to matter by the Human mind, an act which retroactively affirms the producer of meaning as Human.

In Ferreira da Silva's formulation of Kantian spacetime, objects in the world are designated as mechanisms of aesthetic power whose value can be expropriated into the accumulative site of the Human mind. The mind transforms the object and its divergent coordinates of sensation into accumulated juridical and economic value. The World is set in the Kantian schema of spacetime as a zone for the organized displacement of internal Human movements. The force causing all movement in the

---

[4] Denise Ferreira da Silva, "In the Raw," *e-flux* 93 (September 2018), 1, https://www.e-flux.com/journal/93/215795/in-the-raw/.
[5] Ibid.
[6] Ibid.
[7] Ibid.

World is the Human mind. Both World and Human are created by the process of the subjective organization of objects. For Kant, it is this subjective spatiality of the World that produces and registers aesthetics. Aesthetic judgement is not independent of the mind, for Kant; it exists instead as a projective mechanism of being Human. The feeling of beauty, Ferreira da Silva writes in summarizing this Kantian position, does not come from matter, but rather from its form, "which is always already in the subject, since he alone is able to reflect, that is, to consider a representation without referring back to its object, but only to his cognitive faculties (imagination and understanding)."[8]

While these judgements of objects or noumena in the World are necessarily universal for Kant, the universal is not a referent that denotes every living humanoid thing in the lived reality of life on earth. Universal has a particular juridical and historical border raised around its definition. The mind that appeals to the a priori cognitive faculties must have Reason, and Reason, as I have tattooed on my forehead, as I whisper into my bedsheets every night, is inherently white. That is how this genocide began.

The full Human Subject is defined as the "transparent I," who produces reality by registering the perception of objects in a priori categories. The other being, the not-quite, the racialized, the Black, is defined as the "affectable I."[9] The racialized others are

> those whose minds have no access to Reason, which is the cognitive capacity necessary for entertaining the idea of a moral law and the attendant conception of Freedom. For the affectable subject of cultural difference — the racial/global subaltern — is marked precisely by its lack of the minimum requirements for the judgement of taste, which is the rational core of Kant's 'ideal of humanity.'[10]

---

8 Ibid., 6.
9 Ibid.
10 Ibid., 7.

In this schema, it is the whiteness of the white Rational Human that encodes the spatiotemporal situatedness of the city with meaning. Kant moves away from the climatic and strictly geographical racism of earlier modern thinkers. The pre-Kantian concept of race continued in the Aristotelian tradition of aligning all Human sensations and all racial difference as essentially derived from natural and unchangeable categories on earth: cold/hot; wet/dry; soft/hard; top-of-the-world/bottom-of-the-world.[11] In medieval English maps, the Mediterranean is called by the direct translation of its name: the Middle Land Sea. It is so called because it is, in classical geography, the middle of the world; the marker that separates the torrid zones of earth's fiery center from the temperate zones of full life, of Europe.[12]

Kant is one of many foundational modern thinkers who move away from this mystical conception of life's causes to an attempt at rational, universal scientific explanations of causality. Kant's solution is in opposition to both the dominant traditions of his time. In one, the idealists claimed that everything exists only in the Human mind, and in the other, the empiricists claimed that everything exists only in the World. Kant proposed that the World has an existence independent from Humans, and that objects have an internal reason of their own, but it can never be known by Humans. All that Humans can ever know is the Human perception of objects, and the conversion of sensations received from objects into projections of understanding, which is the process of pure Reason.

Space and Time are the archetypal forms imposed on the World by this projective, ampliative logic of Human understanding. Universal concepts are formulated by figuring the sensations of unknowable objects in the a priori forms of space

---

[11] For a brilliant discussion of climate theory, see Ibram X. Kendi, *Stamped from the Beginning: The Definitive History of Racist Ideas in America* (New York City: Nation Books, 2016), 17 ff.

[12] For a critical history of the South of the Mediterranean and North of the Mediterranean divide, see Walter D. Mignolo, "Foreword: Yes, We Can," in Hamid Dabashi, *Can Non-Europeans Think?* (London: Zed Books, 2015), x–xlii.

and time. However, this movement is only possible by full Subjects, by those Humans who are defined as Human by virtue of their ability to perform this fundamentally Human task. And that definition, as Kant makes clear throughout his life, and as Moten and Ferreira da Silva have spent a lot of their lives drawing out and criticizing, also codes those Humans as white, European, and Man. The spatiotemporal form that gives meaning to the matter of the city — its buildings, its built environment — is the condition of whiteness. The city is irreducibly a racist proposition. Since Kant, throughout modernity, urban space is only conceivable through the logics of race. There is no city without whiteness, and there is no possibility of thinking space otherwise without Blackness.

*

It is not because of one particular building or another that I propose the inherent and necessary racism of the city. It is not because of some funky architectural feature, some plastic tunnels, some exposed brick, that I think the implicit position of urban space is white supremacy. It is not because the pointy top of the Shard looks like a Ku Klux Klan hat that I think the kilometers of built environment folding out of London Bridge are the material condition of the British Empire's regime of global racism.

It is, however, because I am white that I have spent two years working obsessively on *Building Black,* dedicating myself to the exposition of why I am fundamentally and essentially a signifier of originary racist violence in the space where I live and work and love. All my love is not undermined by the genocide of my signifying function, but all my hatred is exposed.

*

Postmodernist architects and theorists have explicitly turned away from strict Kantian schemas of spacetime because of its limitations for ideas and practices of radical building.

The trend of architectural manifestoes that reject the traditions before them, instead instigating a joyous futurist utopia, begins at the turn of the twentieth century. In 1920, Bruno Taut celebrates the fall of History's dullness in his manifesto "Down with seriousism!"

> "Oh, our concepts: Space, home, style!" Urgh, how these concepts stink! Destroy them, put an end to them! Let nothing remain! Chase away their schools, let the professional wigs fly, we'll play catch with them! Blast, blast! Let the dusted, matted, gummed up world of concepts, ideologies and systems feel out cold north wind! Death to the concept-lice! Death to everything stuffy! Death to everything called title, dignity, authority! Down with everything serious![13]

The climatic favoring given to Taut's northern European home already presents the possibility of a return to an Aristotelian concept of race as a division between zones premarked for the unequal right to life. It is heat — stuffiness — that oppresses the free urge to build unseriously, and a "cold north wind" that energizes freedom.

There is a more profound aporia in Taut's celebration. On the first of the manifesto's two pages, he calls for the removal of all "title, dignity, authority." It seems to call for the eradication of presupposed forms, and a movement into an undisciplined space of free association and collective creation, not restricted to the dogma of any particular school or tradition. The second page, however, reveals that there is a very clear trajectory for this freedom. "In the distance shines our tomorrow. Hurray, three times hurray for our kingdom without force! Hurray for the transparent, the clear! Hurray for purity! Hurray for crystal!"[14]

---

13 Bruno Taut, "Down with Seriousism!" in *Programs and Manifestoes on 20th Century Architecture,* ed. Ulrich Conrads, trans. Michael Bullock (Cambridge: MIT Press, 1971), 57.
14 Ibid., 57–58.

The lightness of this future is difficult to understand as separate from the history of light's significance in the European imaginary. The dark, hot place beneath the Middle Land Sea [Mediterranean] — on the torrid side of Earth — is always the necessary antithesis to the proposition of Europe's lightness and cool breeze. The fresh force of this manifesto is towards the clearing, the site of openness that Heidegger calls the "Lichtung," the lighting, a patch of sky in a dense forest. The fact that this clearing is in pursuit of a "kingdom" is also troubling to the supposed desire to be ridden of "title" and "authority." How can a kingdom be the spatial and political organization of the coming emancipation of architecture? The pursuit of a King of Light is perfectly analogous with Christianity's pursuit of Jesus Christ, as the Light and the King, and with European History's colonial telos of seeking the light of (white) Reason against the darkness of (Black) barbarism.

Moreover, the declaration of proud unseriousness seems to presuppose a seriousness already given in Taut's status as white, German Architect. It is only by the resolute affirmation of his own position as serious Man that he can so chirpily reject the seriousness of his tradition. An architect forever labelled unserious by the racist language of European ontology and epistemology may not be so eminently able to proclaim herself proudly unserious, as this would only affirm what was already the judgement imposed on her. Taut's proclamation is an implicit acknowledgement of his inherent seriousness. His manifesto for silliness is, of course, taken seriously in his contemporary architectural circles, because his social referents all delineate a semantic assurance of his solid seriousness as a Man of Architecture and Ideas.

In 2002, Rem Koolhaas manipulates a similar delicacy of junk into a more critical formulation of unaesthetic design. "If space-junk is the human debris that litters the universe, JunkSpace is the residue mankind leaves on the planet. The built […] product of modernization is not modern architecture but Junkspace. Junkspace is what remains after modernization has run its course, or, more precisely, what coagulates while modernization is in progress, its fallout."[15]

Koolhaas's critique is focused on the arbitrarily massive, empty, and transparent structures placed without concern for their surroundings into every hegemonic and reproducible city space in the World. The Modernism of modernity has been on display as the spectacle of the last one hundred years, but within that, more profoundly, for Koolhaas, another accumulation has been subtly taking place: the accumulation of junk. Junk is a kind of proudly universal and brutally World-dominating aesthetic of useless crap, buzzing in the brightly lit magnificence of airports and shopping centers, "deploy[ing] the infrastructure of seamlessness," building "not by structure but by skin."[16]

Junkspace has not, historically, been focused on space, but rather "based on an obsessive preoccupation with its opposite: substance and objects, i.e., architecture. Architects could never explain space; junkspace is our punishment for their mystifications."[17] A focus on space, for Koolhaas, would instead be a return to a project that coherently united a global trajectory of time, in a deep but unspoken dedication to Hegel's *Geist*. As Koolhaas puts it, "All architects may unwittingly be working on the same building, so far separate, but with hidden receptors that will eventually make it cohere."[18] It is not the coherence itself that is the marker of this movement's violence for Koolhaas; rather, it is the accumulation of shit happening on the foot of this movement that is his problem.

While Koolhaas is critical of the "old world" imposition of its tired ideological forms on every inhabited and accumulated space, he is still looking for coherent forwards movement in time. "There is no progress; like a crab on LSD, culture staggers endlessly sideways," he laments.[19] This kind of junkspace architecture cannot participate in the movement towards a global

---

15 Rem Koolhaas, "Junkspace," *October* 100 (Spring 2002): 175.
16 Ibid., 175–76.
17 Ibid., 176.
18 Ibid.
19 Ibid., 178.

progression of time because it is chaotic, "a web without a spider," and "flows depend on disciplined movement, bodies that cohere."[20]

A body that coheres, internally and ontologically is a body who is already given to the status of full Kantian Subject, a body that can claim autochthonous constitution as a constitutive body of the World. That is, a coherent body is white. The result of incoherent somatic coordinates in the merged body and building architecture of World is being Black — a non-body that (in)coheres as the antithesis of full Subjectivity in modernity's impossible ethics of observation, its gridlines of ampliative Kantian sight.

The progressive hope of Koolhaas's coherent time leads to a world of buildings beyond the chaotic uniformity of junkspace, of cheap, unimaginative tat. That world, however, is still the World, and still coordinates the coherent internal movements of white bodies.

Deconstructivist Architecture has also attempted to disrupt the Vitruvian establishment of space by eradicating the almost pan-historical affection for symmetry, building instead through disjunctive edges. In the book published on the occasion of the 1988 Museum of Modern Art exhibition "Deconstructivist Architecture," one of the founders, Mark Wigley, with Philip Johnson, writes,

> Deconstruction is not destruction, or dissimulation. While it diagnoses certain structural problems within apparently stable structures, these flaws do not lead to structures' collapse. On the contrary, deconstruction gains all its force by challenging the very values of harmony, unity, and stability, and proposing instead a different view of structure: the view that the flaws are intrinsic to the structure. They cannot be removed without destroying it; they are, indeed, structural.

---

20 Ibid., 179.

> A deconstructive architect is therefore not one who dismantles buildings, but one who locates the inherent dilemmas within buildings.[21]

The proposition begins with the premise that Humans structure objects in space, and the spatial organization of those objects can be performed rightly or wrongly, based on the input agency of Human consciousness. The projection of mind-to-World is not questioned, only the ordering within an a priori projective space.

Reflective surfaces established as self-defying forms are stuck onto empty space, retroactively claiming space as a marker of Human Reason because of its appropriation into the politics of Architecture. Empty space universally comes to signify the pointed corner of a Deconstructivist cone, without its reflective casing. The answer Deconstructivism provides to the problem of space as transcendental ideal is huge metallurgic propositions of Human Reason over the existent gridlines of the city, staggered like a figure playing Twister over colored patches of earth.

Designs that explicitly seek the implementation of a reformulated reality — a reality invariably conceived by paisley-shirt-wearing white men with postgrad degrees from the Bartlett worth about three years of the average British wage — have been surpassed now, and post-∞ architects instead look to some semantic slippage out of temporal signifiers, neither new nor old, contemporary nor traditional, in pursuit of any marker that establishes a visual coding as yet unseen.

The Liverpool trio of paisley white men, Studio MUTT, "believes in engaging with the world as it exists — rejecting the concept of radical newness, instead adopting referencing and sampling as a design solutions [sic] to contemporary issues."[22]

---

21 Mark Wigley, *Deconstructivist Architecture* (New York: The Museum of Modern Art, 1988), 11.
22 Studio MUTT, "What Is Studio MUTT?" https://www.studiomutt.com/mutt-info.

Being new is passé. Now a deeper model of appropriation is the ontological urban practice of Architecture.

Studio MUTT explicitly reject a priori formulas that state the moralizing unity of their projects. They have no prescriptive manifesto like the schools before them. Instead, they "allow each project to respond to its specific site." In this formulation, it is not even the Architects who have agency, but rather their project. It responds, a constitutive will in itself. This response also attempts to coherently merge the Architectural project with the life of the city surrounding it, against the ubiquity of junkspace that just falls out of Architects' thrones onto a space posited as backwards because it was never Architectural before being the pedestal for this glassy throne of mirrors. "Our work seeks to use the extremely familiar to create the perfectly peculiar."[23]

The extremely familiar sets itself into a World with strict spatiotemporal markers that universally signify a Human capacity to inhabit them. The World, in this joyous drive to build for who is already there, is the setting of a deictic scene in which Humans choose every aesthetic and ethical aspect. The site-specific requirements responded to are — as well as being fundamentally economic, based on the profit-expansion of whoever funded the project — necessarily requirements of the resident Humans' experience of space, rather than any earth-focused understanding of space as an organizing concept of Human life; space, instead, is organized by Humans in this formulation, and it is only on the expansion of Human profit and the accumulation of Human coordinates of value that the project of building can be imagined.

Regardless of the desire to respond to the needs of locally-produced knowledge, the projections of Kantian space are the foundational will of building in these Architectural projects. There is a temporal frame of progress inscribed in the semantics of the operation, as well as an ampliative spatial logic that seeks the accumulation of Architectural knowledge from an appropriation of distinct local methods of knowledge formation. As Esther da Costa Meyer interestingly writes, "the overwhelming

---

23 Ibid.

majority of our cutting-edge buildings are de facto, although not stylistically, post-modern because their exuberance expresses a faith in a future that the Anthropocene disavows."[24] Despite the profoundly aporetic possessive referent "our," which is here used to universally subsume all Human life into a group of Architects with da Cosa Meyer herself, the point remains that progressive Architectural projects affirm a temporal logic in which the construction itself — and its attendant industries of extraction and appropriation of raw earth materials — is an accumulator of social history, carrying within its structure the History of Humanity and leading it towards the telos of the future, the Future.

In response to these tangled arms of power in every Architectural suggestion, the Beijing-based WAI think tank recently proposed an antiracist manifesto for architecture, under the hip title "Un-making Architecture." The manifesto begins with vague denunciations of Architecture's reliance on the elusive funders behind each project's necessary massive investment. "Architects should be aware of the programs of the buildings they design," a proclamation most shocking because of its revelation that there are indeed Architects who are unaware of the social, economic, and historic mechanisms that command the possibility of Architecture.[25]

Other sections offer resolute criticisms of Architecture's chirping yea-sayers who defend the "lesser evils" of "sustainable" building practices, working up to punchy aphorisms like, "Racism is a device whose aim is to create walls between people. These walls should not be made. We need to learn to un-make these walls."[26] For one thing, the logic of un-making is a direct antithesis to that of making, establishing it within the same language and impossible ethics of observation as the command to

---

24 Esther da Costa Meyer, "Architectural History in the Anthropocene: Towards Methodology," *The Journal of Architecture* 21, no. 8 (2016): 1216.

25 WAI Architecture Think Tank, "Un-making ARCHITECTURE: An Anti-racist Architecture Manifesto," *The Architect's Newspaper*, June 15, 2020, https://www.archpaper.com/2020/06/un-making-architecture-an-anti-racist-architecture-manifesto/.

26 Ibid.

Architecture itself, the *archē* that marks the origin of solid space as the moment when Man projects his ampliative consciousness onto it. A project based only in reversals of oppressive trends is not a liberatory project.

Un-making a wall is not a particularly challenging threat for a wall. The wall, of course, can fall. Anyone can drive a car into it or kick it down. Anyone can put up posters of a Black fist raised in the air, play some feelgood rap and say that racism's walls have been pulled down in this staged locality of life. But the absence of a wall — in the ubiquity of the World, based on internal borders — still signifies a wall. Entering a house with a side missing is the most immediate way to make everyone acutely aware of walls. Why are there only three? It's cold in here.

The moralizing dictum of "should" adds to the superficial criticism of the antiracist manifesto. A universal proclamation of the requirements of building are still being proposed in this statement. It is not, however, that I am criticizing the operation of morality per se or denying that moral propositions can be made that are conceivably employable by all people, but rather that the position of an Architectural obligation presupposes a universal involvement in the establishment of the immorality to which these moral commands respond. "The walls should not be made" removes the particular Human agency universalized in the making of walls. World as the racializing institution of modernity is the antagonistic and ampliative World-expanding agency of walls. It is, then, the grammar of neutral disguise that hides the violence of this universal should.

The manifesto ends, in the section "RADICAL," with a list of commands that establish the World of another ideology. We must is followed by a set of obligations, structuring a pre-written future of spatial grids; creating perspectival lines leading from the Subject of Architecture, with the agency to inscribe the temporality of World, into a continued temporality that affirms the dominance of Now and of Architecture.

The command to build as History and for Architecture marks the same spatiotemporal constitution of World and its white Man ruler-inhabitant, as any project that is initiated by the World-forming agency of a Subject, affirming the *archē* of Architecture, meaning, as Agamben says, both command and origin.

Noticeable in all of these manifestoes and attempts at radical propositions for new architectures (or the post-post-post rejection of radical newness), against Kantian spacetime and its racializing logics, is a focus on changing space, on reformulating objects into forms that seem more amenable to notions of liberation or equality. These Postmodernist architectural pursuits are based in changing the manifestation of matter in space. None, however, radically confronts the constitutive idea of space itself in Kantian modernity: the Human. It is this formulation of Humanity that designates the spatiotemporal organization of the World as inherently racializing, rather than any particular project of spatial construction in the already-established politics and spaces of the World.

Denise Ferreira da Silva, way beyond, in another earth to all these Worldly Architects and speakers of spacetime's natural ampliative grammar, attempts to propose the eradication of the originary ontological condition of spacetime as the only radical pursuit that will end the World and operate the energy of modernity's ubiquitous violence otherwise. No architectural project that relies on the category of Architecture and its precondition, the Kantian a priori projective logic of spacetime, will ever make any radical difference to the racism of the built environment, nor to the semantic conflation of race and architecture and their mutual genocidal reliance.

It is only the abandonment of spacetime that will finally have initiated the World-ending project of Black radicalism. The abandonment of spacetime is the removal of the World-forming institution of Architecture from the social planning practice of building.

*

Removing Architecture from building takes the Kantian architectonic model of apperception away from politics. The political as a scene of performing ontological struggles in life is a presupposed scene, an order with an over-planned set and script. The political is the space upholding the universe of raciality, gender, and the violent set pieces of our endless peculiar modernity. The act that comes from the withdrawal and denial of Architecture in building removes the material semantics of the city that commands the necessity of syntheses. Buildings in the ideology of Architecture always stipulated their demands as based in an ultimate synthesis: the building and the body, the polis, and the polity, must be synthesized in perfect causal unity; the construction and its foundation — material, geological, social, and philosophical — must develop into a synthesis. A synthesis, in the Kantian schema, is the movement of fitting sensations into the form of preconceived categories that order the Human understanding of reality. The building in Architecture, analogously, must fit into a presupposed form that designates its place in the progressive timescale of the city.

The removal of Architecture is, as Ferreira da Silva seeks, a material and decompositional poethics of Black building, the Black deconstitution of the city.[27] Politics always signifies allegiance to a determinist and teleological creed. It is always presupposed by a set of internal categories that constitute the World-making, ampliative mind of its Human ruler. There is no politics outside of this dynamic. The logic of the polis is the presupposed logic of the polity: the ampliative universality called Human.

A decompositional poethics of Black building is, more than anything else, a practice of always ending buildings by focusing on the opening of their construction, rather than their construction. The creation of a building is a World-ending project if it is practiced as ending-opening. An ending-opening practice is ongoing and disavows its foreclosure by the presupposed category of Architecture, designating it as property, as politics, and a practice that is focused on opening up the building to the congregation of study, which is groups of living.

Outside spacetime, how to conceive of building?

---

27 Ferreira da Silva, "In the Raw."

*

In this global genocide, building is our rejective joy, not an act that attempts or achieves completion. It is an ongoing collective study, a turning of resources into communal forms for the use of the congregation, the congregated groups.

Building without Architecture is a practice that proposes universal moral principles, using the same ampliative logic as Kant. Building proposes a certain formalism of use; it constructs an alternating scene for the congregation of congregations, for the collection of gatherings of life. But, where it moves away from Kantian morality is in this fact: building without Architecture opens itself to poethical decomposition, to eradication, to the townsfolx's manipulation. Building without Architecture proposes itself materially as building on the condition that it can be shifted, changed, and undermined by the study-group of a population that is always an ongoing act of thinking. Building without Architecture is able to build on this condition because the population's city has disavowed Architecture, leaving open the conceptual and material confrontation with buildings that has never been possible from antiquity to late modernity.

Buildings and bodies are separated in their meanings, referring not to each other or becoming synonymous, but rather working in collaboration with one another without the elusive pursuit of syntheses. Buildings and bodies, in the city of building without Architecture, are two constructive antagonisms without relation, refusing the relation that always claims itself above the foundation of an impossible unrelation.

*

Once Architecture is withdrawn as its finalizing telos, building is a praxis of movement in space. It is an external movement of the interiority of the body, a congregation of materials moving as the given-away home of the group, of the Kantian manifold. Building becomes the continuous movement of a collective body in space. Building becomes a dance.

Dance is the manipulation of the lived form(alism) of space — it is the constant reconstruction and decomposition of formalisms; it sets up an infinite proposition of moral spaces — be this way, stand like this, because it is right for this moment, this performance of the movement. However, the morality of dance is always decomposing, reconstituting as something else. The rise is accurate, always, and conforms to the moral proposition of its choreography, but in the next second it changes; a new morality is built and the spatial body is decomposed, recomposed, as another movement of a collective body choreographing space.

Building after Architecture is dance.

Building after Architecture is the act of bringing Kantian intuition — through sensations received from objects in the world — to concepts, provided by the rational internal faculty for understanding of the Human mind, that are continuously changing dependent on the sensations. Building is the endless process of synthetizing the manifold into a decompositional unity that is always in the process of creation, reconstruction, and destruction.

Dance, as building, is the task of always moving, the exhaustion of life, the ever-lasting unity of apperception that breaks the political bonds of causality; nothing came here, nothing made it here — it was here forever and forever is always changing. As Moten riffs,

> exhaustion makes life ever
> lasting. when I dance with
> you I am the moved mover.
> baby, you're a solid sender.[28]

*

---

[28] Fred Moten, *The Little Edges* (Middletown: Wesleyan University Press, 2015), 4.

Dance is a prominent verb and gerund in the grammar of Moten and Harney's collaborative radical optimism. Dance is a feature, in its primary status as the movement of sociality, of the future anterior of forms of life in the undercommons, in the space where the constant reformulation of sociality is conducted within the ethics of planning. And "planning in the undercommons is not an activity, not fishing or dancing or teaching or loving, but the ceaseless experiment with the futurial presence with the forms of life that make such activities possible."[29]

Dance is a mode of exposing the originary sharedness of the manifold before its accumulation into the politics of individuation, which is also the individuation of politics. Dance is the charged energy in the core of the extractive zone, in the hole of the mine, the power of the ferrous weight before its absorption into politics and that oppressive ontological mode's delineation of all life along a teleological line of being-individual. Dance precedes and provides the energy for the condition of organizing the modern life of coherent individuals. Dance is the force that can be found in the planning of a sociality otherwise. "What remains of eccentricity after the relay between loss and restoration has its say or song? In the absence of amenity, in exhaustion, there's a society of friends where everything can fold in dance to black, in being held and flown, in what was never silence. Can't you hear them whisper one another's touch?"[30]

Why trace the lines, like some imperial bespectacled archaeologist, back into the source of seismic shifts between the ruptured fault lines of modernity, in search of what we did, in search of the coagulation that gathers on our palms now, in search of a source of opacity forceful and free enough to undo the entire epistemology we are coordinated inside the gridlines of? And all while the archaeologists of modernity refuse our investigations because we put the prepositions at the end, the sentence of… the punishment.

---

29 Stefano Harney and Fred Moten, *The Undercommons: Fugitive Planning and Black Study* (New York: Minor Compositions, 2013), 74–75.
30 Ibid., 97.

> the unspeakable tower is what they did.
> our shit has some names and sometimes
> they sound good at the bottom of it, therefore proceed
> against that little pill-head fucker that correct people's pronunciation.[31]

*

The social and ontological referent that is race was only recognizable in the training sights of early modern philosophy by the geographical designation of territory. Borders that mark territories physically manifest in the ideological cartography of a previous pronouncement of modernity. Borders were the visible coordinates of race's global organization. As Ferreira da Silva writes in her essay "No Bodies," race was always locked into this prescriptive cartography. This means that what defines the Black person as Black is bound in a stable logic of geography that can be transgressed by the movement of the Black person. If the African moves to Europe, does the African stop being Black? The answer for Kant, of course, is no, but he has to prove it. Prior to Kant, external laws had been the condition on which race was a coherent social referent that marked certain global zones as sites for the extraction of slaves.

> How could Locke's instituted law, which he describes as an exterior (objective) force, become the interior (even if formal) determinant of post-Enlightenment European (political) particularity? The answer requires an account of how universality morphed into the principle actualised and expressed in Enlightenment European bodies and territories.[32]

Kant had to formulate a plan for the internalization of a state of nature that could be grasped and maintained by a racial logic

---

31 Moten, *The Little Edges*, 7.
32 Ferreira da Silva, "No Bodies: Law, Raciality and Violence," *Meritum* 9, no. 1 (2014): 135.

of transcendental reason, allowing a presupposed geographical marker, race, to affirm the internal, ontological supremacy of a certain kind of mind, a certain way of being — and that way is whiteness; an epistemological framework only accessible, through its continuation of the Columbian notion of internal torrid zones and epidermal cartographies, by inheriting the signifying signs of being European.

> When mapping the conditions of possibility of knowledge with certainty, Kant introduces the notion of transcendental reason (pure/formal) as that which provides the understanding with the tools — intuitions and categories — that comprehend the objective and necessary forces at work in phenomena, the modes through which the extent of things of the world is accessible to scientific knowledge.[33]

Universality, in this moment, becomes synonymous with European and white.

The problem with this Kantian model is that universalization becomes a simultaneous process of de-individuation; the being gives himself to the full subjectivity of whiteness/Europeanness by becoming the inherited residue of a regime that supersedes him. The full Subject is then a steward of subjectivity, a laborer within the fields of subjectivity-production. Kant himself foregrounded the ontological status of autochthony, of self-constitution in one place, of rational self-rule. Man must command himself into being as a machinic producer of commandments that make the World in which he lives. However, the formal requirements of universalization — which are, exactly, formalization, or what Ferreira da Silva calls *necessitas* — suspend the World-making step Kant is attempting. This is the movement that Moten simultaneously commiserates as the original scar of philosophy-as-racism and celebrates as the opening of the possibility of Black radical philosophy at length in his 2017–18 trilogy *consent not to be a single being*. This movement establishes

---

33 Ibid., 136.

Kant as the opening into a radical Black ethics at the beginning of the philosophical foreclosure of Black ethics: this is, I mean to say after Moten, what makes Kant such a perfect player in the World-ending project of Black radicalism.

Ferreira da Silva finds the completion — the beautiful *Aufhebung* — of this proto-racializing process in Hegel.

> The second transformation, G.W.F. Hegel's rewriting of formal (transcendental) reason as a living (self-developing) force, resolved *necessitas* into a productive step in the self-revealing (self-representing) trajectory of human consciousness. In Hegel's version, universal reason becomes a transcendental self-determined (interior/temporal) force that is realised in post- Enlightenment European minds and territories. The writing of transcendental reason as spirit, the self-producing, self-knowing, living force, transforms universality (and along with it self-determination [freedom]) into an ontological descriptor, on which signifies (because an effect) a particular spatial/temporal juncture, namely the moment of transparency, where the revelation of transcendentality announces the end of the temporal trajectory of spirit.[34]

Spirit provides a grounding for the spatial exterior of self-consciousness within the same teleological project (of race-formation, of the World-making of a World of whiteness), creating a global whole in which the exteriority of the Human mind is eclipsed within a pursuit of the ideal World, represented formally by the ideal Human (white, European Man) and his ideal territory (industrial, imperial nation-state). World has been completed as a racializing project in the two-step shift from Kant to Hegel.

This defines the Hegelian *Aufhebung* of Spirit's journey through its process of formalization that stands as the skeleton of History; the formal outline of a World defined by its pursuit of becoming-white, moving away from the abhorrent materiality

---

34 Ibid., 137.

of Blackness (in Hegel's "Egypt"). "Under the aegis of historicity, the mode of becoming of spirit, universality, as a principle rules ethical life through and through only because it describes the ethical-juridical totality, figured by the nation and the state — in the late nineteenth century consolidated in the hybrid (ethical-juridical) political entity, namely the nation-state — that marks the end of the trajectory of spirit," Ferreira da Silva writes.[35]

*

The inherent faculty of reason, a priori inside the architectonic mind, is a marker of the Kantian internal cartography of being European. In my loving hopelessness, my long evenings in front of gazing screens, in my dance-off with a thousand friends who do not know me and write the mysticism of my pre-abolished future in a World I was dragged into and forced to rule, I think of dance as a movement that pushes out the internality of space. The movement of dance is a priori, coming already given (*venendo oferto agli altri*) in the sharedness of the show. Dance is already given to the dancer before the logics of dance are coded in the mnemonic rituals of rehearsal spaces. Preceding and presupposing the governance and policy of a show — of a spectacle designated as individual moments of private joy for an audience projecting internal categories of dance-epistemologies, coordinated by the imperial regimes of (anti-)educational institutions and the self-excusing grammar of liberal apology — is a divergent and wayward movement, a form of dance itself as form, that bulges forth from an a priori shift of already given, already shared, always adapting movements that I can only think of calling *love of dance.*

(with this trade, these little fours, your dirty palette, a savory train between in blood sorbet)

let it dry and make a vase out of it. we poured what was in it

---

35 Ibid., 139.

on our greens and blues and ochres, our loud flavors
and the tree we danced around, the tree we made a movie around,
against that little pill-head fucker that correct people's pre-destination.[36]

Dance in this congregation of study movements, this "ceaseless experiment with the futurial presence with the forms of life that make [dancing; love of dance] possible,"[37] is a spatial force underspeaking the grammar of teleology, underscripting the designating language of epidermal cartographies, underacting the ampliative faculty of reason that makes space in the a priori categories. Dancing in this architecture of poethical movement is a decomposition in territory, out of and away from the politics and policies of land; dancing architecture — the structure of antiformal movements, the givenness of movements out of space — is movement into earth, into the form of forms.

Darell Wayne Fields attempts a version of this inwards movement by arriving at such a point of criticism of Hegel that he turns into Hegel. Fields folds into the skin of Hegel, and opens into a form that internally undoes Hegelianism. This begins by moving back to the pre-beginning of the Cartesian *cogito*.

First,
"I think before I am?"
Then,
"Where am I?"
Better yet,
"I think there. I am"

The mind/psyche's I/where?/there formulation speaks for the missing presence preceding the "I think." It is akin to the absence of sound in isolation. No thinking can be done without it. It is being inside. […] The thought recognizes the interior's

---

36 Moten, *The Little Edges*, 7.
37 Harney and Moten, *The Undercommons*, 74–75.

most significant quality, darkness. This darkness is so vast, ubiquitous, and opaque that "I think" and "I am" appear unaware.[38]

What Fields call the "Black Subject" resides in and emerges from a flat, dark, and endless plain inside the fold of History. To that space, History (and its racializing historian) returns constantly, seeking to withdraw a "new" original moment to affirm the progress of History; time goes on — a process constantly established by the creation of an origin within the darkness of temporality's internality.

That space is the epistemological sociality of Blackness, where the Black Subject becomes aware of a repeated scene that is not visible to the external subjects in the telos of time's progress. In the mechanism through which the Kantian Subject posits himself as there (always implicitly saying, in his *cogito, I think [universally], therefore I am [there]*), there is a sociality that exists before and beyond; something precedes the speaking-into-being of the Subject in his act of universal individuation. The antecedent and enduring life of Blackness — in the darkness within, before, and sealed off from Descartes's *cogito,* Kant's transcendental ideality, and Hegel's self-developing *Aufhebung* — is "this black sign system" that uses "arbitrariness in the production of language and cultural artifacts (e.g., poetry)."[39]

The darkness within, which Western philosophy and architecture have feared throughout their history — protected respectively by the obsession with light, Enlightenment, revelation, and outwards movement, and by global urban expansion and the resolute logics of property ownership — is a means of distorting the signifying function of space. The space, however, is not necessarily what Fields seeks to change. Rather, Blackness's poetic sign system of arbitrary distortion collapses the ampliative link between signifier and signified, leaving the

---

38 Darell Wayne Fields, *Architecture in Black: Theory, Space, and Appearance* (London: Bloomsbury, 2015), 5–6.
39 Ibid., 9.

building as it is, but closing the possibility of its urban sign.[40] The meaning of space falls inside the nodal residue of internal, enduring difference, and the building is no longer signified by the ampliative projection of Kantian space. The hegemonic claim to the original — which it endlessly reformulates as the productive novelty — is given over to its antecedent condition, the Black (architectural) sign: what Kant calls *the stupidity of Blackness* and Hegel calls *the dumb mute of Egypt,* Fields recognizes as the internal antecedent condition; the form of meaning itself. "The relegation of being outside history is achieved by being concealed within it. For historical errors, such as blackness, nothing is outside."[41]

There is no outside space to occupy in the Black ethics of building as love of dance. There is instead a faith in the return of the ongoing future, the future anterior that reaches into now and opens lonely eyes, seeing the alternative present that extends into a coming-together of time. This ethics of building against Architecture as love of dance does not exert its force over the undetermined future, but rather reveals the internality of time to itself. There is no outside, there is only the constant sociality of everyone, everything, which is covered up by totalizing violence but ongoing and surviving nonetheless.

The future anterior — future perfect, the coming back of the forwards-thrown — is the temporality of this fugitive dancing movement that breaks the logics of the two-step (goose-step) Kantian/Hegelian constitution of the universal Subject-as-white, the logics of that little pill-head fucker that correct people. It is in the future anterior that the coming-back to a new past of the futurial presence is performed, that which Alexander Weheliye calls *apocatastasis*.[42] In the internality of the dancer as a spatial, architectural form, a form of life in (the always ongoing process of) building, is held not a capacity of pure reason to be imposed

---

40 Ibid., 61.
41 Ibid., 113.
42 For more, see Alexander Weheliye, *Habeas Viscus: Racializing Assemblages, Biopolitics, and Black Feminist Theories of the Human* (Durham: Duke University Press, 2014).

on World as spatial synthesis, but rather a sharedness that came already from the sociality of dance. Dancing itself as a form of sociality — as the condition for moving in the social form — is already given away to the (Blackitectural) home that is always, necessarily, given-away and shared. Moten says in a collaboration with Wu Tsang,

> We live in the gaps between our intentions and the shit that doesn't work out. So many emotions caught in my pipe. I pound my chest to putter it out. The machinations. Glittery enunciation. The first time I heard the sound of your voice it filled me with a sense of future perfect. The friendship I will have had. Getting to know you. Sounding without thinking. Walking. Just walking and heart beating. Out of synch, but in time.[43]

I am sure that nothing has ever described dancing (and therefore building without Architecture) quite as perfectly.

*

What am I saying in this dancing grammar out of World and into earth? I speak like one who says things but the source of opacity that surrounds my reading has obscured the penetrating felicity of my own transparent presence. Fleetingly, it seems, the figure forces upon himself the dancing codes of anticoding, the spectral futurity of coming-back-Black. But what comes out of it? A protocol. Is he planning something? He is registering formal intuitions of policy, calling the police. Naughty naughty. I hope I haven't been so bad that the structure collapses on me. I hope even more I haven't been so good that the collapse restructures me.

*

---

43 Fred Moten and Wu Tsang, *Who Touched Me?* (Amsterdam: If I Can't Dance I Don't Want to be Part of Your Revolution, 2016), 7.

Fig. 4. Giovanni Battista Piranesi, "Frammenti di marmo della Pianta di Roma antica [Marble fragments of the Plan of Ancient Rome]," 1756.

The end of temporal accumulations in the racializing hegemony of time is the ongoing circularity of chasing heat. The collapse of Newtonian spacetime, projected universally onto earth as World in the Kantian transcendental ideality of space, is a dance-away from the production grounds of modernity's policy of individuation. Building to dance. In the ethics of antiracist building — in the home of Black love of dance — the materiality of the construction shifts in split, changes in its adaptive performance, decomposes in its givenness to every inhabitant. Removed from circular spacetime in the marble statues of Newton, Kant, and Hegel, the Black ethics of building seeks a form of heat distribution within its inhabitants, opening its inside to changing days of color and sound, sealing itself off — an archipelagic island against the imperial sea of expansion[44] — from World. Meanwhile, earnest Architects of the Architecture Insti-

---

44 Pier Vittorio Aureli, *The Possibility of an Absolute Architecture* (Cambridge: MIT Press, 2011).

tution of World respond that the Royal Institute of British Architects' (RIBA) regulations on internal insulation do not allow for adaptive dances of heat-distribution. It is impossible to get fire safety certification if the building is dancing, and impossible to approve sufficient access to daylight if it is closed to this "imperial sea." RIBA commands strict policies on "thermal comfort," heat distribution, and access to daylight, conditioned by a building's orientation, physics, and glazing proportions, which seem to somewhat stymie the pursuits of a Black ethics of building in the reality of World.[45]

Fear not, however.

When the non-European thinker Hamid Dabashi asks, "Can non-Europeans think?" another non-European thinker, Walter Mignolo responds, "Yes, we can."[46] Slavoj Žižek, startled by all these non-Europeans thinking, responds first: "Fuck you, Walter Mignolo,"[47] and then second, "Okay, fuck you, who are all these bloody much more interesting intellectuals…? Let's say I was not overly impressed."[48] Philosophy as an institution of World — a strictly and dogmatically European institution that obsessively polices the Europeanness of its borders — has no direct comparison in the lived reality on earth, which it has carefully regulated. But still, there is clearly an imperial, expansive sea in operation in both philosophy and Architecture. Small islands of ruins remain, which, as Pier Vittorio Aureli discusses through the engravings and possible architectures of Giovanni Piranesi, post-Enlightenment urban thought has understood as having "succumbed to the course of time."[49] Aureli instead sees the ruin "as something that has survived both time and the modern city. Through Piranesi these ruins are emancipated to become the latent beginning of a new city whose potential is not yet subsumed by any incipient urban order."[50] The build-

---

45 RIBA, *Plan of Work 2020: Overview* (London: RIBA, 2020).
46 Mignolo, "Foreword."
47 Ibid., xvi.
48 Dabashi, *Can Non-Europeans Think?*, 1.
49 Aureli, *The Possibility of an Absolute Architecture*, 139.
50 Ibid. My emphasis.

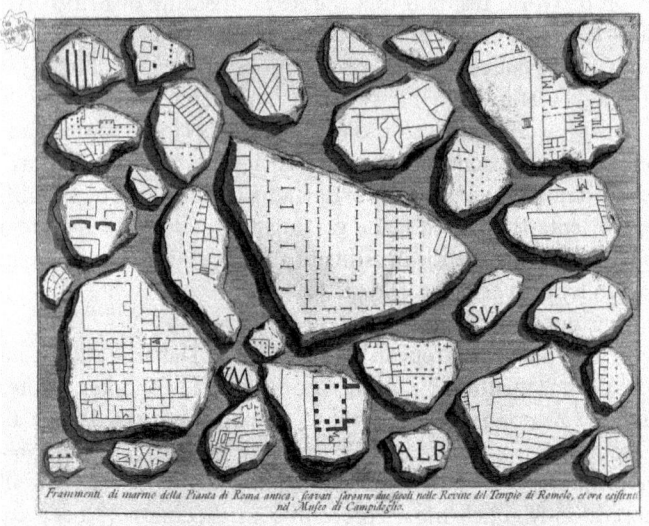

Fig. 5. Giovanni Battista Piranesi, "Frammenti di marmo della Pianta di Roma antica [Marble fragments of the Plan of Ancient Rome]," 1756.

ing—the act of the ethics of building—is separated from its performative part in the totality of urban design.

Instead, the building is singular, attending solely to the precise and peculiar position of its inhabitants and users. RIBA regulations on heat distribution are universalized according to national urban logics and are regulated through the presupposed conduit of property ownership and contract exchanges. The massive cost of satisfying fire safety regulations is chargeable to tenants and leaseholders in order to protect the landowners' and freeholders' profits.[51] Understanding the building

---

51 For more, see Jack Simpson, "Forcing Leaseholders to Pay for Cladding Costs under Building Safety Bill an 'abdication of responsibility,' say MPs," *Inside Housing,* November 24, 2020, https://www.insidehousing.co.uk/news/news/forcing-leaseholders-to-pay-for-cladding-costs-under-building-safety-bill-an-abdication-of-responsibility-say-mps-68710 22.

itself as a ruin, however, opens up the possibility of establishing an island of thinking that moves in the other-space unimaginable to the regulating borders of philosophy and Architecture. The ruin is an absolute architecture that has survived, that has endured the permanent operation of its subsumption into the regulatory framework of the urban totality. It has stood its archipelagic ground,

> demonstrat[ing] that architecture is simply an island within the city, whose urban form far exceeds the possibility of an architectural morphology to accommodate its scale. [...] In this "unplugged" condition of the city, all attributes of urbanity are gone. Rather than interpreting such a scenario as a terminal point of the city, however, Piranesi presents it as a latent beginning embedded within what already exists in urban space — the ruins. The difference between architecture and urban space is radicalized in order to show the architectural clues that allow the critical imagination to rethink the city, not through its managerial practices but as a field of potential possibilities.[52]

Blackness precedes its subsumption in the regulatory ideality of Kantian space and the racializing schema of modern ontology. Blackness is the form — and the condition of another kind of formality, as I have outlined through Darell Fields, Fred Moten, and Denise Ferreira da Silva — of modernity's antecedent and enduring condition. Blackness is the ontological ruin that survives despite the expanding imperial sea. Blackness is the island that carries on.

The multiple institutional manifestations of the abstraction I have called Architecture regulate a border of conceptual integrity. Whatever is not inside these institutions *is not*. But there is a way of building, a way of thinking about space, that exists otherwise.

---

52 Aureli, *Absolute Architecture*, 139–40.

The regulation of heat, light, and color distribution between the sea and the islands continues, but what we — here in the sea — cannot feel, cannot know, is that another kind of heat is happening on the island. Its Black ethics of dance is turned away from us, its walls uninterested in revealing what is inside, in playing the deceptive game of hospitality with the sea that demands a binary of inclusion and exclusion from the wall. But inside, a kind of heat, a kind of light, a kind of color, is given, constantly given, and giving away.

While the sea was comfortably convinced of its inherent universality, the island had been condemned to provinciality. Its languages were unspoken by any outsiders, and its history was ignored as fable and myth. In the process, the sea's blinding conviction of universality made it uninterested in learning about any islands, or anything that is not the sea. Ultimately, the sea became provincial in its lack of interest. The island, meanwhile, forced to speak the language of the sea, learn the sea's history, and smile at the sea so it did not flood the archipelago — while also learning about the island itself, and its neighboring islands — became universal.[53] The ruin survived. It is a sign of survival against the tide that tries to consume its history in the regulating water of the sea.

To build Black is not to build. It is to allow the emergence of what is already there. The ruin itself is internal heat-distribution and the shifting movements of love-of-dance. The ruin is already evidence of building Black.

---

53 Dabashi, *Can Non-Europeans Think?*, 5.

Bibliography

Agamben, Giorgio. *Remnants of Auschwitz: The Witness and the Archive.* Translated by Daniel Heller-Roazen. New York: Zone Books, 1999.
———. *The Use of Bodies.* Translated by Adam Kotsko. Stanford: Stanford University Press, 2016.
Aureli, Pier Vittorio. *The Possibility of an Absolute Architecture.* Cambridge: MIT Press, 2011.
Arendt, Hannah. *Eichmann in Jerusalem: A Report on the Banality of Evil.* New York: Penguin Books, 1994.
Arrighi, Giovanni. *The Long Twentieth Century: Money, Power, and the Origins of Our Times.* London: Verso, 1994.
Bachelard, Gaston. *The Poetics of Space.* Translated by Maria Jolas. London: Penguin, 2014.
Baldwin, James. "Architectural Digest Visits: James Baldwin." *Architectural Digest,* August 1987. https://archive.architecturaldigest.com/article/1987/8/architectural-digest-visitsjames-baldwin.
Baucom, Ian. *Out of Place: Englishness, Empire, and the Locations of Identity.* Princeton: Princeton University Press, 1999.
———. *Specters of the Atlantic: Finance Capital, Slavery, and the Philosophy of History.* Durham: Duke University Press, 2005.

Belly, Lead. "Gwine Dig a Hole to Put the Devil In." Track 2 on *The Lead Belly Legacy, Vol. II: Square Dances, Sooky Jumps, Reels, Blues, Texas, Louisiana, Barrelhouse*. Mach60 Music, 2012.

Benjamin, Walter. *The Arcades Project*. Translated by Howard Eiland and Kevin McLaughlin. Cambridge: Harvard University Press, 2002.

Bentham, Jeremy. *Theory of Legislation*. London: Trübner & Co., 1871.

Bhandar, Brenna. *Colonial Lives of Property: Law, Land, and Racial Regimes of Ownership*. Durham: Duke University Press, 2018.

Booth, Robert. "'Eyesore' London Tower Approved Despite Housing Concerns." *The Guardian,* February 28, 2020. https://www.theguardian.com/uk-news/2020/feb/28/eyesore-london-tower-approved-despite-housing-concerns.

Braddick, Imogen. "Priti Patel Condemns 'Thuggery' of Black Lives Matter and Extinction Rebellion Protests in Tory Speech." *Evening Standard,* October 4, 2020. https://www.standard.co.uk/news/uk/priti-patel-black-lives-matter-extinction-rebellion-protests-tory-speech-a4563016.html.

Bratton, Benjamin H. *Dispute Plan to Prevent Future Luxury Construction*. Berlin: Sternberg Press, 2015.

Bressani, Martin. "Prosthetic Fantasies of the First Machine Age: Viollet-le-Duc's Iron Architecture." *AA Files* 68 (2014): 43–49. DOI: 10.1002/9781118887226.wbcha090.

Brown, Adrienne. "'My Hole Is Warm and Full of Light': The Sub-Urban Real Estate of Invisible Man." In *Race and Real Estate,* edited by Adrienne Brown and Valerie Smith, 178–94. Oxford: Oxford University Press, 2016.

———. *The Black Skyscraper: Architecture and the Perception of Race*. Baltimore: John Hopkins University Press, 2017

Cervenak, Sarah Jane, and J. Kameron Carter. "Untitled and Outdoors: Thinking with Saidiya Hartman." *Women and Performance: A Journal of Feminist Theory* 27, no. 1 (2017): 45–55. DOI: 10.1080/0740770X.2017.1282116.

Cheng, Anne Anlin. *Ornamentalism.* Oxford: Oxford University Press, 2019.

Cheng, Irene, Charles L. Davis II, and Mabel O. Wilson, eds. *Race and Modern Architecture: A Critical History from the Enlightenment to the Present.* Pittsburgh: University of Pittsburgh Press, 2020.

Clark, Michael P., ed. *Revenge of the Aesthetic: The Place of Literature in Theory Today.* Berkeley: University of California Press, 2000.

Colenutt, Bob. *The Property Lobby: The Hidden Reality Behind the Housing Crisis.* Bristol: Policy Press, 2020.

Columbus, Christopher. *The Four Voyages.* London: Penguin, 1969.

Coulthard, Glen Sean. *Red Skin, White Masks: Rejecting the Colonial Politics of Recognition.* Minneapolis: University of Minnesota Press, 2014.

Da Costa Meyer, Esther, "Architectural History in the Anthropocene: Towards Methodology." *The Journal of Architecture* 21, no. 8 (2016): 1203–25. DOI: 10.1080/13602365.2016.1254270.

Davis, Angela Y. *Women, Race & Class.* London: Penguin, 2019.

Davis II, Charles L. *Building Character: The Racial Politics of Modern Architectural Style.* Pittsburgh: University of Pittsburgh Press, 2019.

Derrida, Jacques. *Specters of Marx: The State of the Debt, the Work of Mourning and the New International.* Translated by Peggy Kamuf. London: Routledge, 2006.

———. "'A Self-Unsealing Poetic Text': Poetics and Politics of Witnessing." Translated by Rachel Bowlby. In *Revenge of the Aesthetic,* edited by Michael P. Clark, 180–207. Berkeley: University of California Press, 2000.

Douglass, Frederick. *Narrative of the Life of Frederick Douglass, an American Slave, Written by Himself.* Cambridge: Harvard University Press, 1960.

Equiano, Olaudah. *The Life of Olaudah Equiano, or Gustavus Vassa, the African.* New York: Dover Publications, 1999.

Fai, Roberto. "Giorgio Agamben e l'uso dei corpi." *Kasparhauser,* April 2017. http://www.kasparhauser.net/Ateliers/Filosofia%20italiana/Fai-Agamben.html.

Fanon, Frantz. *Black Skin, White Masks.* Translated by Charles Lam Markmann. London: Pluto Press, 2008.

Ferreira da Silva, Denise. "Before Man: Sylvia Wynter's Rewriting of the Modern Episteme." In *Sylvia Wynter: On Being Human as Praxis,* edited by Katherine McKittrick, 90–105. Durham: Duke University Press, 2015.

———. "In the Raw." *e-flux* 93 (2018). https://www.e-flux.com/journal/93/215795/in-the-raw/.

———. "No Bodies: Law, Raciality and Violence." *Meritum* 9, no. 1 (2014): 119–62. DOI: 10.46560/meritum.v9i1.2493.

———. "Toward a Black Feminist Poethics: The Quest(ion) of Blackness toward the End of the World." *The Black Scholar* 44, no. 2 (2014): 81–97. DOI: 10.1080/00064246.2014.11413690.

Fields, Darell Wayne. *Architecture in Black: Theory, Space, and Appearance.* London: Bloomsbury, 2015.

Foucault, Michel, "Of Other Spaces (1967), Heterotopias." Translated by Jay Miskowiec. *Foucault.info.* https://foucault.info/documents/heterotopia/foucault.heteroTopia.en/.

Frampton, Kenneth. *Modern Architecture: A Critical History.* London: Thames and Hudson, 2018.

Freeman, Elizabeth. *Time Binds: Queer Temporalities, Queer Histories.* Durham: Duke University Press, 2010.

Giedion, Sigfried. *Space, Time & Architecture.* Fifth edition. Cambridge: Harvard University Press, 2008.

Gilroy, Paul. *The Black Atlantic: Modernity and Double Consciousness.* London: Verso, 1993.

Glissant, Édouard. *Poetics of Relation.* Translated by Betsy Wing. Ann Arbor: University of Michigan Press, 1997.

Goldsby, Jacqueline. *A Spectacular Secret: Lynching in American Life and Literature.* Chicago: University of Chicago Press, 2006.

Guyer, Paul. "Kant and the Philosophy of Architecture." *The Journal of Aesthetics and Art Criticism* 69, no. 1, Special Issue: "The Aesthetics of Architecture: Philosophical Investigations into the Art of Building" (2011): 7–19. DOI: 10.1111/j.1540-6245.2010.01442.x.

Grove, Andrew S. *Swimming Across*. London: Hachette UK, 2008).

Halpin, Bryony Jane. *Unsettling Revitalization in Toronto: The Fantasy and Apology of the Settler City.* PhD dissertation, York University, Toronto, 2017. https://yorkspace.library.yorku.ca/xmlui/bitstream/handle/10315/33544/Halpin_Bryony_J_2017_PhD.pdf.

Harney, Stefano, and Fred Moten. *The Undercommons: Fugitive Planning and Black Study.* New York: Minor Compositions, 2013.

Harris, Cheryl I. "Whiteness as Property." *Harvard Law Review* 106, no. 8 (June 1993): 1708–91. https://www.jstor.org/stable/1341787.

Harris, Dianne. "Modeling Race and Class: Architectural Photography and the U.S. Gypsum Research Village, 1952–1955." In *Race and Modern Architecture: A Critical History from the Enlightenment to the Present,* edited by Irene Cheng, Charles L. Davis II, and Mabel O. Wilson, 218–38. Pittsburgh: University of Pittsburgh Press, 2020.

Hartman, Saidiya V. *Scenes of Subjection: Terror, Slavery, and Self-Making in Nineteenth-Century America.* Oxford: Oxford University Press, 1997.

———. *Wayward Lives, Beautiful Experiments.* New York City: W.W. Norton & Company, 2019.

Hegel, G.W.F. *Hegel's Aesthetics: Lectures on Fine Art,* Volume 1. Translated by T.M. Knox. Oxford: Oxford University Press, 1975

———. *The Philosophy of History.* Translated by J. Sibree. Kitchener: Batoche Books, 2001.

Heidegger, Martin. *What Is Called Thinking?* Translated by J. Glenn Gray. London: Perennial, 2004.

"Hill and Peabody Enter into £350m East London Regeneration Joint Venture." *Hill News,* March 30, 2017. https://www.hill.co.uk/news-press/hill-and-peabody-enter-into-%C2%A3350m-east-london-regeneration-joint-venture.

Hobbes, Thomas. *Leviathan, or the Matter, Forme, & Power of a Common-wealth, Ecclesiasticall and Civill.* New York: Touchstone, 1997.

Hyatt, Vera Lawrence, and Rex M. Nettleford, eds. *Race, Discourse and the Origin of the Americas: A New World View.* Washington, DC: Smithsonian Books, 1994.

Jackson, Zakiyyah Iman. *Becoming Human: Matter and Meaning in an Antiblack World.* New York: NYU Press, 2020.

Kaminsky, Ilya. *Deaf Republic.* London: Faber & Faber, 2019.

Kant, Immanuel, "An Answer to the Question: 'What is Enlightenment?'" (1784). In *Kant: Political Writings,* edited by H.S. Reiss, 54–60. Cambridge: Cambridge University Press, 1991.

———. "An Old Question Raised Again: Is the Human Race Constantly Progressing?" In *Religion and Rational Theory,* edited by Allen W. Wood and George Di Giovanni, 297–309. Cambridge: Cambridge University Press, 1996.

———. *Critique of Judgment.* Translated by Werner S. Pluhar. Indianapolis: Hackett Publishing Company, 1987.

———. *Critique of Pure Reason.* Translated by Paul Guyer and Allen W. Wood. Cambridge: Cambridge University Press, 1998.

Kendi, Ibram X. *Stamped from the Beginning: The Definitive History of Racist Ideas in America.* New York: Nation Books, 2016.

King, Tiffany Lethabo, Jenell Navarro, and Andrea Smith, eds. *Otherwise Worlds: Against Settler Colonialism and Anti-Blackness.* Durham: Duke University Press, 2020.

King, Tiffany Lethabo, and Frank B Wilderson III. "Staying Ready for Black Study." In *Otherwise Worlds: Against Settler Colonialism and Anti-Blackness,* edited by Tiffany Lethabo King, Jenell Navarro, and Andrea Smith, 52–73. Durham: Duke University Press, 2020.

Koolhaas, Rem. "Junkspace." *October* 100 (Spring 2002): 175–90. DOI: 10.1162/016228702320218457.

Kuykendall, Ronald. "Hegel and Africa: An Evaluation of the Treatment of Africa in The Philosophy of History." *Journal of Black Studies* 23, no. 4 (June 1993): 571–81. DOI: 10.1177/002193479302300409.

Krivine, Hubert. *The Earth.* Translated by David Fernbach. London: Verso, 2015.

Lacan, Jacques, *Écrits: The First Complete Edition in English.* Translated by Bruce Fink. London: W.W. Norton & Company, 2006.

Leach, Neil, ed. *Rethinking Architecture: A Reader in Cultural Theory.* Abingdon: Routledge, 1997.

León-Portilla, Miguel. "Mesoamerica 1492, and the Eve of 1992." Working Paper 1 in Discovering the Americas: 1992 Lecture Series. College Park: Department of Spanish and Portuguese, University of Maryland, 1992.

Lloyd, David. *Under Representation: The Racial Regime of Aesthetics.* New York City: Fordham University Press, 2019.

Loos, Alfred, "Ornament and Crime (1908)." In *Programs and Manifestoes on 20th Century Architecture,* edited by Ulrich Conrads, 19–24. Cambridge: MIT Press, 1971.

Machiavelli, Niccolò. *The Prince.* New York: Dover Publications, 2000.

Marx, Karl. *Capital: A Critique of Political Economy,* Volume I. Translated by Ben Fowkes. London: Penguin, 1990.

Mbembe, Achille. *Critique of Black Reason.* Translated by Laurent Dubois. Durham: Duke University Press, 2017.

McKittrick, Katherine. *Demonic Grounds: Black Women and the Cartographies of Struggle.* Minneapolis: University of Minnesota Press, 2006.

———, ed. *Sylvia Wynter: On Being Human as Praxis.* Durham: Duke University Press, 2015.

Miessen, Markus. *The Nightmare of Participation: Crossbench Praxis as a Mode of Criticality.* Berlin: Sternberg Press, 2010.

Mignolo, Walter D. "Foreword: Yes, We Can." In Hamid Dabashi, *Can Non-Europeans Think?,* viii–xlii. London: Zed Books, 2015.

Moreton-Robinson, Aileen. *The White Possessive: Property, Power, and Indigenous Sovereignty.* Minneapolis: University of Minnesota Press, 2015.

Moten, Fred. "Manic Depression: A Poetics of Hesitant Sociology." 2017 Northrop Frye Professor Lecture, University of Toronto, April 4, 2017. https://www.youtube.com/watch?v=gQ2kodsmIJE&t=2794s.

———. *Stolen Life.* Durham: Duke University Press, 2018.

———. "The Case of Blackness." *Criticism* 50, no. 2 (2008): 177–218. DOI: 10.1353/crt.0.0062.

———. *The Little Edges.* Middletown: Wesleyan University Press, 2015.

———. *The Universal Machine.* Durham: Duke University Press, 2018.

Moten, Fred, and Stefano Harney. "'Give Away Your Home, Constantly': Fred Moten and Stefano Harney Revisit *The Undercommons* in a Time of Pandemic and Rebellion (Part 2)." *Millennials Are Killing Capitalism,* podcast, July 11, 2020. https://millennialsarekillingcapitalism.libsyn.com/give-away-your-home-constantly-fred-moten-and-stefano-harney.

———. "'Wildcat the Totality': Fred Moten and Stefano Harney Revisit *The Undercommons* in a Time of Pandemic and Rebellion (Part 1)." *Millennials Are Killing Capitalism,* podcast, July 4, 2020. https://millennialsarekillingcapitalism.libsyn.com/wildcat-the-totality-fred-moten-and-stefano-harney-revisit-the-undercommons-in-a-time-of-pandemic-and-rebellion-part-1.

Moten, Fred, and Sondra Perry. "Fred Moten in Conversation with Sondra Perry." *Frieze,* podcast, December 10, 2018. https://player.fm/series/frieze/fred-moten-in-conversation-with-sondra-perry.

Moten, Fred, and Wu Tsang. *Who Touched Me?* Amsterdam: If I Can't Dance I Don't Want to be Part of Your Revolution, 2016.

Motion E10. https://motion-e10.co.uk/.

Ngai, Sianne. *Ugly Feelings.* Cambridge: Harvard University Press, 2005.

Peabody. *Motion: Lea Bridge London E10,* brochure PDF, no date: https://www.peabodysales.co.uk/media/110599/motion-lifestyle-brochure-compressed.pdf.

Perry, Francesca, "'It's like being on an island in the sky': Your Stories of High-rise Living." *The Guardian,* February 24, 2017. https://www.theguardian.com/cities/2017/feb/24/stories-high-rise-living-tall-buildings-skyscrapers-island-sky.

Philip, M. NourbeSe. *Zong!* Middletown: Wesleyan University Press, 2011.

Pitts, Johny. *Afropean: Notes from Black Europe.* London: Penguin, 2020.

Povinelli, Elizabeth A. *The Cunning of Recognition: Indigenous Alterities and the Making of Australian Multiculturalism.* Durham: Duke University Press, 2002.

Preciado, Paul B. *Pornotopia: An Essay on Playboy's Architecture and Biopolitics.* New York: Zone Books, 2019.

Rankine, Claudia. *Just Us: An American Conversation.* London: Allen Lane, 2020.

RIBA. *Plan of Work 2020: Overview.* London: RIBA, 2020.

Robinson, Cedric. *Black Marxism: The Making of the Black Radical Tradition.* Chapel Hill: University of North Carolina Press, 2000.

Robson, Steve. "'In what sense are they going to be Mancunians?'.... The Five-star Flats Where Critics Say Residents Will Be Living in a Bubble." *Manchester Evening News,* June 2, 2019. https://www.manchestereveningnews.co.uk/news/greater-manchester-news/angel-gardens-moda-living-manchester-16306998.

Sexton, Jared. "Afro-pessimism: The Unclear World." *Rhizomes* 29 (2016). http://www.rhizomes.net/issue29/sexton.html. DOI: 10.20415/rhiz/029.e02.

———. "The Curtain of the Sky: An Introduction." *Critical Sociology* 36, no. 1 (2010): 11–24. DOI: 10.1177/0896920509347136.

———. "The Social Life of Social Death: On Afro-Pessimism and Black Optimism." *InTensions Journal* 5 (2011): 1–47. DOI: 10.4324/9781315883700-4.

Simmel, Georg. "Bridge and Door." In *Rethinking Architecture: A Reader in Cultural Theory*, edited by Neil Leach, 63–77. Abingdon: Routledge, 1997.

Simon, Seymour. *Skyscrapers*. Edited by Neil Leach. San Francisco: SeaStar Books, 2005.

Simpson, Jack. "Forcing Leaseholders to Pay for Cladding Costs under Building Safety Bill an 'abdication of responsibility,' say MPs." *Inside Housing*, November 24, 2020. https://www.insidehousing.co.uk/news/news/forcing-leaseholders-to-pay-for-cladding-costs-under-building-safety-bill-an-abdication-of-responsibility-say-mps-68710.

Society for the Humanities. "Nahum Chandler, 'Paraontology; or, Notes on the Practical Theoretical Politics of Thought.'" *Vimeo*, October 29, 2018. https://vimeo.com/297769615.

Sontag, Susan. *On Photography*. New York City: Rosetta Books, 2005.

Studio MUTT, "What Is Studio MUTT?" https://www.studiomutt.com/mutt-info.

Tadiar, Neferti X.M. "The Life-Times of Disposability within Global Neoliberalism." *Social Text* 31, no. 2 (Summer 2013): 19–48. DOI: 10.1215/01642472-2081112.

Taut, Bruno, "Down with Seriousism!" In *Programs and Manifestoes on 20th Century Architecture*, edited by Ulrich Conrads, 57–58. Cambridge: MIT Press, 1971.

Todd, Zoe. "An Indigenous Feminist Take On The Ontological Turn: 'Ontology' Is Just Another Word for Colonialism." *Journal of Historical Sociology* 29, no. 1 (March 2016): 4–22. DOI: 10.1111/johs.12124.

WAI Architecture Think Tank, "Un-making ARCHITECTURE: An anti-racist architecture manifesto." *The Architect's Newspaper,* June 15, 2020. https://www.archpaper.com/2020/06/un-making-architecture-an-anti-racist-architecture-manifesto/.

Wainwright, Oliver, "Welcome to Manc-hatten: How the City Sold Its Soul for Luxury Skyscrapers." *The Guardian,* October 21, 2019. https://www.theguardian.com/artanddesign/2019/oct/21/welcome-to-manc-hattan-how-the-city-sold-its-soul-for-luxury-skyscrapers.

Weheliye, Alexander G. *Habeas Viscus: Racializing Assemblages, Biopolitics, and Black Feminist Theories of the Human.* Durham: Duke University Press, 2014.

Wells, Ida B., Frederick Douglass, Irvine Garland Penn, and Ferdinand L. Barnett. *The Reason Why the Colored American Is Not in the World's Columbian Exposition: The Afro-American's Contribution to Columbian Literature.* Edited by Robert W. Rydell. Urbana: University of Illinois Press, 1999.

Wigley, Mark. *Deconstructivist Architecture.* New York: The Museum of Modern Art, 1988.

Wilderson III, Frank B. *Afro-pessimism.* New York: Liveright Publishing, 2020.

Wright, Michelle M. "Black in Time: Exploring New Ontologies, New Dimensions, New Epistemologies of the African Diaspora." *Transforming Anthropology* 18, no. 1 (2010): 70–73. DOI: 10.1111/j.1548-7466.2010.01072.x.

Wynter, Sylvia, "1492: A New World View." In *Race, Discourse and the Origin of the Americas,* edited by Vera Lawrence Hyatt and Rex M. Nettleford, 5–57. Washington, DC: Smithsonian Books, 1994.

Wynter, Sylvia, and Kathrine McKittrick. "Unparalleled Catastrophe for Our Species? Or, to Give Humanness a Different Future: Conversations." In *Sylvia Wynter: On Being Human as Praxis,* edited by Kathrine McKittrick, 9–89. Durham: Duke University Press, 2015.

X, Malcolm, and Alex Haley. *The Autobiography of Malcolm X, as Told to Alex Haley.* New York: Ballentine Books, 2015.

Zingman, Alon, dir. *Shtisel*, Season 2, Episode 5, "Love Pains," written by Yehonatan Indursky and Ori Elon, first aired November 28, 2015 on *Yes Oh,* https://www.yesstudios.tv/shtisel .

www.ingramcontent.com/pod-product-compliance
Lightning Source LLC
Chambersburg PA
CBHW071001160426
43193CB00012B/1868